Africa Now

Africa Now is an exciting new series, published by Zed Books in association with the internationally respected Nordic Africa Institute. Featuring high-quality, cutting-edge research from leading academics, the series addresses the big issues confronting Africa today. Accessible but in-depth, and wide-ranging in its scope, Africa Now engages with the critical political, economic, sociological and development debates affecting the continent, shedding new light on pressing concerns.

Nordic Africa Institute

The Nordic Africa Institute (Nordiska Afrikainstitutet) is a centre for research, documentation and information on modern Africa. Based in Uppsala, Sweden, the Institute is dedicated to providing timely, critical and alternative research and analysis of Africa and to cooperating with African researchers. As a hub and a meeting place for a growing field of research and analysis, the Institute strives to put knowledge of African issues within reach for scholars, policy-makers, politicians, the media, students and the general public. The Institute is financed jointly by the Nordic countries (Denmark, Finland, Iceland, Norway and Sweden).

www.nai.uu.se

Forthcoming titles

Prosper B. Matondi, Kjell Havnevik and Atakilte Beyene (eds), *Biofuels, Land Grabbing and Food Security in Africa*

Mats Utas (ed.), *African Conflicts and Informal Power: Big Men and Networks*

Titles already published

Fantu Cheru and Cyril Obi (eds), *The Rise of China and India in Africa: Challenges, Opportunities and Critical Interventions*

Ilda Lindell (ed.), *Africa's Informal Workers: Collective Agency, Alliances and Transnational Organizing in Urban Africa*

Iman Hashim and Dorte Thorsen, *Child Migration in Africa*

Cyril Obi and Siri Aas Rustad (eds), *Oil and Insurgency in the Niger Delta: Managing the Complex Politics of Petro-violence*

About the authors

Iman Hashim is an assistant professor at the Department of International Relations, Istanbul Kültür University. She has worked on children's independent migration from rural north-eastern Ghana to rural and urban central Ghana. Her current work builds on long-term child-centred ethnographic research undertaken in a farming community in north-eastern Ghana, which examined how boys and girls spend their time, the work that they do and their experiences of education. It paid particular attention to the role that children play in households' livelihoods strategies, the nature of inter and intra-generational relations, and the negotiations and decision-making processes associated with boys' and girls' various activities. She has also worked for national and international non-governmental organizations as a programme and research officer.

Dorte Thorsen is a teaching fellow at the Department of Geography and Environmental Science, University of Reading. She has done ethnographic research with children and youth migrating from the Bisa region in south-eastern Burkina Faso to Ouagadougou and Abidjan and with their rural families in some twenty villages. Raising methodological questions about the way in which children's and youth's agency can be studied beyond a narrow focus on verbal negotiations, her research theorizes decision-making processes linked with young migrants' performance of identities, urban labour relations and the enactment of relatedness. She has published book chapters and policy papers based on this research, and articles in the journals *Migrations & Hommes, Forum for Development Studies* and the *Journal for Comparative Family Studies*.

Child Migration in Africa

Iman Hashim and Dorte Thorsen

Nordiska Afrikainstitutet
The Nordic Africa Institute

Zed Books
LONDON | NEW YORK

Child Migration in Africa was first published in association with the
Nordic Africa Institute, PO Box 1703, SE-751 47 Uppsala, Sweden in 2011
by Zed Books Ltd, 7 Cynthia Street, London N1 9JF, UK and Room 400,
175 Fifth Avenue, New York, NY 10010, USA

www.zedbooks.co.uk
www.nai.uu.se

Set in OurType Arnhem, Monotype Gill Sans Heavy by Ewan Smith, London
Index: ed.emery@thefreeuniversity.net
Cover by Rogue Four Design; cover photographs copyright Dorte Thorsen
Printed and bound in Great Britain by the MPG Books Group, Bodmin and
King's Lynn

Distributed in the USA exclusively by Palgrave Macmillan, a division of
St Martin's Press, LLC, 175 Fifth Avenue, New York, NY 10010, USA

A catalogue record for this book is available from the British Library
Library of Congress Cataloging in Publication Data available

ISBN 978 1 84813 455 3 hb
ISBN 978 1 84813 456 0 pb
ISBN 978 1 84813 457 7 eb

Contents

Maps

Preface

This book addresses the issue of children's independent migration in West Africa. The term children's independent migration is increasingly used in the literature, including our own, to refer to the movement of individuals who are under the age of eighteen, and who are not coerced or tricked into moving by a third person, but who migrate voluntarily and separately from their parents. This definition, however, incorporates a number of concepts and ideas that require some scrutinizing. First, questions arise regarding when children are 'children' and when they are 'youth', as well as whether girls and boys are labelled as 'children' or 'youth' in the same way. International conventions, such as the United Nations Convention on the Rights of the Child (CRC), define anyone below the age of eighteen as a child. However, labelling in legal definitions, which for practical reasons is tied to chronological age, is one thing, but how appropriate is this for rural peoples in the West African savannah, whose conceptualization of age is embedded in social relations and generational hierarchies?

Second, the idea of children migrating independently and separately from their parents brings up two significant issues when speaking of societies where kinship and social networks are important parameters in people's lives. One concerns who child migrants' 'parents' are. The implicit assumption is that they are only the birth parents, but is this necessarily the case in societies where several adults may behave like fathers and mothers and have claims on and obligations to children? The inquiry into parenthood also necessitates a consideration of who the 'parents' are if a child is left behind when birth parents migrate, and who they are if children travel with an adult who may not be a birth parent but may be considered a parent, or even one who is not. The second issue relates to the voluntary nature of the migration; is the implicit corollary of not being coerced or tricked into travelling that children migrate autonomously? The notion of 'voluntary' foregrounds children's agency, but this poses the question: to what extent can they choose to migrate or not – especially if parents in the larger sense take charge of their journey or ask them to come? Other questions concern what constraints children experience if they wish to migrate, and whether girls and boys have the same opportunities for moving and/or for staying.

Finally, the concept of migration may suggest a narrow focus on geographical relocation, and/or on numbers and flows of child migrants. Conceptualizing migration as one among several forms of mobility leads us to raise a set of questions that move us beyond dichotomies frequently evident in the analysis of spatial movement; in particular those of rural versus urban, forced versus voluntary, and traditional versus modern. Our questions touch on how children and young people themselves understand child migration and on children's experiences as migrants, on how adults understand it, how these understandings and experiences by young and old are gendered, and how they are enacted and contested. Importantly, the concept of mobility also compels us to interrogate sedentarist approaches to social life that lead to assumptions regarding children's migration resulting from family rupture and/or social breakdown.

In order to explore the many facets of children's independent migration we use the stories told by young migrants, who were either under eighteen or had left on their first migration before they were eighteen (insofar as we can gauge this, since many children did not know their precise chronological age). These stories were produced in interviews and conversations with children at migration destinations in Ghana, Burkina Faso and Côte d'Ivoire, and with children in rural villages in what was then the Bawku East district of the Upper East Region of Ghana and Pays Bisa in the Région Centre-est of Burkina Faso. Adults in these locations also offered their views on children's migration and on childhood in general in interviews and conversations. In addition to these child-centred and multi-sited research activities, which we carried out in Ghana in 2004 (Iman Hashim) and in Burkina Faso and Côte d'Ivoire between 2005 and 2008 (Dorte Thorsen), we have each carried out ethnographic fieldwork in the rural communities from where some of or all the child migrants in our subsequent studies originate. In Ghana, this involved child-centred research in a farming village in the north-east in 2000/01, which examined how boys and girls spend their time, the work they do and their experiences of education, as well as the negotiations and decision-making processes associated with boys' and girls' various activities. In Burkina Faso, the research was with married women and men in a small farming village in the south-east in 2001/02. This field study explored how rural women strategize, choose and make decisions, and brought to light many invisible facets of the multiple social arenas that are important sources of symbolic and material resources as well as sites of obligation for women at different points in their lives.

Our approach to social relations, negotiation and decision-making processes is rooted in feminist work on conceptualizing household behaviour, power relations and gender differences, among others. It also stresses an important aspect of post-structural qualitative analysis, in that we do not represent only a generalized picture of why and how children migrate, because this would only reveal part of the story. There is a tendency to theorize poor children from developing countries, and especially those such as independent child migrants, who are in circumstances particularly challenging to universal ideals regarding what children should properly be doing, as muted victims; just as 'Third

World' women were theorized in the past. Adopting a feminist approach helps us deconstruct such representations in order to present a more nuanced and multifaceted understanding of children's lives in West Africa. While children's and youth's stories about their migration are at the core of our analysis, the feminist approach encourages us to interrogate what these stories tell us about the range of choices children have, how girls and boys are constrained and enabled differently, and how childhood is socially constituted locally.

Listening to what young migrants have to say about their own circumstances and refuting the almost automatic presentation of child migrants as victims does not imply romanticizing their lives. Rather it requires representing the complexities of their lives and foregrounding their concerns, actions and strategies. This is especially important because powerful normative ideals regarding what childhood is shape outsiders' views of children's independent migration. Through this lens, children are viewed as victims, not as migrants in their own right. This often accounts for our own experiences when presenting material showing children's participation in decisions surrounding migration and work, where we are often practically accused of advocating child trafficking and the exploitation of children. Another allegation encountered, when talking about young male migrants in their teens, is that when we describe how they deal with being cheated of their wages, we offer a naive representation of innocence, when it is assumed they are likely to engage in criminal activities and gangs.

In this book, we would like to tell a story that challenges people to rethink these preconceived ideas. For those readers who are already aware of the multiplicity of childhood, and the capacities and capabilities of children, we hope to add to the growing body of research that illuminates this.

Our objective is to unpack children's migration and show the different ways that young people can be migrants. Exploring how the categories of children and youth are demarcated among the rural communities with whom we work in West Africa leads us to discuss gendered notions of childhood and youth and the identity constructions children and youth engage in and negotiate with adults as well as with age-mates. Such negotiations concern individuals' self-image and how they are labelled by people around them. Interrogating the category of 'parent' results in a broader conceptualization of the family and of relatedness that more accurately reflects the fluidity in household composition in societies with a high level of mobility, and which highlights the multi-sited dimension of families as well as the normality of movement. This leads us to look at how 'cultures of migration' in the West African savannah shape children's, youth's and adults' perceptions of migration and its outcomes. It also leads to exploring how kin and other relationships are negotiated and how they may facilitate or hinder children's migration and shape their experience. Although we primarily analyse the migration of youngsters aged ten to eighteen in relation to ideals of childhood and not to ideals of youth, we are not thinking about a sixteen- or seventeen-year-old as a child but rather as a 'young youth'. This subcategory of youth is marginalized in the child literature as well as the youth literature, which tends to focus on youth up to somewhere in their thirties. We have chosen the analytical angle of childhood because of the emphasis on children and migration in much of the policy and advocacy addressing trafficking, and because youth and migration is not perceived as a problem.

Writing this book and doing the multi-sited research presented in it has been possible only with the economic and institutional support of the Nordic Africa Institute, the UK's Department for International Development, the Development Research Centre (DRC) on Migration, Globalization and Poverty at the University of Sussex, the Economic and Social Research Council in the UK and the Danish Research Agency. We gratefully acknowledge this support. We are grateful too for the help and support of Richard Black, Saskia Gent and Meera Warrier at the DRC, Birgitta Hellmark-Lindgren and Sonja Johansson at the Nordic Africa Institute, and Ken Barlow at Zed Books. We each of us owe a huge debt to Ann Whitehead, who has mentored us over the last few years with wisdom and brilliance, and challenged as well as inspired us always to think and to scrutinize and to question. The comments of Laura Hammond and an anonymous reviewer also pushed us to rethink some of our arguments and to go deeper into theoretical debates, which made the work with the book all the more interesting.

Individually, we also have many people to thank. During both phases of her research, innumerable people provided Iman Hashim with their time, their help, their friendship and their moral support, in Ghana, the UK and Turkey. Thanks are due to the capable assistance and translation of Lawrence Asambo, and especially Peter Asaal, as well as to the people of Tempane Natinga, whose generosity and trust made her research possible. To the children who participated in the research, special thanks for teaching her so much, and for bringing immense joy, if sometimes sorrow, to the process; and to her family, for their love and support, not to mention patience. Finally, to Burak Ülman, thank you for everything. Dorte Thorsen would like to express her deepest gratitude to all the children, youth and parents who have responded to endless questions, narrated their journeys, even when they brought back disheartening memories, and shared with her fun moments. She also wishes to thank her research assistants, Nombré Damata, Bidiga Assita, Dindané Mahamadou, Kéré Ousseni and Kéré Sanhouba, for additional insights into and interpretations of children's and youth's migration. Finally, she thanks friends and family in Burkina Faso, Côte d'Ivoire, Denmark and the UK for love, support and inspiring discussions.

This book is dedicated to Emir, Nadir and Natalie,
and is in memory of Fanta.

1 | Introduction: interrogating childhood and migration

'We discovered yet another child today who had not appeared during the first household survey. She is the daughter of the household head's daughter and had been staying with her paternal grandparents while her parents were working in the south. They had both since died so her maternal grandfather decided to bring her to live with him until her parents' return, as there were only the father's brothers left in the house and he was concerned that they wouldn't care properly for her. Moving on to the next house we discovered that Laadi [aged seventeen] was back from Kumasi but her brother Moses [aged fourteen] was not, and nor will he come soon. [...] She has been helping her aunt with her catering business as well as hawking oranges. Moses, she thinks, is working on contract for a cocoa farmer.' (Field notes from Ghana, 7 February 2001)

'I approached the village imam specifically to ask about his daughter, Yarassou, as I remembered her mother telling me in 2002 that despite the fact she had not yet reached school age, Yarassou had started school the previous year. One of the school teachers in the village loved the child and had asked for her when she was posted in a rural town some 55 miles away. As the imam and I were chatting about children, family relations and, of course, Yarassou, I learned that she had only stayed with the teacher two years before her father brought her back. In his view, Yarassou was helping the teacher and had not left because of schooling. At one point, someone had sent a message to let him know that his daughter was not treated well. The problem was that Yarassou did not always do the work required of her, the teacher then tried to force her and after that, she beat her severely. After hearing this, he waited until the school holidays because he did not want to disrupt Yarassou's schooling and then went to see the teacher and, anxious not to anger her, reclaimed the child by explaining that her mother needed her help after having given birth. As soon as she was back in the village, he enrolled her in school.' (Field notes from Burkina Faso, 16 February 2005)

This book addresses children's migration independently of their birth parents. The extracts from our field diaries give an indication of the extent to which children in rural West Africa do move around independently of their birth parents. Some move to help out in the household or on the farm of the person to whom they move and/or to learn a trade, go to school or pursue other forms of learning, such as apprenticeships. Others move to find paid work – in other words, they become labour migrants. Another point both diary extracts illustrate is that children's movements are not necessarily due to parental neglect. In the West African context, parents and grandparents worry about children's immediate and future welfare, and encourage moves they believe will benefit the child, whether the moves are away from them or bring children into their protection and care. Moving about has long been central to West Africans' welfare strategies, especially those of the poor, but the frequency and normality of such strategies can be difficult to grasp when one is from a society where individuals' lifestyles are more sedentary. Similarly, strongly held preconceptions of childhood and the appropriate relationship between children and their (birth) parents can be a hindrance to seeing the different ways of being a child and of parenting. The last couple of decades have seen the rise of child-centred studies in which childhood – rather than being seen as a natural given – is understood to be lived and experienced contextually (James and Prout 1997). The claims to universality in Western studies of child development had received an early challenge from anthropologists carrying out detailed ethnographic studies in diverse societies (see, for example, Margaret Mead's (1928) *Coming of Age in Samoa*; Meyer Fortes's (1938) 'Social and psychological aspects of education in Taleland'; and Ruth Benedict's (1938) 'Continuities and discontinuities in cultural conditioning'). Moreover, it is not merely in 'other' societies that children's experiences do not conform to this idealized model of childhood. Children in the 'West' who do not conform to this model – for example, by being involved in child labour, being the primary carers of incapacitated parents, or being considered out of place by spending much time on the streets or living outside the family realm – are frequently labelled deviant or simply not recognized (Evans 2009; McKechnie and Hobbs 1999; Terrio 2008). Despite this evidence-based push for the multiplicity of childhood, child development and parenting (Lancy 2008; LeVine and New 2008), as we shall discuss in detail later, there is still a tendency to treat the category of childhood as a universal one. Consequently, children's migration in developing[1] countries is rarely understood in terms of how childhood, socialization, work and education normally crystallize in their local context.

The book thus addresses not only children's migration independently of their birth parents but argues for the importance of interrogating strongly held ideas about childhood in order to fully apprehend as well as comprehend children's movement. The issues at stake in rural West Africa will become clearer through the course of the book as we explore the different paths young migrants follow – whether they do so intentionally, happen to be pushed in that direction by adults, or seize upon an opportunity when it arises.

Universalizing ideals of childhood

Powerful ideas regarding what childhood consists of inform child protection work and legislation surrounding family relations, as well as many scholarly analyses and media representations of social practices involving children (Boyden 2001). Yet, childhood as a social concept did not always exist. In the early 1960s, the French historian Aries claimed that the very institution of childhood did not emerge until the sixteenth and seventeenth centuries; even later among the working classes. It has not always been the case, for example, that children and work were viewed as incompatible. The first campaigns against child labour in Britain did not take place until the 1830s and 1840s (Hasnat 1995: 424). Many historians trace the rise of this in Britain to the period of the Industrial Revolution of the nineteenth century. Industrialization created a huge demand for labour, which children were instrumental in filling. Children moved out of the home and into factories and mines. However, in doing so they also became more visible. The harsh conditions and long hours their work involved jarred with elite sensibilities at the time, which dictated that individuals needed protection and guidance through their early years. The result was protests and demands for legislation against child employment (Hendrick 1997). Factory owners, and parents who resented state interference in their lives, resisted this. However, this initial resistance to legislation limiting children's involvement in work and to compulsory schooling gradually gave way, owing primarily to rising wages for men, the increasing engagement of women in the labour force and technological advances that reduced the demand for children in factories (Cunningham and Viazzo 1996). State intervention in the family in the form of compulsory education in response to the need for educated wage labourers eventually extended children's dependency into adolescence. Their cost to the family soon became considerably greater than just that of their forgone labour, so that 'children have subtly but rapidly developed into a labour-intensive, capital intensive product of the family in industrial society' (Minge-Kalman 1978: 466). These processes, combined with a dramatic drop in birth rates, also resulted in changing ideals about childhood, and a view emerged of the child as a purely emotional and affective asset. The economic and sentimental values of children increasingly came to be seen as incompatible, resulting in the view that only callous or insensitive parents violated this boundary, while properly loved children belonged in a domesticated, non-productive world of lessons and games (Zelizer 1994). This affective transition is summarized well by Kabeer, who notes how the transition from an old to a new mortality pattern in Britain was associated with a series of interdependent changes. These included:

> improved chances of child survival, greater resort to contraception, changing perceptions of human life, personhood and individuality, the emergence of affective relations within the family, more personalized parent–child, particularly mother–child relationships and a new reproductive strategy which entailed giving birth to fewer infants and investing more heavily (emotionally as well as materially) in each one from birth onward. (Kabeer 2000: 468)

Protests and subsequent legislation against children's employment in Britain were mirrored in other industrialized countries, with the result that moves were made to adopt international legislation against child labour. In 1919, the first of such legislation was instituted with the International Labour Organization's (ILO) Convention on Minimum Age in Industry (No. 5) (ILO 1996: 23). Between 1919 and 1998 a further ten conventions on or related to child labour were adopted by the ILO. The most far-reaching of these is the 1973 Convention Concerning Minimum Age for Admission to Employment (No. 138). This convention obliges ratifying states to fix a minimum age for admission to employment or work and to undertake to pursue a national policy designed to ensure the effective abolition of child labour (ibid.: 24–5).

However, the resistance to child labour legislation witnessed in the industrialized world was mirrored in the developing world. In this instance, in addition to accusations of cultural imperialism, the motives behind moves to prevent the import of goods produced by child labour were questioned. Some argued that the protection of Northern workers' jobs and trade protectionism, rather than child protection, were the key factors (Hasnat 1995; see also Rosemberg and Freitas 1999, Tan and Gomez 1993). For instance, Panicker notes, 'their hearts started bleeding for the poor children of the south only after the liberalization process began and today practically all nations of the south are caught in the web of globalization. The "free market" is what set the agenda and the priorities' (Panicker 1998: 284–5).

The overall effect was that by the late 1990s the debate about child labour had reached something of an impasse. As a result, much attention is now directed at the worst forms of child labour, such as prostitution, child 'trafficking' and children's involvement in armed conflict, since there is consensus that these are patently harmful and exploitative (Myers 1999: 24). This is reflected in the drawing up of the latest convention on child labour, ILO Convention No. 182 – Worst Forms of Child Labour Convention (1999). This convention, which is more widely ratified than the Minimum Age Convention, obliges ratifying states to take immediate and effective measures to prohibit and eliminate practices such as slavery, the commercial sexual exploitation of children, the use of children in illicit activities, and work which, by its nature or circumstances, is likely to harm the health, safety or morals of a child.

Even more widely ratified is the United Nations Convention on the Rights of the Child (CRC), adopted by the General Assembly in 1989. Developed over ten years, with input from representatives of all societies, religions and cultures, the CRC brought together, in a single legal instrument, all standards concerning children. It is the most widely accepted human rights treaty and is significant in its claim to the universality of a particular model of childhood, which we refer to as the universalizing ideal. We use this term to underscore that this model of childhood is one that not only is not the reality in many contexts, both in the developing world and the industrialized world, but is also frequently one that is contested. Our aim is to reiterate that there is not a static category of childhood, even though international legal instruments may give the illusion of constancy and permanence, but there still exist very powerful normative ideals of childhood, which emerged as a result of the affective transition described above.

Undoubtedly, the CRC was an important advance in many respects, and it certainly aimed both to protect and empower children by defining them as a category apart from adults. However, it has also been criticized for precisely the same reasons. By treating children as right-holders in their own right, the CRC has expanded the reach of the state into the family by empowering outside professionals to represent the interests of the child, displacing the child's family as the primary advocates of a child's interests (Pupavac 2001: 100). While on the one hand the lack of enforcement of the CRC means that the rights it guarantees are rarely enacted in practice, its almost universal ratification has meant that it has become central to international principles and policy. The African Union's (AU) Charter on the Rights and Welfare of the Child (AU 1990) is a case in point, which we shall return to below.

Other criticisms of the CRC are that it has trivialized certain rights (Ansell 2005; Ennew et al. 2005). Entitlements to government protection and services have received more attention than children's rights of empowerment. Critics have suggested that 'this leaves children *more* vulnerable because it reinforces the idea that they are wholly dependent on adults and reduces their capacity for autonomy' (Ennew et al. 2005: 32, emphasis in original). Moreover, the emphasis on children's dependency contradicts the reality of many children's lives because it ignores children's role as producers and therefore places working children on the margins of what is perceived as proper childhood, despite the necessity or normality of their contribution to family activities (Ansell 2005: 230; Boyden 2001; Punch 2001a: 805; Robson 2004b: 241). A different critique addresses the aim of the CRC's Article 12(1), which assures a child's 'right to express [his or her own views] freely in all matters affecting the child, the views of the child being given due weight in accordance with the age and maturity of the child' (UN 1989). The idea that underlies the right of free expression draws on a Western understanding of decision-making as a verbal, discursive process. This contrasts with societies where notions of respect govern everyone's speech and stipulate what can be discussed openly and by whom (Ferme 2001: 7), and where the expression of ideas and aspirations entails acting upon them in strategic or tactical ways to get away with specific actions or to indirectly convey opinions (Thorsen 2005). These critiques are pertinent to understanding children's migration, and the lack of attention to the conceptualization of childhood explains why there exist tensions and contradictions within the debates around the issue (Hashim 2004: 13).

Another ideal of childhood is the one presented in the AU's Charter on the

Rights and Welfare of the Child (AU 1990). As pointed out by de Waal (2002), many of the articles in the charter are almost identical with the CRC. The African Charter diverges from the CRC in one important respect, in stressing not only children's rights but also their responsibilities towards their family. This it does in Article 31, which reads: 'The child, subject to his age and ability [...] shall have the duty to work for the cohesion of the family, to respect his parents, superiors and elders at all times and to assist them in case of need' (ibid.). Research carried out with African parents in Nigeria confirms the importance parents place on children's participation in activities that would be considered work in the global perspective, as part of children's socialization process (Ajayi and Torimiro 2004). It illustrates how different constructions of childhood prevail in diverse contexts. In this model, children are allowed a productive role while still being kept as juniors in the social hierarchy. Having rights and duties complicates the categorization of children as mere dependants, as well as their being thought about in terms of being autonomous individuals. They are neither; the African Charter affirms the importance of social personhood and thus of being embedded in social units (Ansell 2005: 230; Cheney 2007).

The fact that African leaders felt the need to formulate an African model for children's rights illustrates the diversity of understandings of childhood, and yet there continues to be a tendency to regard childhood as a universal category, rather than perceiving it as an empirical question (Boyden 2001; Jenks 2004: 5). As we have noted, such ethnocentric attitudes may hinder an under-standing of the motivations and justification for particular practices because they fail to accept that people may have other ways of doing things and other ways of living their lives. This inevitably raises the issue of cultural relativ-ism – especially when it is a question of children's welfare – since it raises questions related to whether we should seek universal measures of quality of life for all or 'defer instead to the many different norms that traditional cultures have selected' (Nussbaum and Glover 1995, cited in Jackson 1997: 146). It is for this reason that cultural relativism is often posited as the op-posite of ethnocentrism. However, as Eriksen (1995) points out, they are not binary opposites since the former does not in itself contain a moral principle. Rather, cultural relativism is a methodological and theoretical necessity if one is attempting to investigate societies and understand their own inner logic and workings (ibid.: 13). This is precisely what this book seeks to do; to unfold the material, social and cultural dimensions of children's migration in the West African savannah without moral prejudices about local notions of the child, parents, family and home. This, however, does not imply an uncritical view of practices that may result in suffering or distress for children. Rather, our aim is to examine how children, themselves, experience various practices and how they act upon these experiences.

Childhood and its constituting concepts

In the previous section, we noted that while childhood is often seen as universal and constant, in actuality it is a category made of a bundle of concepts that far from being static are subject to negotiation and change. Furthermore, this is so not only in the European context, as shown above, but also in African communities (Nyamnjoh 2002). In this section, we want to explore in greater detail the key concepts relating to childhood; which is especially important as changes and the negotiated nature of social categories, culture and tradition are not always reflected in the way children, and especially poor children, are represented (Malkki and Martin 2003).

A child, in most international legal definitions, is any individual below the age of eighteen years. Such a wide category inevitably begs differentiation, since the needs and abilities of a toddler and a teenager are very different. This is the first area where there are evident differences regarding what characterizes children in different phases of childhood and their transition from one phase to another. In what we term the universalizing, dominant or 'modern' Western model, childhood is structured around chronological age and cognitive development.[2] Although subtle distinctions are made between babies and toddlers based on their sensory and language development, and birthdays are celebrated elaborately, the first major transition for children is linked with entering into formal education at the age of five or six years. Leaving school and starting work is also a major transition, but it is not linked with any particular age as children can pursue different educational paths, which results in some being in education well beyond the age of eighteen while others go into vocational training or leave formal education entirely, possibly to work. Transitions in late childhood may also be blurred by the possibility of their intersection with one another. These include children being labelled – or labelling themselves – teenagers from the age of thirteen, youth from the age of fifteen, and various legal transitions specified in national legislation,[3] such as passing the minimum age for paid employment, achieving the age of majority for voting or engaging in sexual relations, being allowed to drive a vehicle, or to marry, and so on (Valentine 2003). In addition to these types of transitions linked with chronological age, childhood is also seen as a process of gradually gaining independence, implying that a five-year-old and a fifteen-year-old are not being treated as dependants in the same way. For example, while the parents of a five-year-old may restrict his or her freedom to roam around in public places, the parents of a fifteen-year-old may impose few constraints on their child's everyday mobility but be concerned about the time of the day the child goes to different places. The parents of the five-year-old may also cook all the child's meals, while the fifteen-year-old is asked to help with food preparation. Children thus have liberties or constraints imposed on them that reflect common discourses in a given society about age-appropriate behaviour. Variations may exist within these; for example, some children may be permitted to return home by 9 p.m. at age fourteen, while others may have this restriction imposed until they are aged sixteen; and clearly gender may be a factor in this, reflecting how childhood itself intersects with other issues, such as ethnicity and socio-economic status, as well as gender. Nevertheless, these liberties and constraints reflect more general ideas regarding childhood transitions, whereby children are perceived to be in need of care and protection for survival, well-being and guidance in order to develop in the right way irrespective of age.

These ideals of childhood and their expression in national legislation contrast to those evident from empirical work in a number of societies. For one, in the societies in which we work, as well as in other West African societies, chronological age is not central to childhood. Nevertheless, childhood does also have different phases; for example, babies and very young children are considered positioned between the worlds of the living and the spirits, and if they are not satisfied with the conditions in the living world, they may *choose* to return to the spirits. Children, thus, are perceived to be in a liminal phase in the first years and need persuasion to stay in the world of the living (Gottlieb 1998; Samuelsen 1999: 76–7).[4] Later transitions within childhood are rooted in social personhood and children's gradual incorporation into the social, spatial and material arenas of their community through learning different tasks, rituals and practices of how to do things. The pace at which the child becomes skilful in the various areas varies according to how much their participation is needed and their willingness to take part, their gender, sibling order, the number of people calling on their services, and whether they are raised in a rural or urban setting (Hashim 2004; Katz 2004; Nyamnjoh 2002; Reynolds 1991; Robson 2004b; for other geographical contexts, see Nieuwenhuys 1994; Leinaweaver 2007; and Punch 2001b). Children suggest how they should be perceived – by behaving maturely, for example, or by absconding from work – and this also shapes others' views of them (Hashim 2004: 81–3; Johnson-Hanks 2002; Thorsen 2006; Valentine 2003: 38). Thus, how children are perceived in terms of maturity and ability is relational and relative: it depends, for example, on the presence of older and younger children and on their gender rather than on their chronological age. Moreover, education outside the home, marriage, having children (within or outside marriage) and a variety of other rites of passage may influence how a child is conceptualized, as these transitions also do in the Western model. Children of all ages are perceived to be part of the social relations surrounding the family because this provides them with material, social and symbolic safety and well-being. Their inclusion requires active participation by children and gives them the responsibility of rendering services to seniors.

Any model of childhood involves ideas about who parents are, as well as what parenting entails, and how this is tied to notions of family and home. In the universalizing model of childhood, the relationship between parents and children is usually conceptualized as a unidirectional one involving the provision of basic needs, protection, socialization and adults' emotional attention to children, and in particular from birth mothers to their offspring. This emphasis on children as having needs and parents meeting them is linked to the development of the family as a unit of two to three generations in which material transfers and care-giving emanate from people categorized as producers to people categorized as consumers (Malhotra and Kabeer 2002). Empirically our research finds that West African children also stress how a good parent is one who provides them with support. However, the relationship between parent and child is seen also as a reciprocal one where children have obligations to their parents (and other significant seniors) (Hashim 2004: 76). Equally important is that, rather than parents being producers and children consumers, in the West African context they are all producers and children are frequently responsible for covering the costs of some aspects of personal consumption, such as clothing and schooling costs.

Despite the fact that Western family patterns are becoming more and more complicated owing to women's and men's reproductive trajectories stretching over more marriages and increasingly common practices of shared parenting after divorce, the notion of parenthood is still linked primarily with the two birth parents. What is changing in the Western context is the constitution of the family, not the ideas about who should be care-givers or about the need for children and youth to be protected up to the age of eighteen. The family, by and large, is equated with the birth parents, or those legally designated as parents. In contrast, in many African societies, while birth parents also provide care, there are many more parents who are or who want to be involved in raising a child and thus contribute to its care and who feel they have certain claims on the child (Vischer 1997). These additional parents – classificatory parents – are a product of how the kinship system works; among the Bisa, for example, in addition to the birth mother, her co-wives, the wives of her husband's brothers and her own sisters, are considered mothers. Likewise, the birth father's brothers are considered fathers and, although not being designated as a mother or a father, the mother's brothers and the father's sisters are important kin for a child because they have a particular set of responsibilities for and claims on the child. Within this structure of child–parent relations there is an ideal of a child belonging to everyone and, thus, of all children being treated equally within a household. Yet, in reality, distinctions are made based on social and affectionate closeness, but also on the context in which the relationship is invoked, since the language of kinship can be used to create a particular type of relationship within the extended family and, occasionally, outside (Bourdieu 1977; Carsten 2000; O'Laughlin 1995).

The existence of several mothers and fathers also means that children may live with different parents for shorter or longer periods of time. This possibility disrupts the idea of a residentially bounded, nuclear and essentially sedentary family because children may move between family members in several locations who are willing or feel obliged to take on parental responsibilities. While they cannot criticize the parent(s) they live with openly, as long as they have other mothers or fathers with whom they can live, this flexibility may permit them to negotiate indirectly who is a parent and what parenthood should encompass (Notermans 2008).[5] Thus, another important difference between the universalizing model and the reality of childhood in other places is the narrow focus on the two birth parents in the former and the negotiated relationships within and outside extended families in the latter, which give children a wider set of social relations and an active influence in the decisions that make and sustain these. Equally, and related, is that, rather than the home being the place in which the birth or adopted parents reside, if one has a range of individuals across different spaces that one can call as a 'parent' and make a claim to live with, the home is not the sedentary unit of the universalizing model.

Finally, as noted earlier, because of the economic, social and political transformations associated with late industrialization, which institutionalized 'modern' childhood as a category separate from adulthood, childhood and formal schooling became intimately connected, such that education came to be seen as the proper activity for children, while work is not. As a result, education has come to be seen as commensurate with schooling, although, in its broadest sense, it refers to any process of teaching, training or improving.[6] For a great number of children, however, going to school is not a normal part of childhood, while work is. Some argue that their education is more like a socialization process, whether when working at home, with people outside their home and when learning particular skills in an apprenticeship (Chauveau 1998: 42). Others have suggested that even this argument is based on a normative understanding of childhood, since it rests on an assumption that childhood is defined primarily as a period of 'becoming' and, as a result, all experiences are regarded as being education (Schildkrout 1981: 93). Children's work activities thus become recast as a means of learning, part of being taught to become an adult, rather than being seen as what they actually are, and lost in the process is the fact that children are working because that is what children properly do (Hashim forthcoming).

In a number of ways, then, West African children's experiences are far from the normative globalized ideals of childhood, in which childhood is a period of dependency, involving education, play and leisure; where the only legitimate places for growing up are the 'sanctity of the nuclear family on the one hand and the school on the other' (Nieuwenhuys 1996: 242). In this idealized version, the home is perceived as a sedentary unit that offers a safe framework for children's lives, with the 'proper' place for children being within the bosom of a loving family.[7] The only mobility offered to children in this model is movement associated with formal education, as when they go to boarding schools or to live with kin to enable them to go to good schools. In this way, too, West African children challenge the normative model.

The mobility–migration nexus in West Africa

Sustained high levels of population movement in West African communities over several generations comprise many different types of moves. Migrations, for instance, include widespread rural movements in order to gain access to fertile land or areas of greater agricultural potential; long-term rural movements responding to changes in rains; seasonal livelihood migrations; movements to towns as people seek employment in the formal or informal sector or entre-preneurial opportunities which are mainly available in towns. Such migrations may be circular in the short or long term or of a more permanent nature. Mobilities, on the other hand, encompass all types of movement over short or longer distances, of different duration and frequency; from everyday travel to seasonal transhumance, migration, tourism, occasional pilgrimage and indeterminate forced displacement. Importantly, mobilities go beyond move-ment from A to B and focus on 'how mobility is engrained in the history, daily life and experiences of people' (de Bruijn et al. 2001: 1). Until recently, most movements were studied in a migration paradigm that produced a number of dichotomies – rural versus urban, subsistence versus market economy, and traditional versus modernity. De Bruijn et al. raise the critique that such dichotomies and the idea of bounded spaces that goes with them are less than useful after years of economic and social transformations. In their view, the focus on mobility is more pertinent because it allows for 'a close reading of people's own understanding of the spaces and places in which they move and the experiences these movements entail' (ibid.: 2). Moreover, rather than conceptualizing movements as a social rupture, the concept of mobility helps us unpack how different forms of mobility are ingrained in livelihood strategies and in people's social lives, how sedentary lives may actually result in defaulting on social obligations (ibid.) and mobility in creating and consolidating social relationships (Klute and Hahn 2007). We therefore need an analytical frame that captures the fluidity of families and homes, and explores people's sense of belonging to places and to social groups.

A number of scholars within the disciplines of anthropology, sociology and geography have explored notions of travel and mobility to critique and move beyond a deep-seated sedentarism in social sciences. Sedentarism, they argue, reiterates a narrow focus on discrete communities, a compartmentalization that hinders an understanding of how places and communities are bounded spatially and temporally, and how cultural and social practices may be con-joined spatially and historically. The result has been that stability of location and people's practices in that location is seen as normal, while mobility and change are presented as pathological. Not being 'at home' is perceived as being uprooted, thereby linking travellers', migrants' and displaced people's identities to 'the home' without considering how movement may influence identities (Clifford 1992: 96; Malkki 1992: 31–3; Sheller and Urry 2006: 208–9). To explore the dynamic links between places and cultures, Clifford suggests looking at what practices and ideas of home and dwelling people bring to a new place from their prior location(s), and how they are maintained and transformed in the new place (Clifford 1992: 115). Additionally, he points out that it is important to pay attention to the ways in which outside influences shape the discourses and practices in local communities, even if travel is not literal but through radio, TV, commodities, visitors and structures of the state (ibid.: 103). In this sense, mobility is both about those on the move and those staying. Apart from dynamics of change and continuity in particular locations, those who stay may enable others to be mobile by providing the necessary infrastructure and institutional moorings (Hannam et al. 2006: 3).

The analysis of children's migration in the following chapters draws on the analytical insights gained from the mobilities paradigm, which does not underestimate or trivialize the extent and significance of movements in people's lives. The insights of such an approach are particularly pertinent to an analysis of children's movement. For one, sedentarism underpins many policy approaches to children's welfare, especially so because of the perceived sanctity of 'the home' in the idealized version of childhood and because these strongly held ideas regarding what childhood should properly entail inhibit us from imagining children moving on their own account. Second, the historically high degree of mobility in West Africa means that migrants very often move within cultural contexts and social relations stretching over numerous places. Although ideals concerning childhood as expressed in the African Charter on the Rights and Welfare of the Child refer to children's responsibilities to their families, and although many people implicitly accept children's movements within the framework of extended families, the more abstract issue of conceptualizing families and homes that extend to multiple locations has not been addressed. To apprehend children's movement in the West African context we need to analyse their movement on a par with adults' movements rather than categorizing children as a group apart. This does not mean that we see children as miniature adults but rather that their movements cannot be understood in isolation. In the analysis of children's migration, these considerations are important for understanding children's aspirations regarding the outcome of migration, the roots of their wanderlust and differences in ability to travel linked with gender, sibling order and family size. Furthermore, they are important for understanding children's choices at the destination regarding their dwelling, work and social network, the types of constraints on their choices and how their views may change in the course of time. Finally, they are helpful for working out adults' relationships with migrant children, be they relatives or strangers, and how adults' views are interconnected across localities.

Our focus is children's migration *and* their mobility, especially their spatial mobility at the destination and the social mobility they gain from migration or, at least, hope to gain. Although migration is one form of mobility, we wish to highlight the fact that these children's journeys are not day trips but may entail movements of several hundred miles and may cross international borders. Moreover, their journeys often imply living in other places for one, two or more years before visiting the homes in which they spent their early years. Prior to going into our own findings on children's migration, however, we shall look at how children's movement has been explored in the literature to date.

Children's migration

Children's migration is not new (Hertrich and Lesclingand 2007; Lambert 2007; Le Jeune et al. 2004; Punch 2009: 1); however, attention to it is relatively new within both the policy and the academic literature.[8] This is because until recently women and children were typically imagined as merely tagging along behind the 'primary' male migrant (Gugler and Ludwar-Ene 1995; King 2002; O'Connell Davidson and Farrow 2007; Thorsen 2007a); consequently migrant women's and children's perspectives were rarely heard (Punch 2009: 1). Recent studies have shown that women are migrants in their own right (Anarfi et al. 1997; Sudarkasa 1977), and it is now more widely appreciated that the reasons for and experiences of migration differ for women as compared to men (Elmhirst 2002; McKay 2005; Mills 2001; Muzvidziwa 2001). Female migrants now receive more attention in the literature, but migration scholars, with few exceptions, have continued to focus their work on adults (Mahler and Pessar 2006: 35). Beyond the literature on the impact of parental migration on health and education outcomes for their children, on those limited occasions where children's experiences of migration have been considered, the assumption has been that children move with one or both parents. Primarily here the focus has been on immigrant children's experiences in schools, as transnationals and as second-generation immigrants (ibid.).

What limited attention has been directed to children who move without their parents has tended to focus on children in particularly difficult circumstances, such as street children, AIDS orphans, child soldiers, child refugees and children forced to work in exploitative, abusive and/or dangerous conditions (Whitehead and Hashim 2005). Trafficking in children – where those under eighteen years of age are recruited, transported, transferred, harboured or received for the purpose of exploitation (UN 2000) – in particular receives a huge amount of attention, especially trafficking for the purposes of commercial sexual exploitation. Though the cases of trafficking that have been documented are extremely disturbing and warrant attention and concern, they are also very much outside

13

the norm (O'Connell Davidson 2003). Nevertheless, the issue of trafficking is receiving significant attention globally, as well as in West Africa (cf. Dottridge 2002; IOM 2003; SCF Canada 2003; UNICEF 2002).

Across the region advocacy and intervention programmes were launched in the late 1990s and early 2000s by the International Labour Organization's (ILO) International Programme on the Elimination of Child Labour (IPEC) and the 'Lutte contre le Trafic des Enfants en Afrique de l'Ouest' (LUTRENA, the Fight against Child Trafficking in West Africa). In most accounts of children's movement without their birth parents, the difference between migration and trafficking is barely distinguishable. For instance, the ILO seems to suggest that these practices are now merging into one, when it states, '[c]entral to the phenomenon of trafficking in Africa is abuse of the tradition of placing children with extended families or other care-takers when they cannot be cared for by their parents' (ILO 2002: 3). Similarly, the International Organization for Migration (IOM) views child trafficking in Ghana, in part, to be related to child fostering, as made explicit by Ernest Taylor of the IOM Accra who commented that: 'Traditionally it has been a common practice for poor parents to hand over their children to be looked after by relatives and friends. Traffickers are now exploiting this age-old tradition resulting in parents inadvertently but effectively selling their children' (cited in Anarfi and Kwankye 2003: 24). In both Ghana and Burkina Faso rural children's migration has been a subject of national public and media concern in the last few years, and it has increasingly come to be equated with the trafficking of children. Alternatively, the migration of children is seen to be the result of pathological situations, such as conflict, abuse or poverty, and automatically to result in vulnerability to high levels of exploitation, harmful working conditions and/or abuse.

The practice of child fostering deserves a more elaborate discussion; both to show how the analysis of fostering has changed within the social sciences and to provide nuances to the simplified association of children's independent migration with trafficking. Fostering, where children reside in households other than their birth parents' and/or circulate between different social parents, has been common in many societies in Africa for a long time (Fentiman et al. 1999; Goody 1982; Meinert 2003; Notermans 2004; Pilon 2003; Verhoef 2005). This practice has been linked with migration and children's well-being in different ways in both the policy literature and in academic research. It is perceived to facilitate the international migration of adults, and especially women, because children can be left behind safely with close relatives. Fostering also accounts for children's local, regional and international migration for care and/or for their education, when they move to other households when their own cannot provide for them (Isiugo-Abanihe 1985: 55). Particularly in the literature on rural African societies, staying with kin at migration destinations is generally seen as beneficial and a safety mechanism for children who migrate because of parents' poverty or because of crises in the family linked with illness, death, divorce or fear of witchcraft (Einarsdóttir 2006; Isiugo-Abanihe 1985, 1994; Pilon 2003). Other researchers find that staying with kin is likely to result in children's abuse or exploitation (Ansell and Young 2002). Although these diverging views reflect the great variation in children's experiences and lived realities, they also reflect different methodological points of departure. The way fostering is described depends on the questions asked, whether they were directed at senior males, women or children, and how family relations in general are perceived. Thus, it is imperative to unpick the notions of childhood, children and families lying beneath quick references to 'traditional fostering practices' as a motivation for children's movement because these notions shape the interpretations of the empirical material. The notion of traditional practices is problematic in itself because it presents African communities as static and backward, denying the dynamism of and changes in the economic, social and cultural life of Africans, which have resulted in change and diversification in practices of child fostering.

Goody (1982), Isiugo-Abanihe (1985) and Jonckers (1997) outline how anthropologists and demographers have conceptualized the main features of fostering within a structural-functionalist paradigm as the need to reallocate resources within the kin group to increase survival and strengthen social ties, and to create and strengthen alliances with other lineages or important religious and political leaders. In this perspective, children are seen simply as resources on a par with other resources, and there is no discussion of family decision-making processes or relations between parents and children. These dimensions recur in many economic and demographic studies working with larger statistical data sets to model different effects of fostering practices – for example, on the availability of household labour or children's education. Some of these studies argue that fostering arrangements are linked with adjustments of the household structure to cope with risks in the form of exogenous income shocks or to satisfy labour demands within the household (Akresh 2004a, b). Alternatively, children are seen as important human capital assets in mitigating or preventing risks in poor families who lack other assets (Kielland 2009: 260). While Akresh (2004a) argues that fostering may have a positive outcome on children's education, Kielland and Sanogo (2002: 10) are more sceptical and argue that fostering today, especially of girls, often conceals exploitation of these children as domestic servants and, further, puts them at risk because they are not given love, protection and education. Fostering also is misdescribed by household economists who treat the family analytically as a black box and therefore assume that decisions within the household aim at maximizing the collective welfare, whether decisions are governed by joint altruism or by a benevolent household head (Smith and Chavas 1999: 4–5). From this perspective, it is not necessary to know how fostering decisions are made.

A shift of focus in kinship studies from the rigid understandings of genealogies and kinship in structural-functionalism (anglophone) and structuralism (francophone) towards a focus on relatedness and the making of kinship has pushed anthropologists to explore the motivations and decision-making processes involved in a foster child's relocation. This shift has shed light on women's, and especially elderly women's, diverse interests in fostering arrangements. Alber, for example, describes changes in fostering practices among the Baatombu in northern Benin, where women used to have strong rights in their daughters' second child and assumed full responsibility for the upbringing of fostered grandchildren from meeting their basic needs in childhood to ensuring their transition into adulthood and finding them a husband or wife. Her study shows a change in parents' willingness to accept fostering requests, which is rooted in aspirations of formal education for their children. As a result, the circulation of children has become more unidirectional from rural to urban areas, whereas previously urban-based parents would also accept sending a child to a grandmother living in a rural area (Alber 2004). This change indicates an ongoing shift in Baatomba notions of childhood as a period of learning skills in school but not necessarily in the home of a child's birth parents. In other words, the family is not conceptualized as a sedentary nuclear unit but as a multi-spatial group of people, who may offer children different possibilities.

Only in the past decade have children's perspectives on and experience of fostering been considered by anthropologists, sociologists and geographers. Child-centred research draws attention to children's choices in building or refusing kinship. A study in Indonesia, for example, shows how children act out their resistance to fostering arrangements in which they do not feel well treated by refusing to address their foster parents as 'Father' and 'Mother', even if it causes them to be punished because they transgress the code of respectful behaviour (Schrauwers 1999). Adolescents pursuing formal education in Sierra Leone may call on their birth parents to challenge maltreatment in the hope that they will be treated better or will be allowed to move to other foster parents. They are not always able to elicit support, however, and may be told to stick out hardship in order to advance their education (Bledsoe 1990). These studies show that, even if children cannot choose their residence freely, they may have a say in decisions, and they certainly try to negotiate the situation to their advantage with varying degrees of success. Notermans's work focusing on children's fostering trajectories and their experience of fostering bears witness to their active participation in the processes of making kinship – for example, by asking permission to join kin who might support their formal education. However, her study also highlights children's vulnerability when the circumstances in a household change and negatively affect their status within the household – for example, if jealousies and conflicts within the conjugal unit spill over to other household members. Such changes often compel children to move to other 'fathers', 'mothers' or 'grandmothers' on their own initiative or to be sent by the parent with whom they lived (Notermans 2008). The dynamic between moving on one's own initiative as opposed to being sent by an adult is an important one to highlight. All too often, children's relocation is described in terms of being sent.

Conclusion

Child-centred studies offer insights into the complex ways in which children respond to the circumstances of their everyday lives, inevitably influencing how we understand fostering arrangements and children's moves between different family or household members. Throughout the book, we will come back to this inquiry into children's use of kinship as one avenue for increasing their options in our bid to understand their choices.

Exploring children's choices and engagement in decision-making, we argue, is crucial to understanding their migration in a manner that neither romanticizes their strengths nor presents them as passive victims. It is especially important as missing from many accounts are what children themselves think about their movement and what role they play in their migration. Yet children themselves may play a big part in the decision to move (Andvig 2000). Indeed, the very possibility that children might be capable of exercising choice about whether or not to move is rejected in many perspectives, including in a number of legal instruments. One example is the Protocol to Prevent, Suppress and Punish Trafficking in Persons, Especially Women and Children supplementing the United Nations Convention against Transnational Organized Crime (often known as the Palermo Protocol), which distinguishes between smuggling and trafficking. Smuggling refers to the movement of individuals where the individual has consented, while trafficking involves the threat or use of force or other forms of coercion, abduction, fraud, deception or abuse of power. However, Article 3 of the protocol makes it explicit that in the case of those under the age of eighteen the issue of consent is irrelevant if their movement is considered to be for the purposes of exploitation (ILO 2002; UN 2000). The implication is that those under the age of eighteen are incapable of exercising meaningful choice, in the process inextricably linking the status of 'child' with that of 'victim' or 'potential victim' (O'Connell Davidson 2005). Hopkins and Hill make a similar point in a discussion of the difference between the category of unaccompanied asylum-seeking children and that of separated children. Unaccompanied children are 'defined as those who are younger than 18 years old who have been separated from both parents [and] are not being cared for by an adult who, by law or custom, has a responsibility to do so' (UNHCR 2005, cited in Hopkins and Hill 2008: 258). In contrast, the Separated Children in Europe Programme prefers to use the term 'separated' to highlight the fact that the children may not be unaccompanied, but may actually be travelling with others, such as a trafficker or sibling (ibid.: 258). The reason the term 'separated' is preferred, apparently, is because it 'better defines the essential problem that children face, which is that they are without the care and protection of their parents or legal guardian' (Save the Children (SCF) 2004: 2, cited in Hopkins and Hill 2008: 258). Hopkins and Hill argue, however, that 'the term "separated" implies passivity and overlooks the children's agency, since some of the children may have chosen to move' (ibid.).

This presentation of childhood contrasts with those in different African societies, where children are conceptualized as agents, even as babies (Gottlieb 1998; Nyamnjoh 2002). We would also point out that underlying both terms is an assumption that a child moving without their birth parents or legal guardian is *automatically* vulnerable.

Overall, as researchers have pointed out, dualistic categories such as adult/ child, forced/voluntary, and so on, smooth out differences in the experiences, needs and circumstances of migrant children, while obscuring the interplay between structure and human agency in shaping those experiences (Hopkins and Hill 2008; O'Connell Davidson 2005). An important link exists between agency and age, which has legal, developmental and social dimensions and needs to be considered; and thus the issue is not simply about agency but structure too. As Vandenbroeck and Bouverne-de Bie suggest (2006: 140), 'the analysis of agency on the psychological level may benefit from a structural point of view, just as the structural analysis needs to take the personal agency into account'.

Thus, throughout the book, we attempt to move back and forth between children's roles in their own movements, and how these are curtailed or facilitated by their environments, and the social relations in which they are enmeshed. At the core of the book are our own two studies with independent child migrants. Although there are many similarities between our communities of origin, such as the high rates of inter-household mobility that are a feature of many West African savannah communities, the differing research strategies we adopted, as well as the different settings to which migrants moved, make direct comparisons impossible. This in any case is not our purpose. Rather, our aim is to contribute to the growing body of child-centred studies that not only question the normative assumptions and discourses in many of the approaches to issues related to children, but which try to foreground children's own views.

The rest of the book is organized as follows: in Chapter 2, we consider the nature of the economic and social relations in the places of origin and how these influence girls' and boys' aspirations to move and family members' incentives to permit or discourage their children's movement. The theme of the importance of context and how it influences why children move continues in Chapter 3, which explores how poverty and its gendered dimensions impact on the range of options girls and boys have. In Chapter 4, we explore children's journeys and how they make kinship relations and use them as a means to become migrants. In this chapter, we also pose the question of how migrant relatives feed the imagination of children and thus bear on their motivations to become migrants.

In Chapter 5, we examine migrant children's lived realities at the destination and explore the activities in which they engage and through which they enact different identities, reflecting how they interpret their position in society, within their family and/or their peer group. In Chapter 6, we explore in more detail what our empirical work contributes to investigating children's migration in a manner that enables both negative and positive aspects of children's mobility to be considered, which in turn leads us to examine, in this concluding chapter, the key question of how we conceptualize children's agency.

2 | Contexts of migration

'We arrived at the household of Ayaraga Mbilla at about 9 a.m. to begin the detailed questionnaire. The household head wasn't ready for us so we sat and waited under a tree. There was a man in his 30s sitting outside in the shade (the brother's son I think), who said he was "resting small" as he had spent all morning on the farm. A little apart, the young girl with the limp (polio I suspect) whom I'd noticed before, as usual was looking after the baby. She must be about ten or so. A boy a little older was husking maize and two other boys were just hanging around. A girl of about 15 came out of the compound with a basket of millet and started to winnow it. A group of about ten young men then arrived and grabbed sticks that were lying outside. They jostled and fought for the best ones, and then went inside with the household head's brother's son. There were pounding noises and occasionally they would burst into song. They were threshing rice. Two tiny children in the distinctive purple uniform of the nursery school arrived. We asked them why they had come back from school. They were so shy they were barely able to bring themselves to talk to us. Apparently, the teachers had a meeting in town so had sent the children home. They went inside and then reappeared minutes later, minus uniforms, and disappeared off; to play presumably. Even now, I still can't get used to how such young children are free to move around unsupervised. A young woman then appeared and started breastfeeding the baby. She said something to the teenage girl who went off, after fetching a large basin from inside. She came back about 15 minutes later with water, I assume for the threshing party since it was not from the nearby well, but from the borehole. The household head then arrived and apologised for keeping us waiting. He commented that he had forgotten we were coming today and that the household's women "had escaped early" for work, since it is harvesting time, so they were not available to be interviewed. Nor were his brother's granddaughter and grandson, who were at school.' (Field notes from Ghana, 15 November 2000)

This extract from one of our field diaries represents a typical morning during harvest time in farming households of the savannah areas of West Africa, where we have undertaken our research. It illustrates how children are occupied with a variety of activities that include work, in addition to learning and play. These dimensions of rural childhood contrast with the universalized ideals of childhood discussed in the opening chapter, which portray childhood as a 'work-free, dependent, vulnerable and care-receiving phase of life' (Abebe 2007: 78) and one consisting of school or playful leisure (Boyden 1997; Robson 2004b: 239). Undoubtedly the extent and nature of children's work varies according to a variety of factors such as age, gender, household wealth and whether they are raised in a rural or urban setting (Punch 2001a: 806). Nonetheless, for many children work can and does occupy a significant amount of their time (Hashim 2004; Katz 2004; Nieuwenhuys 1994; Reynolds 1991).

Significantly, work is a central part of children's identity formation and both self-perceptions and others' perceptions of them as 'a good child' (Hashim 2004: 83). This is well illustrated in a conversation that took place in the Upper East Region of Ghana with fifteen-year-old Aduma, as he built a protective mud wall around his onion seedlings planted on land 'begged' (borrowed) from a neighbour whom he had repaid with onion seed.

> If they send you [to the farm] and you go, your parents will note this and help you. Those that don't go will be seen as a bad child. When I'm free I go to my own work. I decide myself. If I don't and sit down, how will I get to eat [...] All that children do in the household is important because it brings money to the household and the children can even get money and give it to the landlord [household head] to drink *pito* [millet beer]. [...] My work for my family is important because it is where they will get their food to eat. It is also good for me because I'll get food too and get strength that will allow me to go to my own work and get money [...] Because of my work for them, if I have friends to help me with my rice farming, they will fetch millet for me to prepare food for them. [...] And when I marry my father will give me the animals for my bride-wealth.

Adamu's narrative introduces the general discourse on children's position in their household in his community and underscores our argument that a narrow conceptualization of childhood as a period free from work does not capture the reality of childhood in the West African context. His description and understanding of his work, its role in acquiring practical and social skills, as well as its economic significance, and the role it plays in creating interdependencies between different categories of people inside and outside of the household, demonstrate how the universalized ideals of childhood are entirely inadequate for understanding many children's lives. We argue, therefore, that it is imperative to pay attention to the set of ideas and practices that constitute childhood in a particular context and acknowledge their validity, even if they differ from the universalized model. Only through addressing the specific forms of childhood experience that are the context for migration decisions is it possible to understand children's migration. In this chapter, we lay the foundation for a situated understanding of the young migrants who are the primary focus of the book by providing information about the rural areas from which they originate. This is important for following our arguments in the subsequent chapters but, at the

Map 2.1 The research areas in West Africa

Legend:
- ★ Area of child migrants' origin
- ● Destination area where child migrants were interviewed
- ○ Significant town
- ⌇ International boundary

MALI

BURKINA FASO

◉ Ouagadougou

PAYS BISA ★

○ Bobo Dioulasso

Bolgatanga ○

★ BAWKU EAST DISTRICT

○ Korhogo

○ Tamale

CÔTE D'IVOIRE

GHANA

TOGO

Yamoussoukrou ○

Abengourou ○

Kumasi ◉

LIBERIA

Abidjan ●◎

○ Aboisso

○ Accra

Sassandra ○

○ San Pedro

Gulf of Guinea

0 — 150km
0 — 75 miles

abstract level, the chapter also raises questions that are imperative to examine in every context where children's mobility is scrutinized.

Communities generating child migrants

Although the children we have undertaken research with come from communities located in different countries and colonial language zones and are comprised of different ethnic groups (Bisa in Burkina Faso and Kusasi in Ghana[1]), as is evident from the map above, they are located only some 125 miles apart and share many social, cultural and economic similarities. Historically, the two communities are linked through the resettlement during colonial rule of Bisa families in the area inhabited by Kusasi without subsequent ethnic conflicts. In this section, the similarities between our communities will be laid out, which will also facilitate a discussion at the end of the chapter of the differences in migratory trajectories evidenced in the two contexts, particularly along gender lines, despite these similarities. This will serve to illustrate further the importance of in-depth knowledge of the context from which children move when attempting to comprehend fully children's independent migration.

The communities in which we work are among the poorest in Burkina Faso and Ghana. In Burkina Faso, Pays Bisa is located in Province du Boulgou, Région Centre-est, where the proportion of the population earning an income below the national poverty line of 82,672 CFA francs per year (approximately US$0.36 per day) was 55.1 per cent in 2003 (INSD 2008a). Asset-based well-being indicators also show that 23.4 per cent of the households in this region are poor and 34.0 per cent very poor – values that are somewhat higher than those for the entire country, which are 21.5 per cent and 23.3 per cent respectively (INSD 2008b). Levels of poverty are comparable to those of the Bawku East district[2] of the Upper East Region of Ghana, from where the children in the Ghanaian research originate. The region was identified as the poorest in the country and one where poverty had got worse when Canagarajah and Pörtner examined the regional trends in poverty in Ghana on the basis of the 1991/92 and 1998/99 rounds of the Ghana Living Standards Survey (Canagarajah and Pörtner 2002: 22).

Both communities' principal livelihood strategy consists of farming, which is rain-fed and has a low level of mechanization where ox-ploughs substitute for the hoe – for those who can afford an ox or its hire. They are also both located within a large belt of West African savannah in which households on average are quite large, and inheritance and kinship affiliation is patrilineal. The communities are exogamous, with wives moving to live in their husbands' communities on marriage. One other important common feature of these societies is the way in which households are organized as intricate layers of sub-units through which individuals are linked with one another and make claims on resources. What this means is that, normatively, household heads have a heavy responsibility for ensuring sufficient food for all household members ('dependants' or 'juniors') and for managing livestock, so larger expenses for healthcare, funerals and young men's marriage can be met (Whitehead 1998: 22–5). To do this they use the labour of all household members, who are expected to contribute to production on household farms. By working in this way, household members make implicit claims on food, shelter and other collective resources. Household heads are also concerned about maintaining a web of social relations to facilitate good marriages for children of both genders, and to access resources and assistance if need be (Thorsen 2005: 96–101).

In addition to their work on the compound farms, all household members are allowed to farm independently, organizing the work and controlling the crops or income realized. The extent to which they are able to spend time on these independent economic activities, however, depends on the gender, age and status of a dependant. We found that, as was the case in earlier years (see Whitehead 1996)[3], among the Kusasi, young male youth, for example, spend considerable time in household fields and may be 'sent out' to communal work parties. In contrast, a middle-aged but junior brother of a household head may have his own granaries and considerable independent income and largely be providing separately for his wives and children. He may work on his older brother's farms only on certain symbolic occasions. The household head will still call on his wives and children, and in return each wife will have a share in the periodic distributions of grain from the household head's granaries (ibid.). Similar patterns for the organization of male labour exist among the Bisa, but here women have a more significant role in household food security. In Zéké village, for example, married women's independent farms accounted for around one third of the cultivated land in 1997/98 and much of their land was planted with millet, the main staple (Thorsen 2002). Although girls and women work in the household fields[4] and attend working parties on behalf of the household head, they sometimes negotiate and are allocated time to work on their own farms for the entire day, especially in households where many women are the wives of absent migrants or are widowed (Thorsen 2005).

Women's obligations are demanding, given both the nature of labour hierarchies in these contexts and the arduousness of domestic tasks. In addition to their roles in farming, they are responsible for processing foodstuffs and for providing ingredients for the soups that accompany the staple porridge. They are also responsible for other domestic tasks, such as childcare, water collection, cooking and cleaning. In contrast to their responsibilities in farming, however, Kusasi women do this work only for their husbands and children (Hashim 2004; Whitehead 1996), while age-based hierarchies among Bisa women imply that young married women carry out much domestic work for their mother-in-law and often serve an elderly household head food and water (Thorsen 2005). The hierarchical system of control and command over labour means that a successful household head is one who manages the balance between the various kinds of activities of household members and who is successful in the social management of negotiations and tensions around this (Whitehead 1996: 111–12).

From a young age, children are encouraged and expected to contribute to the household's subsistence. This is a theme we will treat in more detail below; here it suffices to offer a quick overview of what is expected of children growing up in these farming communities. From when they are first able to toddle around, children are helping with tasks such as caring for their siblings and running errands. From age seven onwards their activities begin to make a contribution to the running of the household and to its livelihood activities. By the age of fourteen, they are carrying out all those tasks that adults of their gender are able and expected to do. Children's tasks are gendered to the extent that few activities are undertaken both by boys and by girls. Adolescents are significant labour assets. Girls are essential to the domestic running of most households, since domestic labour is both arduous and time-consuming. Most women farm and/or engage in income-generating activities, such as the brewing of beer or trade, so they benefit from the additional labour of young girls or their taking over of domestic tasks so the mother has more time on her hands (Hashim 2004: 58). As we have noted, male youth, too, are significant labour assets, and the part they play in communal work parties secures their household heads' moral claims on labour when they require their own reciprocal labour, which is important in contexts such as these, given the labour-intensive nature of particular farming tasks (Whitehead 1996: 253).

Unpredictable rainfall coupled with highly depleted soil fertility and increasing demands on land in the face of a growing population has meant that it is difficult to secure subsistence through farming (Awumbila 1997; Devereux 1992; Dietz and Millar 1999; Mazzucato and Niemeijer 2000; Reenberg and Lund 1998; Roncoli et al. 2002). In both areas, cotton and rice have been introduced as cash crops. Although rice is an important cash crop in the Bawku East district, in Pays Bisa long delays in the provision of grain for seeding and payment for cotton crops, as well as falling prices, have undermined the economic potential of these crops. Even in the Bawku East district, despite this diversification, making a living from farming is a stressful and arduous task. Consequently, as we have noted, most households in both areas are very poor, and, like other farming households in such circumstances, they engage in multiple activities to secure their immediate as well as long-term well-being (see Whitehead and Kabeer 2001). These livelihood activities include the rearing of livestock, hand-irrigated gardening and off-farm activities, such as petty trading or artisan production. The other key livelihood strategy for both communities is that of migration.

Histories of migration

The literature on migration frequently presents the movement of individuals away from a household as a means of reducing demand on scant resources and/or of diversifying potential sources of income (Cordell et al. 1996; de Haan 1999; Hoddinott 1992). Certainly, for many years, large numbers of people have travelled out of rural areas to take up seasonal or longer-term work (Cordell et al. 1996; Breusers 1998; Zongo 2003). The migration system from the West African savannah to the plantations in the coastal countries has been comparable in importance and duration with the system of labour migration to the mines in southern Africa (Cordell et al. 1996). The communities in which we work are no exception. When addressing the migration of children independently of their families, it is important to take into consideration these scales of migration, as well as their history, to understand how people of all ages think about relocation, the status of migrants and the effects of migration on well-being.

In the Upper Volta (now Burkina Faso), the movement of people, especially of young men, soared in the years of colonial rule, when the French developed a system of taxation and labour conscription to pay for the costs of the administration and to develop the Ivorian plantation economy (Breusers 1998: 102; Şaul and Royer 2001: 88). These policies were similar to those of other colonial powers; the difference being the degree of force imposed on the local population to make them comply with the colonial rulers' objectives. While the French coerced their subjects to work on French-owned plantations in Côte d'Ivoire, the British colonial administration pursued a policy of underdeveloping the north of the Gold Coast (now Ghana) precisely to promote its role largely as a labour reserve for the south (Thomas 1973). Migrants from Burkina Faso also moved to the cocoa-growing areas of the Gold Coast, in part to evade labour conscription and in part to benefit from the higher wages. However, when the cocoa economy declined in the late 1950s, along with northern Ghanaians, they increasingly shifted their migration from Ghana to the thriving cocoa farms in Côte d'Ivoire (Anarfi and Kwankye 2003; Finnegan 1976).

Earlier sources describe migration from the savannah as occurring during the long dry season, when there was little or no farm work to be done (Caldwell 1969); however, by the 1970s most labour migration was much more long term, with men staying away for several years (Cordell et al. 1996; Whitehead 1996). By the late 1980s, long-term migrants from northern Ghana also shifted their destinations from cocoa-growing areas to work in rural Côte d'Ivoire because of the adverse economic situation throughout Ghana. By 2000, adult male migrants had been joined by significant numbers of women and children and were working and living away, and more migrants were once again working in the cocoa-growing regions of Ghana, which by then had expanded from the south into the centre of the country. Migrants of rural origin did not limit themselves to plantation work but also spread into the cities to take up various kinds of trades, piecemeal work and other income-generating activities, especially when world cocoa prices declined throughout the 1990s, making its production less profitable (Amanor 2001).

The history of female migrants is not described to the same extent and in the same detail as past male migrations. However, a few studies in francophone West Africa have examined panel data on migration to shed light on gender differences among migrants aged twelve to twenty-five. A study in Burkina Faso showed that whereas in the 1950s female first-time migrants were either family helpers or enumerated as 'unoccupied', their occupations had become more diverse by the late 1980s and 1990s. By then 39 per cent of the young female migrants were self-employed, 15 per cent were students, 2 per cent apprentices, 2 per cent private sector employees and the remaining 42 per cent family helpers or 'unoccupied' (Le Jeune et al. 2004: 161–6). Another study from Mali combining census panel data and interviews shows that while boys' labour migration rose steadily in the 1940s and 1950s, girls' labour migration picked up only in the early 1970s. By the 1990s, boys mostly travelled to other rural areas to work as farm labour and herders, while 90 per cent of the girls travelled to urban areas to become domestic workers. This migration is particularly important for girls, argue the authors, because they build up a material and symbolic capital that enables them to assert themselves in a more personal way and increases the way they are valued by their peers, but also by young men (Hertrich and Lesclingand 2007). Lambert's historical analysis of young Jola women's migration in Senegal shows that some girls and young women migrated to the Senegambian groundnut basin in the 1930s, where they helped their brothers and received a small remuneration in kind for their work. Jola women became independent migrants in the 1950s and 1960s when increasing urbanization opened up possibilities for domestic work (Lambert 2007).

In spite of the civil war in Côte d'Ivoire, which escalated in 2002, migration to the country remains a source of livelihood for both rural populations. This is especially so for the Burkinabé migrants who, in 1998, comprised 56 per cent of the migrant population in Côte d'Ivoire, whereas a mere 3.3 per cent were Ghanaian migrants. About half of the Burkinabé migrants and one quarter of the Ghanaian migrants were born in Côte d'Ivoire (Bredeloup 2003: 90–91). Although many were forced to leave the country early in the civil war, many also remained, either because they were too poor to return or because they had invested all their savings in property or businesses with a view to remaining permanently. The accounts told by people in Pays Bisa in 2005 revealed that, throughout the civil war, both men and women continued to travel to and from Côte d'Ivoire because the wage levels and income from trade were still considerably higher than in Burkina Faso, in spite of the deteriorating employment opportunities.

Thus, the historical roots of migration in both areas have continued as a dominant experience for most households in the region, to the extent that the 2000 Population and Housing Census found that of the 379,007 Kusasi indigenous to the Upper East Region of Ghana, only 192,360 were residing there (GSS 2002: 23). Surveys we each undertook in our communities of origin indicate similarly high levels of migration. For example, 68 per cent of household heads in the village of Tempane Natinga in Ghana's Upper East Region reported that they had at least one adult male migrant and 13.5 per cent had four or more in 2001.[5] Similarly, in Zéké village in Pays Bisa, 85 per cent of the households had at least one adult male migrant and 12 per cent had four or more in 2005.[6]

Children may also have spent their early years in towns or villages in Côte d'Ivoire or southern Ghana or have seen their mothers travel abroad to spend a couple of years with their father before returning to the village. With few exceptions, the current generation of fathers and grandfathers in Pays Bisa and Bawku East district have been migrants to the central and southern regions of Ghana or to Côte d'Ivoire, as have some mothers and some grandmothers.

27

At social gatherings, stories about migrant life and urban lifestyles in Accra, Abidjan, Kumasi and Ouagadougou often crop up, both to reinforce the social status attained as migrants and to obtain information about current migrants. Children see older relatives leave the village and return looking fatter and more smartly dressed, and bringing gifts and money to invest in livestock, housing, consumer items and other desirable objects.

Clear, too, is that children's migration without their parents is also extensive. For example, in Tempane Natinga, 51 of its 96 households reported having at least one independent child migrant. Moreover, the total is probably higher, given the sex-ratio discrepancy between girls and boys (190 to 257 respectively), which is likely to be due in part to the under-reporting of girl migrants. Moreover, migration was not only out of the village but also into it; the polio-inflicted girl in the opening extract being one example. The normality of children's movement between households is well illustrated in the following case study of just one household in Ghana's Upper East Region.

> A young man, Paul, who is aged 30, heads this farming household. Paul is the most junior of five brothers, the other four brothers being migrants, three in the south of Ghana and one in Côte d'Ivoire. Other household members include Paul's aged mother, his wife and their baby daughter. In addition, Paul's wife's teen-aged sister lives with them to help with childcare and domestic work while her elder sister carries out some petty trading and trains as a seamstress. Another teen-aged girl living in the household is the second-born brother's daughter who helps her grandmother with her domestic work. Also in the household is one of Paul's eldest brother's sons, aged about 17, and the third-born brother's 14-year-old son, who was sent back by his parents in order to receive 'traditional' treatment for the epilepsy from which he suffers. The 17-year-old moved into the household a few years earlier to assist Paul by looking after the livestock and to carry out farm work. Prior to this, his older brother had lived in this household for a number of years for the same reason. He had then moved to the third brother's household, in Côte d'Ivoire, to look after this brother's family and property while the brother was away on long trips, trading in kola and other goods between Ghana and Nigeria.

Children's worlds and work

Children in the majority world undertake a myriad of work tasks. Girls and boys of all ages work in rural locations in agriculture, in domestic tasks and as cattle-herders (Abebe 2007; Hashim 2004; Katz 2004; Nieuwenhuys 1994; Punch 2001a; Reynolds 1991), as well as in fishing (Anarfi and Kwankye 2003; Caouette 2001). They work in the informal economy of urban areas as hawkers, shoe shiners and porters (Agarwal et al. 1997; Anarfi and Kwankye 2003; Beauchemin 1999; Castle and Diarra 2003; Khair 2005; Kwankye et al. 2007; Thorsen 2007b), as garbage collectors (Khair 2005), as well as assistants to market women (Robson 2004a; Schildkrout 1981). They can work as carers (Robson 2004b) and be employed in factories (Cauoette 2001; Nieuwenhuys 1995), in shops, restaurants (Castle and Diarra 2003; Thorsen 2009c) and hotels (Iversen 2002), in mining (Bøås and Hatløy 2008), the construction industry, commercial agriculture (Bastia 2005; Punch 2007), and as domestic workers (Camacho 1999; Jacquemin 2004; Khair 2005; Somerfelt 2001) and in the commercial sex industry (Caouette 2001; Montgomery 2001; O'Connell Davidson 2005).

These various studies of children's work indicate that children's tasks can be paid or unpaid, that they can work for themselves, for their families or for others, and that the work in which they participate involves a wide range and varying degrees of hazard (Hashim 2008). The majority, though, are more concerned with children working in abusive and exploitative situations, primarily because they are oriented towards advocacy or policy issues, often responding to the huge attention that the issues of child labour and child trafficking have received in the last decade or so. This international advocacy has been effective in highlighting the plight of those children in particularly difficult circumstances. However, it has also resulted in a totalizing discourse where the diversity of children's experiences and work situations becomes treated as equivalent, reducing all working children to the status of victims, and serving to shore up a characterization of them as without agency (O'Connell Davidson 2005; Whitehead and Hashim 2005).

It has also had a number of other repercussions. For one, certain aspects of children's work have remained largely unconsidered. Katz, for instance, bemoans the paucity of data on children's labour in rural areas, especially in domestic work, arguing that even when it is discussed it is rarely documented systematically, which she suggests reflects the metropolitan concern with remuneration and the market (Katz 2004: 279). It is also the case that work for one's own household has tended to be considered as 'helping out' and not genuine work (see, for example, Bequele and Boyden 1988; ILO 1997); consequently, little attention has been given to children's work in the domestic arena (Hashim 2004: 16). This is despite the fact that many children work as unremunerated members of their families' labour force (Nieuwenhuys 1994: 203); the majority of the 90 per cent of child labour in Ghana, for example, being unpaid family workers involved in family farms and enterprises (Canagarajah and Coulombe 1997: 10). Zelizer, for her part, argues that the dominance of attention to child labour and its representation as a corrupting force has inhibited careful examination of children's economic activity, little consideration being given to children as authentic economic agents (Zelizer 2002: 377). Whitehead et al. suggest that this is largely due to perceptions of children as economic dependants in the family (Whitehead et al. 2007: 37–8).

Third, a very austere picture of children's engagement in tasks that contribute to production and reproduction has been painted. In contrast, many child-centred studies present an alternative picture. Katz, for example, refers to how play and work intertwine in children's lives in a village in the Sudan where she carried out her research, where children 'worked at play and played at work. They worked while they played and played while they worked, they worked around their play and they played in the interstices of their work' (Katz 2004: 60). In our own research, we frequently found that this was the case too, even when the work was tough, as three young cattle-herders made evident when they were observed taking turns to chase the cattle away from the crops, between times playing and wrestling and swimming in the dam.

This morning at 8 a.m. we found two young boys sitting under a tree while another boy was chasing some cattle away from crops. They were Michael, who is nine, Luke, who is ten or so, and Abugre, who is old for a herder at about 13. As usual, after some initial shyness, they were eager to tell me about their experiences. Apparently, they bring out the cattle at about 7 a.m. to graze and then take them down to the dam at around midday to drink, before finding a shady area to rest until sunset, when they take them home and pen them. They were looking after about 30 cattle in total and they take it in turns to chase the cattle away from the crops, starting with the most junior. When I asked them how they decided who was the most junior they told me it was decided by wrestling. They drank water from a well as we went down to the dam and took the opportunity to have a dip, although the respite didn't last long as other herders arrived and the animals got mixed up, so they chased their cattle, whacking them to separate them from the others. (Field notes from Ghana, 30 October 2000)

Girls in Pays Bisa used the occasion of work parties as an opportunity for gossip and banter.

Four adolescent girls, one of whom had recently married, had entered a small rotational work party arrangement with a woman in her mid-30s; this day, when we were working along, they were harvesting her bambara groundnuts and in the following days they would harvest each girl's field in turn. During the work we chatted and the girls were accusing the Fulani herders, who had settled in their village, of being sorcerers because one of them had beaten a pregnant woman from the neighbouring household during a quarrel. At another much larger work party to harvest millet, where all the participants had been sent by their household heads, young girls were gossiping about a married woman whose husband was in Côte d'Ivoire. Although they were made up beautifully, with coloured dots on their foreheads and cheeks to attract the attention of young men at the work party, they echoed adult gossip and disapproval in their own manner by noting that it was frightening how that woman applied make-up. (Field notes from Burkina Faso, 15 October and 10 December 2001)

What these examples illustrate is the risk of separating activities from their meanings if we look at children's work in isolation. As a result, we fail to understand that, in addition, for example, to constructing an identity of being a good child through work, the social context of the work, of running an errand or participating in ceremonies on behalf of an adult, gives children the opportunity to develop other identities through observing, reflecting and participating. Thus, it is not just play which is integrated with work in this way, but also the learning of a variety of practical and social skills.

Work is a central part of children's lives and reflects the high value placed on hard work in the West African savannah. The principal greeting from a passer-by to those engaged in any activity, for instance, in Kusasi vernacular is *tom'e tom'e* and in Bisa vernacular *zibeu-zibeu* – terms that literally translate as 'work work' and signify that the passer-by wishes the worker good luck. However, people never compelled young children to work, but children were present in all work spheres and were encouraged to take up small tasks by their parents and older siblings, such as collecting water or caring for younger siblings. Tasks were usually carried out in the company of other children and under the guidance of adults, and children took significant pride in their participation in work, in the rewards for their work or in the purchasing of small items from the proceeds of their work.

> Five-year-old Pascal was very proud that he had participated in a work party in his own right that day. It was a work party called by one of the old women in the household and before setting off to her farm, he had told his mother that she didn't need to call him when the meal was ready for he was off to a work party and would eat there. (Field notes from Burkina Faso, 1 October 2001)

Although young children in the village in the Upper East Region of Ghana also were not compelled to work, they sometimes were accused of being lazy if they refused to work. Expectations grew, though, as they became older, and sanctions could be more severe, in extreme cases with the withholding of food or beatings (Hashim 2004: 90). Thus, by the age of twelve or thirteen, as was the case among the Bisa, children were increasingly expected to contribute, and so became integrated into all tasks and obliged to take part in agricultural work.

Our findings are in keeping with other studies of children's work in both developing and industrialized countries, which indicate that the amount and type of children's participation in tasks increase as they get older and that the tasks they perform increase in complexity and responsibility (Punch 2001a: 806). Work thus becomes more important to children's sense of self as they get older and is as central to being a child as it is to being an adult. Children's development is often measured in terms of their embracing a positive attitude to work (Hashim 2004: 78), as reflected in Adamu's story above.

Although parents and grandparents are concerned that children become

31

skilled at various economic and social activities, also important was that children adopted a sense of self-reliance, as nicely described by Lamisi in the village of Tempane Natinga. 'As children grow they follow you to the farm but then they grow enough to see that they, by themselves, want to start doing something for themselves. You pull back small and then they are responsible for themselves' (ibid.: 78). Similarly, in Pays Bisa, Minneta's mother often told anecdotes about her youngest children, among others about her seven-year-old daughter's dream of selling the harvest from her tiny rice field to pay for her school enrolment. Some weeks later, she helped her daughter buy school clothes, adding a little extra money to the revenue from the rice (Thorsen 2005: 143). Children are expected and encouraged both to contribute and to provide for themselves by engaging in economic activities, usually by being allocated a small field. Among the Bisa, most boys and some girls have a rice field from an early age and older boys also tended to have a millet field, while the girls had a groundnut field. In Tempane Natinga almost all boys and girls from age ten and sometimes younger had a small rice field, although younger children did not produce enough to earn very much from their farming. In the dry season, older boys in their mid to late teens farmed onions if they had access to the land, but older girls did not. This, in part, accounts for the differences we found in the likelihood of girls migrating, as we shall explore later.

Children did not always spend their money in ways of which their parents approved – spending it on sweets, for instance; but what is clear is that children in these contexts exercise autonomy[7] over their own income. Among the Kusasi, children tended to buy things like soap and, their income supplemented by their parents as a means to encourage and reward them, cloth to be made into clothing for celebrations. However, as they get older and are able either to produce more or to pursue other income-generating activities, in addition to cloth and soap, children begin to purchase those items that are necessary for their progression into adulthood; namely pots, basins and bowls, in the case of girls, and livestock to rear, in the case of boys. If they are students, they often take on some of the costs associated with their schooling. Older children also give gifts to seniors who have assisted them with land or labour. In so doing, they are demonstrating an understanding of the nature of social relations in this context (Hashim 2004: 81).

Thus in the contexts in which we work, children's core pursuits are, at all ages, doing many domestic, farming and livelihood tasks. Moreover, it is not simply that children have to work – for example, because of family or community poverty – but that work is seen as correct behaviour for children. Both children and adults define a good child by conformity to such behaviour. Undoubtedly, there are differences in children's working roles on the basis of age and gender, but, crucially, work is fundamentally implicated in the identity of a child and working is viewed as part of her or his 'healthy' development.

Children's worlds and learning

As discussed in Chapter 1, childhood and formal education became inextricably linked during the changes in the industrialized world in the nineteenth century. As a result, one of the key concepts that has become intrinsic to the definition of 'average' or 'normal' childhood is formal education (Boyden 1997: 200). There is a tendency, consequently, to view children's inability to access schooling as an opportunity denied (Hashim 2007), both because it is seen as a precondition for economic growth and social development, and importantly because of its role in individual self-realization (Kabeer 2000: 463). Although the normalcy of schooling rarely comes into question, constantly under debate is formal education's purpose (e.g. to prepare children to join the workforce or to facilitate them to pursue their unique strengths and interests), its most appropriate content (e.g. basic skills acquisition or critical thinking) and the best means of providing it (e.g. teacher-imparted information or student-led learning). Policy-makers nevertheless do perceive universal formal education as important, because it is seen as vital to economic development and to the proper functioning of the social and political process (Boyden 1997; Cheney 2007; Kabeer 2000). Consequently, national governments, as well as organizations such as the World Bank and the IMF, pursue a policy of increasing school enrolment and attendance rates in the belief that only through increasing formal education will countries be able to develop. In particular, the United Nations Educational, Scientific and Cultural Organization's (UNESCO) initiative of Education for All (EFA) in 1990 established an international commitment to bring the benefits of formal education to every citizen in every society; this was reaffirmed in 2000, when 189 countries adopted two of the EFA goals among the eight Millennium Development Goals (MDGs).

Owing in part to EFA, both Ghana (see GME 1999) and Burkina Faso (see Ministère de l'Enseignement de Base et de l'Alphabétisation)[8] pursue the principle of free primary schooling. However, although in theory primary schooling is free, we both found that schools usually demanded levies for a range of items, such as equipment, extra teachers, lunches and other items and services, some of which benefit the schoolchildren while others do not. These costs, in addition to others, such as for uniforms, textbooks and notebooks, are significant in a context where most families are poor or very poor and family sizes large, placing formal education for all household children out of the reach of many.

This is reflected in the relatively low rates of school uptake in both our communities of origin. In the village of Tempane Natinga in the Upper East Region of Ghana, for example, only 62 per cent of school-aged children were enrolled in 2000/01. It is important to note, too, that these children were concentrated in the early stages of the formal educational system, with 47 per cent being enrolled in primary school, 10 per cent in junior secondary and just 5 per cent in senior secondary school. This contrasts with the national gross primary enrolment rate of 73 per cent for boys and 71 for girls,[9] between 2000 and 2007 (UNICEF 2008: 134).

Across the border to the north, in the Bisa region, the formal educational take-up rates were even lower. In 1999/2000, the primary school uptake was as low as 24 per cent at the district level (Koné 2001) but 35.1 per cent at the regional level and 43.0 per cent at the national level. By 2007/08, the enrolment rates had increased to 69.8 per cent and 72.5 per cent at the regional and national levels respectively (INSD 2008a), but it is difficult to say whether this increase is also reflected in more remote rural villages. Even within the Bisa region, school development differs significantly. Some villages had schools built in the 1970s and early 1980s, while others still do not have any school buildings. The primary school in Zéké village where we lived opened only in 1988 and served three small villages. In 1992/93 it had 160 pupils (44 girls and 116 boys) (Berthelette 2001) and the number increased slightly in 1999/2000 to 176 pupils (55 girls and 121 boys). It decreased again in 1999/2000, when only 109 children attended (28 girls and 81 boys) (Koné 2001). This decrease reflected the disillusionment felt by parents when the teachers pleaded with the school authorities to be moved to schools in rural towns or, at least, to larger, less remote villages. Nonetheless, in both our cases most parents, even in the poorest families, enrolled at least one child in primary school, only thirteen households in Tempane Natinga, for example, having no children enrolled in school.

Despite the difficulties associated with schooling, some children were not only successful in completing schooling but went to extraordinary lengths to do so, as exemplified by the story of one teenaged boy, who was in the first year of junior secondary school in Tempane Natinga.

In 2000, David was 14 years old and lived in a large household of 18 people. His father, Abanga, who was in his 50s, was the head of the household. Overall, David's family was very poor. His father had no education and described himself as a farmer, but produced very little. He was also a well digger and earned some income from this. David's mother grew a little rice, but, because she was sickly, was unable to do much. David, for his part, was very active. In fact, it took two weeks of us trying to interview him before he was available because he was so busy with a variety of different activities. In addition to farming rice, he farmed bambara groundnuts and onions. David also engaged in other income-generating activities. Along with two friends, he contracted himself out to work on people's farms during the rainy season and to build mud walls around onion farms in the dry season. In the school holidays, he pushed a donkey cart and sold water in the district capital, Bawku. David spent his income on school levies, books, pens, eggs to rear guinea fowl, ingredients for his mother to cook for a work party to weed his father's farm and, because he had no time to collect this himself, grass for roofing the compound's rooms. Although David's mother had paid most of his school costs until Primary Six, since then he had covered all expenses himself, except for his uniform, which was bought for him by his senior brother; himself a migrant to the south.

It is clear from David's story that he was working incredibly hard to put himself through school; not only by covering his school expenses, but also by securing the necessary labour to ensure that vital farm work was done. However, by 2004 David had dropped out of school and was working in nearby Garu, operating a grinding mill. He was, though, using some of his income to help with his younger siblings' school costs. Whether it was his decision to drop out or he was encouraged by his elders to do so is not clear. Among Bisa families with access to more labour, seniors sometimes encouraged their juniors in secondary school to find paid work outside the family to meet some of their own educational expenses, as did the elderly household head, Nokwende, in January 2005.

One of my [grand]sons has [attended] secondary school in Tenkodogo [for] three years. When he returned home at the beginning of the holidays, I advised him to find a temporary job in town rather than hanging about in the village. My son was lucky and found work in a bar, but after some time he came home for a visit and this time he complained about not having enough sleep. I told him that life is like that and asked if he preferred to come home or wanted to continue working. In fact, my son is still working and he will only stop once the new school year starts!

Children's own role in pursuing schooling in this way is rarely addressed in the literature. It tends to be assumed that parents decide to fund or not to fund children's schooling, and that if they do, then children go to school (Hashim 2007). These examples clearly show how this may not be the case; David's account shows the ends to which children may go to remain in education if they believe this will benefit them in the longer term, and Nokwende's account shows that some elders support this type of strategizing. In an important sense, the aspiration to go to school, to continue schooling and to get through school is as much an individual commitment by the child, and children demonstrate this commitment by contributing to the costs of their formal education, especially when and if parents cannot meet them (Hashim forthcoming).

In contrast to children like David, other children clearly doubted the value of school. This was especially so as, although there are some jobs and opportunities in the local labour market which require formal education, these are very limited, so that children's chief ways of earning incomes locally did not require formal education. Also relevant is that dominant modes of securing resources in these areas are through patronage relations and communal labour; for which, again, formal education has no relevance. A further disincentive to schooling was that formal education was rarely considered to be beneficial unless a child completed secondary school, since formal job opportunities were uncommon without a senior secondary school certificate (Hashim 2007). Also relevant is that the benefits of education are evaluated not only in terms of its merits for an individual child, but in terms of securing a household's well-being, as made explicit in the following, when one elderly father explains why he struggled to send one of his sons to school: 'If they do well they can get jobs. By the time they finish I will be old and they can feed the younger children' (Hashim 2004: 76). This comment reinforces how relational is well-being in this context; as will be taken up later in later chapters. In this sense, decisions related to schooling involve multiple considerations related to a number of individuals' well-being, and are not simply an evaluation of the educational benefits for an individual child.

Thus, even when they could technically afford the costs of schooling, parents still did not usually send all their children to school. Some researchers suggest this is due to parents' ignorance of the benefits of schooling (Ike and Twumasi-Ankrah 1999), while others have suggested that parents prefer to send their children to work rather than school, believing their role as parents is to prepare their children for adulthood – for example, by teaching them a trade early (Boyden 1997: 212). Alternatively, in contexts such as ours, wealthier households may have more incentive not to send their children to school, since in those households which are successful in farming, children's labour is needed and is more 'productive'. This is related to a further vital factor in determining whether formal education is considered a viable option for the poor in rural areas, which is the perception of the benefits of formal education compared with other available opportunities (Punch 2002a: 126). These considerations are particularly important if the labour market 'is structured such that there is a market for children's work and for unskilled adult labour, but a limited market for semi-skilled labour offering limited improvements in returns in addition to poor quality education' (Moore 2001: 8). Some economists, in particular, pursue the idea that 'formal education makes very little difference, given limited formal sector opportunities, and most skills are acquired by the "learning by doing" principle' (Grootaert and Kanbur 1995: 193), reflecting the ideas of Rogers and Standing, who queried the dichotomy between work and education itself. They suggest that commentators should not 'make an automatic assumption that work by children impairs education and intellectual development [...] work itself may be an important component of "education" especially in household-based production systems' (Rogers and Standing 1981, cited in Akabayashi and Psacharopoulos 1999: 121).

We too have highlighted how children's work is partly about their learning; both how to undertake their principal roles in domestic, farming and income-generating activities, and learning about the nature of social relations in context.

This is especially so, as formal education in the area is either perceived as of too poor quality to be worth the investment or not likely to provide livelihood opportunities on completion. However, we also caution against seeing all children's work as the process of acquiring the skills necessary for their advancement into adulthood. Children also work because, in contexts such as these, work is an age-appropriate behaviour (Hashim 2004).

Also significant is how households in contexts such as those in which we work, where there is considerable agro-climatic difficulty and uncertainty, adopt a range of strategies to secure immediate and long-term security, including both crop diversification and diversification of livelihoods (Whitehead and Kabeer 2001: 8–9). Migration itself is a diversification strategy, in that it expands potential sources of income (Cordell et al. 1996; Hoddinott 1992). Formal education is also one means of potential diversification, with households investing some resources as it represents the *possibility* of future alternative livelihoods (Hashim forthcoming). However, because formal schooling is not a guarantee of security, it remains, for most households, just one of a range of activities, and parents often express the need to balance out the various strategies to secure present and future well-being, as well expressed in the comments of one household head in Ghana, himself educated: 'If you have four boys, you send two to school and two will stay to care for animals and help you on the farm. That way you can care for those in school. If you have girls, you give them vocational training, such as sewing or hairdressing.'

In the Bisa region, the mother of a young boy who was approaching school age explained their educational strategies for him and for two older half-brothers, whose mother had remarried and left the village. None of the parents was formally educated and only two daughters had been enrolled in school earlier, but one had dropped out when her father died and the other died in her first year of school.

> Of the three boys, the oldest is helping his father on the farm. He is the one to lead the oxen when they plough. The second one will be sent to a Koranic school in a village near the Ghanaian border when he gets a bit older. Eventually that will give him work, for someone who knows how to read the Koran can teach others and he can also perform ceremonies. The youngest – my son – will go to the school here in the village. He is too soft to endure a Koranic school.

This comment also illustrates how there is diversification within strategies for learning. In addition to the formal education system, which in Burkina Faso include state- and mission-run schools, parents, and in particular fathers or male household heads, sent children to different types of Koranic schools. Mostly they sent one or two boys to a rural Koranic school, where the children worked on their master's farm in addition to learning the Koran.[10] Some children were sent to a '*franco-arabe*' school in Tenkodogo, where the system resembled the formal school system in the sense that the children lived with kin and were taught French, mathematics and the Koran at regular hours. Finally, some were sent to masters in town, where their training would include begging and working for various employers to get food. Another strategy was to find an apprenticeship for a son, usually with kin, as otherwise it would require a large fee to be paid to the patron. This diversification of learning strategies diminishes competition between children and also increases the chances that some are successful and can support others (Thorsen 2007b).

The ability to adopt learning diversification strategies, of course, is dependent on the opportunities available locally, and one contrasting aspect of our sending communities is the availability of formal and informal education. In the village of Tempane Natinga, the recent addition of a senior secondary school to the existing primary and junior secondary schools meant that children were able to complete their school education without leaving home. Nevertheless, many still preferred to go to other schools owing to the village school's relative newness and perceived deficiency, especially as the village had no electricity, limiting the operation of the school and its appeal to good teachers. Limited opportunities to carry out apprenticeships locally meant children had to travel farther afield to pursue opportunities in the apprenticeships they preferred. In both our areas, favoured apprenticeships were as vehicle or moped mechanics and in carpentry for boys, as well as tailoring in Pays Bisa. Girls in both our areas preferred tailoring, followed by hairdressing apprenticeships. In Pays Bisa, however, all learning strategies outside farming meant that children had to leave home before the age of eighteen. Secondary formal education required that they moved into the nearest rural town at the age of twelve or thirteen; some attended Koranic school from the age of seven or eight but often started when they were a few years older, and apprenticeships were usually initiated when children were in their mid-teens. Thus, in the contexts in which we work, schooling is not intrinsic to childhood. Parents view formal education as just one among a variety of ways of preparing their children for adulthood and ensuring their ability to secure a livelihood, which is also tempered by perceptions of what types of learning are more appropriate for girls and for boys and by a child's perceived interest and ability. Adolescent children also begin to make conscious decisions regarding which form of learning to pursue.

Conclusion: the importance of context

In the opening chapter of this book, we discussed how the universalizing ideal of childhood may not capture the reality of children's lives in diverse contexts. This chapter has illustrated just how different are the local ideas and practices related to childhood in the areas in which we work. For one, in contrast to the global model, clearly work in these contexts is intrinsic to childhood. Moreover, schooling is not. We argue, as a result, that when trying to comprehend

38

childhood, it is necessary to explore this situationally. The importance of this is made clear through a comparison of our studies in two rural communities, which despite many social, cultural and economic similarities have significant differences in children's migratory trajectories.

The most significant difference between the areas of origin in our studies concern girls' opportunities to migrate. Although Bisa girls are just as keen to migrate as boys, the girls are far more constrained socially in their movement compared to boys, who set off on their first migration in their mid to late teens. Parents are generally reluctant to allow adolescent girls to migrate independently of relatives, hence only six of fifty-nine young migrants interviewed in Ouagadougou and two rural towns in the south-east in 2005 were girls. This, moreover, was not a methodological bias emerging from the more hidden nature of the work that migrant girls tend to do, as it was supported by household composition surveys in the area of origin in 2001/02 and 2005 that showed that teenaged girls primarily moved to join their husband. This contrasts with the findings from the research in Ghana, which showed that girls were migrating independently in larger numbers than were boys, with thirty-six boys compared to forty-one girls living outside the village at the time of a migration survey in March 2001, while eighteen boys and thirty girls migrated into the village. Moreover, as noted earlier, the sex-ratio discrepancy between boys and girls is likely in part to be accounted for by the larger number of girls migrating.

A further difference was that, although in both cases boys were found to take matters into their own hands and run away from home if parents did not give permission for them to migrate, Bisa girls seemed more reluctant. In contrast, as we shall discuss in more detail later in the book, in the Ghanaian research, girls as well as boys were reported to have 'run away', and three of the four runaways interviewed in southern Ghana were girls. Both of us found that one tenet of the discourses surrounding girls' migration was the imagined benefit of acquiring trousseau items. For girls in Pays Bisa, someone 'who has acquired most of this herself has a better standing vis-à-vis her in-laws, and in the case the marriage broke she will not have to start anew' (Thorsen 2010: 273). The paradox of adolescent Bisa girls wishing to migrate and see the world, and yet having their movements constrained, was actually pushing them not to delay marriage, and to preferably marry migrants who more readily guaranteed to take them abroad.

These kinds of discourses linking girls' migration with the acquiring of a trousseau are common in other contexts too, and referred to in a number of academic and policy-oriented studies of children's migration in West Africa (cf. Beauchemin 1999; Castle and Diarra 2003; Kielland and Sanogo 2002; Riisøen et al. 2004). For instance, one study which looked at *kayayoos* (head porters) in Accra, Ghana, found many of these girls to be migrants from the north, who see their migration 'as the short-term cost to be paid for a long-term gain – change to a better occupation, marriage, or the purchase of capital goods necessary for training for a better occupation' (Agarwal et al. 1997: 257). Casely-Hayford's work with the Dagomba of the Northern Region of Ghana found that 'in the last few years young girls and women have begun migrating to the cities on a seasonal and yearly basis to find work and improve their income. Girls interviewed stated that they went on "*kayayoo*", to "have their eyes opened" and also buy the necessary items for marriage' (Casely-Hayford 1999: 16). An interesting longitudinal perspective of this is provided by Lambert, in his analysis of young Jola women in Senegal. Lambert argues that, in the beginning, the mobility of the early urban migrants in the 1950s and 1960s was circumscribed by their elders' fears of losing control over their domestic capacity in the day-to-day and longer-term running of the household. Nevertheless, young women were able to overcome the opposition to their urban activities by returning each farming season and by justifying their migration with the need to amass a trousseau, a practice that had become increasingly widespread during the 1950s. According to Lambert, this justification has been transformed in the course of time to entail, in the 1970s, girls providing some or all of their own clothing and, by the 1990s, girls aspiring to be urban residents. Part of this transformation, he argues, was rooted in the development of new youth styles associated with school and modernity and enacted through clothing and visits to dance halls. Older girls were able to orient their identity construction towards these styles only after working in domestic service and, in turn, spurred the material desires of their younger sisters (Lambert 2007). Limitations on Bisa girls' ability to migrate in turn pushed boys to migrate because otherwise they might have had a hard time finding a wife. Marriage was also a factor in boys' movement among the Kusasi in the Upper East Region of Ghana; however, in this case it was related to the need to earn an income, as there appears to be increasing pressure on boys to have certain items, such as furniture, in order to marry (Hashim 2005: 50). Consequently, while in both our cases children and youth expressed the desire to see a bit of the world outside the village, along with other migratory aspirations, in Pays Bisa this put pressure on girls to marry early, while in the Upper East Region the effect was to delay marriage.

Thus, in spite of some parental concern, in the Upper East Region of Ghana girls appear more able to migrate, while just a couple of hundred kilometres north, in Pays Bisa, despite the many similarities in economic and social relations, girls are far less able to move away from home except as wives. As females farm more actively in Pays Bisa, this may be significant. Because of this, Bisa girls were more able to earn an income in their home villages from the sale of the proceeds of the crops. In contrast, girls in the Upper East Region of Ghana, who were less able to farm privately yet still had a need for an income, used this as leverage when negotiating with their seniors to migrate in order to acquire either an income or what they hoped to purchase with it – for example, by being gifted it by a relative whom they 'helped out'. Also crucial are strong taboos against having children outside marriage and elders' fears that their daughters will fall pregnant if they migrate independently. Parents also feared that daughters might marry a man from a different region at the migration destination and thereby decrease the parents' ability to call on married daughters' help and on the labour contribution that was part of their son-in-law's lifelong obligations to them. Kusasi elders are similarly concerned that girls may not marry a Kusasi man if they are migrants, as this might mean the loss of valuable bride-price cattle; however, as we shall see later, the pressures brought to bear by girls to be allowed to migrate can be quite significant.

While this discussion of migration may be somewhat pre-emptive here, it is useful to make these comparisons in order to illustrate the very important point that the economic and social dynamics of a place make possible or constrain girls' and boys' mobility in diverse ways, such that children's migratory paths and trajectories cannot be assumed but need to be established.

3 | Choosing to move: the reasons for rural children's migration

'Akuka was 18 when we interviewed him in a village in the Ashanti Region of Ghana. He had never attended school and had been a migrant since the age of 14, working always in rural areas in farming, for both a relative and a non-related employer.

'"It was poverty that made me come here. I wasn't in school and I was suffering [in my village] so my senior brother brought me here. I did not want to come, but poverty forced me out. [...] I am working with my brother farming maize, and tomatoes too."

'Just six weeks after his arrival in Ouagadougou in February 2005, we interviewed the 16-year-old shoe-shiner, Seni, whose brothers introduced us. As it were, we also knew his father from a visit to his village a few weeks earlier; the snow-balling strategy to find street-working child migrants was introducing us to a large, multi-local network of people and livelihoods.

'"This year, instead of working on the irrigated rice farms at Bagré with my father, I came to the city because I wanted to be familiar with the city too. [...] I've come to Ouaga to get money! When I go back to my village, I'll give some to my parents to receive their blessings and I'll also buy a bicycle to travel to the village [from the nearest town twelve miles away]."'

The above remarks, made by child migrants whom we interviewed, begin to convey the reasons why the children from our areas migrate. In both accounts poverty and the desire to earn money figure large in the boys' reasons for moving, as they do in much of the literature addressing children's migration, especially the advocacy literature (cf. ILO 2002; SC UK 2005, 2006, 2007; Terre des Hommes 2003). How poverty exactly influences migration decisions needs to be unpacked and examined in more detail. For example, Beauchemin, in a report for UNICEF and Catholic Action for Street Children in Accra, Ghana, states that 35 per cent of the children registered in a street children's programme in Accra cited poverty as their reasons for leaving home (Beauchemin 1999: 15). Other studies suggest that although migrants may come from poorer families, they do not necessarily represent the poorest. One survey of child labour migration from rural Burkina Faso based on interviews with parents, for instance, shows that differences in household and village wealth were a much weaker factor than anticipated. The analysis was premised on children's relocation being an outcome of household decisions, and the authors conclude that poorer households lack the information, the social networks and the resources to organize their children's migration, even if they desire to send them to the city or to neighbouring countries (Kielland and Sanogo 2002: 30–33). Another study conducted in Laos, Myanmar and Thailand finds that the expenses associated with migration may be beyond the reach of the very poor, and the risk of not finding work may also discourage movement (SC UK 2005: 30). These findings reflect research focusing on adult transnational migrants travelling much longer distances. While these trends may be valid for the children in our studies who migrate to destinations farther away, notably to Côte d'Ivoire, travel costs to destinations closer to home are often within the reach of everyone (discussed in more detail in Chapter 4).

As with our research, other more child-centred, qualitative studies also provide testimonies regarding the role of poverty in children's independent migration. A study led by Sumaiya Khair on independent child migrants in Bangladesh finds that poverty was the major reason why children move (Khair 2005), as we found in our own research.

Khair also finds that maltreatment at home was one of the many implications impoverishment carried for children (ibid.). Similarly, Beauchemin's study in Accra finds that children ran away to escape abusive home environments. This is an important point, as it illustrates the ways in which reasons for migration can be interrelated. For instance, domestic violence and family breakdown, which might compel individuals to move, are often linked to economic decline and political and social destabilization (O'Connell Davidson and Farrow 2007: 16). However, it is equally important to remember that children run away because they have information regarding where they can run to and the possibilities of being able to survive should they do so (Hashim 2008: 8). Such a strategy, consequently, may be more common in areas where migration has long been perceived as a rite of passage for adolescent children, as was found by Castle and Diarra (2003) in Mali and Lambert (2007) in Senegal, or where there are historically high rates of adult migration, such as is the case in much of West Africa (our studies; Bredeloup 2003; Castle and Diarra 2003; Lambert 2007; Lesclingand 2004; Zongo 2003) and in other places, such as Bolivia (Bastia 2005; Punch 2002b), to name but a few examples. Individuals' movements, thus, are not simply due to push or pull factors, as neoclassical models of migration would suggest. Rather, as O'Connell Davidson and Farrow succinctly put it, they are:

> the outcome of an extremely complex interplay between macro-level structures, micro-level institutions and individual agency. Broader social, economic and political structures provide the context in which individuals and groups must decide whether or not to migrate. Their decisions, however, are strongly influenced by their own personal histories, identities and resources; their connections with social networks in a destination country [...]; and by the extent to

which out-migration from their country or region is institutionalized. (O'Connell Davidson and Farrow 2007: 16)

The communities in which we work are poor in many ways. There is very little local employment and farming productivity is very constrained; basic food supplies are insufficient and insecure, and people go hungry; incomes are uncertain and low; people have few clothes or possessions; they lack access to basic services and amenities; and the quality of and opportunity for education are very low. Individual households are on a continuum from being destitute through varying degrees of serious poverty to being poor, but having a limited number of assets that enable a household to withstand shocks to food supplies or to income sources (Whitehead 1996). Children migrate from households at all these different socio-economic levels, but it is likely that different children are responding to different aspects of this multidimensional poverty. In this chapter, we explore what these different motivations may be.

In addition, we focus closely on what the motivations to move are from the child's point of view. Attention to children's own perspectives, as well as how best to access these effectively, is an important issue for a number of reasons and thus warrants a more detailed discussion. Consequently, before we move on to consider what children actually tell us about their motives for moving, we shall consider these issues, which are fundamentally related to the methods and methodologies used.

Researching with children

In the opening chapter of this book, we noted how a mobilities paradigm assists us in better understanding children's movement. The importance of the mobilities paradigm extends beyond challenging the sedentarism underpinning the universalized ideals of childhood and the family, which hamper our apprehension of children moving on their own account without necessarily breaking with their family or their social context. It also challenges the social sciences in terms of the objects of inquiries and the methodologies for research (Clifford 1992; Malkki 1992; Sheller and Urry 2006). Until recently children, by and large, have been invisible from the field of social science inquiry (Hirschfeld 2002), and even when their migration is acknowledged it tends to be subsumed within the literature on family migration (King 2002). Where children's movement without their birth parents is recognized, it is frequently pathologized. As a result, the focus is on the role of adults in the decision-making process, thereby stressing the degree of compulsion or coercion involved. This focus, by and large, underplays children's own motivations to migrate.

The methodological implications of the mobilities paradigm – of considering how movement may influence people's identities and trying to understand how migrants and non-migrants make sense of and experience the spaces and places characterized by movement – require a multi-local research strategy. Likewise, the recognition that children have been left out of the research agenda also has implications, just as it did for research and theory that ignored women, subsequently recognized as impoverished and misleading (Hirschfeld 2002: 613); hence the growing attention to children as a research category.

However, a number of authors have noted how researching with children presents unique challenges (Notermans 2008; Punch 2002b). Age-related societal arrangements frequently result in powerlessness for the young. This can be the basis for perceptions regarding the necessity for special measures to protect them, but may also end up being a source of vulnerability, since the very idea that children need protection can inhibit actually listening to what they have to say, or giving it any credence. As Leinaweaver (2007), drawing on Ardener's work, points out, in this regard children truly represent a subaltern or 'muted group', whose voices are effectively silenced. As Ardener himself points out in relation to women as muted groups, this is not a matter of women's position but rather the methodological and theoretical problems raised by women in relation to research (Ardener 1977). In other words, it is because women may be difficult to engage in conversation that they are muted, and the same applies to children, whose worlds, like women's worlds, are more difficult to access and explore.

At their most basic, age hierarchies may prevent children openly or freely speaking to adults and thus constrain them from even expressing their views, never mind having them heard. The methodological challenge, thus, is to find ways to discover and represent how children make choices and act upon them in less visible and audible ways (Thorsen 2006: 94) without labelling them indiscriminately as transgressions of social or familial norms. This is one of the reasons why we adopted an ethnographic approach in our research, since such a methodology is particular important given the inaccessibility of children's lives and, importantly, their views. This is especially so as the research is concerned with interrogating normative ideas (including our own) regarding childhood and parenting – as well as very powerful dominant policy discourses on a highly emotive issue – that of children's welfare. Moreover, because of our interest in children's migration, we adopted what Sheller and Urry describe as 'mobile ethnography', or participation in patterns of movement and transition between a number of different localities (Sheller and Urry 2006: 217), in our bid to better understand young people's migration.

A final crucial factor, we argue, when it comes to working with young people, is the need to privilege their voices. The work of postmodernist, post-structuralist and feminist theorists has made a significant impact on our understandings of how the production of knowledge is not an apolitical process (Abu-Lughod 1993; Harding 1987; Lather 2000; Mani 1992; Mohanty 1991). The result has been a growing focus on the participation of research subjects in the process of research and a privileging of their views. Such approaches have been mirrored in initiatives concerned with children and their welfare. As Grover puts it when referring to researching with children, social scientists can be sensitive 'by giving a voice to the vulnerable, rather than by creating images of those studied which are infused with the political and social agendas of the power elite' (Grover 2004: 83). These 'child-centred approaches', thus, have increasingly placed a high priority on the participation of children in research and policies aimed at their welfare, as they discourage stereotypes of children as helpless victims, and instead facilitate their involvement in decisions and activities concerning their lives (Myers and Boyden 1998: 12). This does not solve all problems because, as Reynolds et al. point out, the very practice of giving voice asserts power hierarchies. The listening to subaltern voices does not automatically change the frame; indeed, the fact of *giving* voice affirms that the listener has the power to do so (Reynolds et al. 2006: 294).

We are of the opinion that listening to the views of children is vital in order to provide insights into their subjective worlds. We are therefore convinced of the necessity to recognize children's subaltern status and the need to work towards overcoming their muted position by actively involving them in challenging others' representations of them and their best interests (Leinaweaver 2007). Attention to gender and age as sources of additional vulnerability notwithstanding, the failure to listen to child migrants has led to an underestimation of the extent to which a child's gender and age impacts on their decision to move, as well as their ability to do so. Although we privilege children's voices, we also refer in this chapter and throughout the book to the views of significant adults, and especially children's kin. As we argue that childhood cannot be seen as an abstract concept but must be understood contextually, by the same token it is vital that we consider significant adults' (as well as peers' and siblings') views, since in these contexts they are significant relationships in children's lives. In other words, children do not live in isolation but are embedded in often complex and extended webs of kin and other social networks, which, as will become even more evident in this chapter, have a significant bearing on the decisions children make about their migration, even if they are made independently.

Moving to find work

As we saw in the previous chapter, in Ghana's Upper East Region and in Pays Bisa children are embedded in family-based household relations that are a complex mix of dependence, independence and interdependence in which there are significant economic dimensions. While growing up, children increasingly work for their seniors and contribute to their households' production and reproduction. This work contributes to their upkeep and enables them to make claims on seniors. In addition, from early adolescence children begin to be expected to earn an independent income, which they are encouraged to spend on clothes and other necessities for themselves and on inputs to generate more income.

Opportunities to earn an income, however, are limited in the communities of origin, and this is a significant motivation to move. In the Central Region of Ghana in June 2004, we spoke to eighteen-year-old Sibo, who was orphaned and had been a migrant in a farming village for four years, and who depicted the process of deciding to migrate in terms of material poverty as well as of poverty of opportunity. When we asked him why he had come he said:

> Poverty! I wasn't in school so I when I was in the house, I was suffering and I didn't have any handiwork [apprenticeship] so I decided to come to see if I can get small, small. [...] I spoke to my senior brother and he agreed that I should come as he had no money to help me. [...] After three years, I will return home because by then I will have enough to help me in the house.

This kind of trajectory seems to be common for adolescents in the West African savannah and supports our findings that migration becomes an important means for children to engage in independent economic activities and for their parents and elders to allow them to do so, albeit at times reluctantly. It is clear from Sibo's story that, although he was motivated to migrate on his own, he was supported by his family, which, like most other families in our areas, has connections with households in multiple locations. It is between these households that many children and young people, as well as adults, move, among other reasons because it may facilitate the access to more rewarding labour markets. Thus, the long histories of migration from areas of origin mean that children know of alternative locations and labour markets where they can earn an income, as is expected of them by members of their family, even when it is not necessary for their households' subsistence.

Another motivating factor in Sibo's desire to move is the lack of opportunities to access symbolic or material resources that will enhance his status and/or future opportunities, as mirrored in his quest for an apprenticeship. Among the young migrants from Pays Bisa in Ouagadougou, the material aspects of working in the city were reiterated discursively. While explaining why he had migrated at the age of fourteen, Seni, whom we met at the beginning of the chapter, presented the dominant view among adult migrants about learning from travelling. As important to him was being integrated in the gift economy, where social relationships are consolidated through reciprocating gifts and receiving approval, often enacted through sacrifices and prayers to the ancestors, God and/or Allah. However, he soon started to talk about the more immediate desires of an adolescent boy who had never owned anything.

> The only thing I want is my bicycle. [...] It is different here than in the village because to find money is not so easy. I don't feel being in Ouagadougou changes me, the only thing that could change me would be to earn money. If I had money, I would change completely!

47

Almost one year later, when we met Seni in his village, he was cycling. Despite the fact that he had returned because of an illness that prevented him working and required indigenous medicine, he had been able to buy a bicycle. Not just a second-hand bicycle or a cheap Ghanaian bicycle, which in 2005 would cost 25–30,000 CFA francs, but a better-quality blue Peugeot bicycle that must have cost 45–50,000 CFA francs, and which was still wrapped in protective cardboard to highlight the fact that it was brand new (Thorsen 2007b).

Seni and Sibo are just two among many children who are motivated to migrate because of the lack of economic opportunities in rural areas. Unless children and youth from Pays Bisa planned to migrate to rural areas where they would undertake farm or plantation work, they had only vague ideas about the work they would do to earn the desired income. Their primary objective was to become a migrant, and they were willing to take up whatever job they were offered. Although they knew they would not get employment that required literacy, since only four of the seventy-five children and youth interviewed had left primary school with a certificate, the boys were optimistic about the wages they would earn and the ease with which they would find work. Bisa girls, on the other hand, expected to work for kin, usually classificatory mothers or older sisters, and were realistic about being remunerated with small gifts and clothing. Nevertheless, they still thought migration would be ideal for them (Thorsen 2007a). Although Kusasi girls from the Upper East Region also often went to work for relatives, their experience contrasted with that of the Bisa girls, in that they appeared freer to move to work for non-related employers. In addition, they tended to receive more remuneration if they worked for non-family members, and for this reason they *sometimes* preferred this. A good example here is that of two teenaged sisters interviewed in Tempane Natinga in 2001. The youngest, thirteen-year-old Barakeso, said of her work on a commercial farm in Côte d'Ivoire, 'Here you won't get so tired, but you won't have anything for yourself. There you are tired but you get money.' By comparison, her sixteen-year-old sister, Fostina, who had gone to an aunt's in a town in the central area of Ghana, said that she preferred life in Tempane Natinga because 'here I can do my own rice farming but there I couldn't'. Rice farming is one of the few means by which young children, and especially girls, are able to earn a private income, which they use to buy personal items and those related to their trousseaux, so the inability to do so is a significant setback. Nonetheless, Fostina was not unhappy about having been a migrant since her aunt had presented her with some items on her return. Also significant was that Fostina was happy about her migration experiences because she now 'knew there', illustrating the multiple ways in which children perceive their communities to be lacking. Thus, labour migration is not simply about earning an income. It is also about attaining knowledge and status, and the empowerment children and youth achieve through the social status ascribed to migrant identities in their contexts (Aitken 2007; Punch 2007; Thorsen 2007a).

Moving and education

Constraints on resources allocated to schools by the state, the availability of teaching materials, and infrastructure related to school education in the majority world can lead to a lack of confidence in the benefits of schooling among young people and their families (Boyden 1997; Grootaert and Kanbur 1995; Kabeer 2001; Myers and Boyden 1998). This is especially pertinent in rural areas, which often suffer greater disadvantages than urban regions (Albornoz 1993, cited in Punch 2004: 163).

Certainly, paucity of learning opportunity is often presented as an explanatory factor in children dropping out and migrating. For example, Castle and Diarra's work in Mali finds that there is a statistical link between not going to school and the propensity of rural children to migrate to work (Castle and Diarra 2003), while Beauchemin's study in Ghana finds that children migrate because they are disappointed that their parents will not send them to school (Beauchemin 1999). Equally, studies such as Kielland and Sanogo's in Burkina Faso found that school attendance reduces the likelihood of children migrating (Kielland and Sanogo 2002), while children's testimonies in Castle and Diarra's study consistently reiterated that pupils had long-term goals and seemed less susceptible to peer pressure to obtain material items (Castle and Diarra 2003). An interesting account is given by Ping and Pieke (2003) in their review of children's migration in China, which suggests that because rural–urban migrants enter a strongly segmented labour market, there is little incentive to acquire an education beyond elementary literacy. Consequently, in villages where outmigration is widespread, pupils frequently drop out of school before the completion of compulsory education to migrate to cities (ibid.). Other more negative aspects of the relationship between migration and education relate to the differential value placed on schooling in different regions resulting in regional inequalities within a country. In Ghana, for example, formal education is more highly valued in southerly parts of the country (GSS and World Bank 1998), and its acquisition provides more opportunities there. As a consequence, children, and especially girls, may be encouraged to migrate from the north to relatives in the south to substitute for the labour of relatives' own children, who are attending school (Hashim 2007).

There are these more negative correlations between migration and learning. However, these do not necessarily always obtain, and, certainly, any negative impact needs to be established rather than assumed. That is in addition to the need to question assertions regarding schooling *necessarily* being a positive force; assumptions regarding the negative impact that migration has on children's education arise partly because there is a tendency to see learning as synonymous with schooling (ibid.: 911). Thus, children's migration is often viewed negatively since it is assumed to undermine children's opportunities to go to school. However, there are alternative and more positive linkages between migration and learning. For instance, for many young people living in rural areas only primary education is available near by; consequently they have to migrate to access secondary education (Ansell 2004; Punch 2004). Alternatively, schools in rural areas can be under-resourced and the teaching quality poor, which may lead young people to migrate to access better schools (Bey 2003).

The twelve-year-old daughter of one of the teachers in Tempane Natinga in the Upper East Region, for example, was 'worrying' her father to allow her to move to a relative's home in a town to attend school since she deemed her school in the village (which did not have electricity) to be inadequate. Her father was unsure whether he was going to acquiesce as he was not convinced of the suitability of the environment for her learning and because he was somewhat reluctant to establish those sorts of reciprocating linkages with the household in question. Migration of this type, where a child goes to a relative who will send her or him to school, is common in Cameroon too (Notermans 2008) and was so among the Mende in pre-war Sierra Leone (Bledsoe 1990). Bledsoe argues that fosterage facilitating children's formal education is woven into their integration in the web of kin and, additionally, possibly facilitates their learning new skills that birth parents cannot teach. The Mende believe that children need to develop and earn their knowledge through struggle; hence the sometimes harsher treatment of foster children is viewed as having a positive influence on their learning (ibid.). Although many Kusasi and Bisa parents subscribe to an ideology of hardship similar to that of the Mende in Sierra Leone, they oppose frequent and harsh punishment of small children and evaluate in each case whether a child can cope with educational relocation.

Rural discourses on the quality of formal education, which may encourage migration to other places, are shared by children and by adults, even those without any formal education, who are often portrayed as 'traditional' and 'ignorant' of the perceived benefits of schooling. An elderly household head, Nokwende, who remained faithful to his animist traditions and played an important role in most sacrifices, also took great care in securing the schooling of those of the children in his household who had lost one or both of their birth parents. In January 2005, he described succinctly the feeling of being marginalized in rural villages in relation to the state provision of formal education.

> The real school is in Ouaga! When children go to the village school, everything must arrive from Ouaga, if a child is in Ouaga he is at the source of things. It's better like that. Someone educated in Ouagadougou and someone educated in England are the same – if a child is educated here in the village, it's completely different. I wanted to enrol this child in school [Nokwende pointed to a young child] but the teachers wouldn't accept the child. Here, it is difficult. My neighbour sent his child to school but one day the teacher beat him so badly that the child fainted. It's okay to pull their ears once in a while to make the children learn but today it's better to egg on the children.

As illustrated by the example of the teacher's daughter above, migration to learn is arranged also by children, who initiate different types of moves for a variety of learning opportunities. They may migrate in order to earn the money with which to pay fees, either over vacations or dropping out for a year in order to do so. This is especially the case because higher costs of schooling (senior secondary fees[1]) and/or the taking up of vocational training (usually after the completion of junior secondary schooling) coincide with the period when children are expected to be more self-reliant and are increasingly able to earn an income (Hashim 2007). Interviewed in the Ashanti Region of Ghana in June 2004, eighteen-year-old Ashikoba described how he interwove schooling with work to finance his studies.

> [Three years ago] I was in school up to JSS2 [junior secondary school class 2] but when I was to register [for JSS3] I had no money so I came here to find labour work to get money and go back but I got contract work so I registered here to write my exams instead. [...] I was just coming alone to find work but I met another Kusasi man on the bus and he said because I didn't know the place it would be better to follow him. [...] I worked on Saturdays and Sundays because the man I am staying with is good, so I got to eat in the morning and I closed work and ate in the evening. [...] I registered and passed some of my exams which enabled me to continue [to senior secondary school] but because of the financial problems I stopped, as I am getting small, small to support myself and help my parents. [...] I am still staying with him but working on contract for an Ashanti for the last months. I will be paid ₵650,000[2] [£41] at the end of my year [...] I usually help the Kusasi man on Sundays when the Ashanti man goes to church.

It is not only for formal learning opportunities that young people may wish to move. Interviews with young migrants illustrate that young people migrate to access other types of learning opportunities. Vocational training and apprenticeships may be particularly valued, and indeed formal schooling may be far less valued than vocational training. A Ghana Statistical Survey study found that the Upper East Region had the lowest number of children who were not interested in training; a mere 1.1 per cent (GSS 2003: 43). This was in contrast to the findings on interest in schooling, as the Upper East Region had the highest number of children not interested in schooling at 12.6 per cent (GSS and World Bank 1998: 26). What the GSS study also revealed, however, was that the overall percentage of children who were receiving any form of training was low at only 2 per cent, and that the region had the highest proportion of children who could not afford training (56.6 per cent). Thus, moving to areas where training opportunities were more readily available or where the money to cover the costs could more easily be acquired is also a significant motivation for children's migration. Seventeen-year-old Awintim'e had several experiences of migration. Following her first migration to the south, when she moved to the household of a married (classificatory) sister, and was rewarded with a sewing machine for her input into the household's reproductive work, she is likely to have begun to cultivate aspirations to become a tailor. We interviewed her in the Brong Ahafo Region in June 2004, where she described what had happened to her over the previous few years.

When I was in the house, I asked my mother to find me something [an apprenticeship] but she couldn't so my brother asked me to come here and learn some work. I didn't have anything in the house so he said I should come and he would get somebody I could stay with. [...] He paid for my ticket [...] He was involved in illegal timber logging and was caught and imprisoned so I am staying with my uncle. I am learning tailoring work and helping my uncle by preparing food, collecting firewood and caring for his children. [...] It's my brother who got me this work; the master is his friend [...] When I was about ten or twelve my sister came and took me to Kumasi[3] to look after her child while she helped her husband with cocoa farming. I stayed with her for two years and she bought me some clothing and a sewing machine. [...] It is this machine I'm using in my work. I still have problems as they ask us to sew a uniform or buy sandals or tracing paper, and I have no money for that. [...] Sometimes I go by-day and get ¢12,000 to ¢13,000 [£0.75–0.81] to buy my things with. [...] [but if] I don't have money for tracing paper, then I don't go to work [in the tailor's workshop] and that is bringing the work [learning] back.

In total four female and four male migrants interviewed in Ghana were apprentices, while a further six girls interviewed were hoping that the relatives with whom they were living and/or working for would help them with apprenticeship fees; illustrating how training opportunities figured highly in children's calculations. The way in which Awintim'e spoke about her tailoring apprenticeship as work is indicative of the significant point that, from the perspective of many children, work and learning are not dichotomous concepts. They are not necessarily even discrete but intertwined concepts. These activities, which frequently need to be defined as work *or* learning because of the manner in which education and childhood have become intimately connected in the industrialized world, are more appropriately described exactly as she portrays them – learning work.[4] These processes of learning work are equally evident in the learning of work at trading, food preparation or brick-making, as a fifteen-year-old daughter of a widow, whom we have known since 1997 when the girl was still in Côte d'Ivoire, described in February 2005.

My mother's younger sister brought me to Côte d'Ivoire because I was suffering at home after my father had died and my mother struggled to feed us all. In the beginning, I looked after her baby and when the child had grown a little older, I bought cooking oil and sold that in smaller quantities and I also sold eggs. As

I was only small when I went to Côte d'Ivoire, I don't know exactly how many years I spent there but I often wanted to see my mother again. I came back home because she had problems with her foot and could barely get up to cook for my brothers. That's the reason why I came back. I was happy in Côte d'Ivoire but as it was a health problem that made my mother ask me to return, I can't say that I wasn't happy to return. It had become an obligation. Anyway, I would have come back sooner or later because I would return to get married here. [...] For me it's easier, I still remember how to calculate and trade. Just after my return I always spoke Dioula, but my friends here told me that I offended them and often we didn't get along well.

Solange's account thus underscores how informal learning is implicated in a variety of ways in children's movement, and the skills to which children ascribe value are instrumental not only in income generation but also in broadening their knowledge through knowing more languages and feeling at home in several places.

Moving to 'help'

Solange is a good example of another category of children who may move away from home – children who go to relatives to help during periods of particular need. These children are significant in number, particularly among younger children. Many of the children from the Upper East Region too had migrated to help a relative, and girls especially figured quite high among them. This is because many adult Kusasi migrants in the south are in the early years of family formation and consequently do not have older girls to help with the housework. Hence, there is a high level of requests from migrant families for girls from their communities of origin to move south to live with relatives. Parents acquiesce, sometimes reluctantly, because of the collective or plural view of parenthood in this context; as expressed in one father's view that 'if your brother asks for your child you can't refuse because it's his child too'. Similar views were expressed among the Bisa, Solange's mother explaining that 'if you decline sending your child, you kind of suggest that your relationship with the person who asked is problematic, or that you do not value this person. Moreover, if you send your child, you can ask the other person for a favour at another moment.' Nevertheless, demands on a child were sometimes turned down, especially to very poor women. Topka had several times asked her brother for one of his daughters, but the first time he said no because the girl was only four years old; a couple of years later he declined because Topka had lost her sight and was alone and therefore would not be able to supervise the girl properly (Thorsen 2005: 126).

It was not just girls, though, who moved in this way; boys may too, as Sedu's story makes clear. He was interviewed in a farming village in the Central Region of Ghana where he had lived and worked for four years.

My father didn't send me to school or [get] money to send me to handiwork. He asked me to come south to find work in order to help them. One of my brothers-in-law came to visit and my father asked me to follow him. Home is more interesting for me but if you can't get money and you can't get to eat you can't stay. We can't all be in the house because of the poverty [...] When I first came I was working for my brother-in-law but he was not giving me enough to do the work I wanted to do [which is] to be a mechanic or something that will give me an income when I am old so I can support my children. [...] My father sent a message that because I am not in the house to help him farm my brother-in-law should help him, so he sent the money to him.

The picture developing here could be seen as one in which younger children and/or girls may appear as pawns, either in relation to the various needs that adults have for their labour or to wider social needs to maintain active kin relations. Such an interpretation is in line with many of the approaches to children's trafficking in the policy literature, where what is foregrounded is younger children and girls' relative powerlessness in their movement between households and the ease with which they can be coerced to migrate. Again, however, we argue that these issues are context specific, thus the degree of compulsion to move needs to be established. Importantly, as we noted at the start of the chapter, only by accessing the views of children themselves is it possible to assess this. For example, in the description of a sending household in the previous chapter, we saw a number of children being moved into Paul's household to assist the adults, and with no access to their views these children *appear* to be pawns in strategic decisions made by adults. However, this contrasts markedly with our findings that child migrants mostly view their mobility as their own choice.

Among the children interviewed in Ghana, only three children had not wished to migrate, while the other sixty-seven said they had wanted to move. It was the case that a significant number of children had been asked to move by parents or other seniors, and often in response to a request from other relatives. This was particularly the case for children in the younger age category of seven to thirteen, who rarely initiated their move themselves. However, they also rarely stated that they did not wish to move. These younger children frequently talk about how 'it was decided' that they should move, but also about how they decided to move. This is not necessarily contradictory and should be respected as telling us something important about the decision-making process. As we noted earlier, children's obligations, expectations and responsibilities vary in different contexts; and in the contexts in which we work in West Africa, being a good child involves understanding and fulfilling their role in the production of the household's food, in the production of cash crops and in the reproductive labour necessary to secure the household's subsistence. Thus, in addition to often wanting to see beyond their home villages, as illustrated by fourteen-year-old Awpwaka in the Ashanti Region in June 2004, children are happy to migrate because they are fulfilling their obligations to kin, merely in a different context, since many relatives are themselves living as migrants.

> My sister [father's brother's daughter] collected me three years ago to care for her child and because I thought it would be better here I chose to follow her. [...] My father came here to Kumasi nine years ago and never returned nor was he found when he was searched for so we don't know where he is. My mother is alone in the house and there is a lot of suffering in the house. It was my uncle who decided I should come but I chose to come because if I stayed in the house I would be suffering. [...] Now my sister has delivered again and she went home and brought another young girl to care for the child, so now I am following her to the farm. [...] My sister said that after the harvest she will send me to learn work [...] Hairdressing. [...] Because she is my sister she is not paying me [but] when I go home she will buy me something to send me with, [such as] clothing or a sewing machine. Or she will allow me to enter an apprenticeship. [...] Last year I worked for my sister [farming] and she gave me one bag of corn that I sold for ¢120,000 [£7.50] and I saved that money. [...] If I learn work [enter an apprenticeship] I will stay another three years. [...] Last year my mother sent a message that I shouldn't come home if everything is fine for me [because] if I go home I will suffer.

Since the domestic economy includes the pursuit of private endeavours, notions of being a 'good child' also involve the adoption of a sense of self-reliance, and for children migration presents an opportunity to seek out alternative learning or economic possibilities. Consequently, children have their own interests in links with a wider range of relatives from whom they seek to get a commitment for support, and from quite a young age boys and girls search for small forms of assistance from a range of relatives and build up relationships with a variety of people.

Thus, children have a complex set of reasons of their own for going and staying in households in different locations and, even when adults are apparently making the decisions about children's movement, children, even when young, may have a say.

Moving and family crisis

Children do frequently move, therefore, when they are needed by kin elsewhere, often as a result of a minor family crisis, such as illness, or a change in circumstance, such as the birth of a child, that may elicit the need for an extra pair of hands to farm, care for a young child or help out an elderly person. Alternatively, the changing circumstances may be in a child's own home and mean that only another household can meet their basic needs and/or cover the costs of their schooling. In the scholarly literature, these crises are frequently seen as evidence of family breakdown, with the result that family dysfunction figures large in discussions of children's migration. Bledsoe, for example, has pointed out that in this body of literature African parents are often perceived to be unsympathetically indifferent to their children. This view is rooted in presumptions that parents send away children because of high child mortality and fear of emotional attachment, that parents neglect children's emotional and physical distress because of poverty, that parents believe that their children will mature through experiencing hardship, or because the parents assert their own autonomy at the expense of their children (Bledsoe 1990: 72). Explanations in the advocacy literature often follow the same line of reasoning. If the focus is on the children, their movement away from the immediate family is often seen as signalling that the child is either delinquent or reacting to insufficient care by parents or guardians. If the focus is on the parents, the presumption is frequently that the family is broken because parents are no longer providing a child with supervision, affection and economic support since the child is no longer living with them (Whitehead et al. 2007: 7).

Beauchemin's study of street children in Accra is an example of this kind of argument. His analysis suggests that parents may find the strain of caring for numerous offspring too great, and so neglect some or all of their children, leading them to leave their homes (Beauchemin 1999: 28). The exodus of children from rural areas to the urban centres of Ghana, he argues, is 'linked to the breakdown of the nuclear family' (ibid.: 15). Other studies, however, cast doubt on the too easy equation of child migration with family dysfunction or breakdown (Whitehead et al. 2007: 7). From the Upper East Region in Ghana, seven children (three boys and four girls) moved for reasons of neglect and/or not being cared for sufficiently in their households in the north – some 10 per cent of the children interviewed. Most of these children were orphans or children who had lost their father, and some of them had run away. It is important to note, though, that being orphaned by no means inevitably results in a child being neglected and ill treated. Some of the children had moved in order to be better cared for elsewhere because of a crisis in their households in the north and were being well looked after in the households to which they had moved. In fact, twenty-five of the seventy children interviewed were orphans or had lost their father, although they did not give this as their primary motivation for moving. Thus, losing one or both parents might be instrumental in the movement of children to another household, as it was for fifteen-year-old Solange and fourteen-year-old Awpwaka, quoted above, but this does not inevitably equate with neglect, and nor does it necessarily signal family breakdown. Indeed, we both found instances of older children who migrated when orphaned of a father to help their mothers cover the expenses associated with younger siblings' formal education, or just because they felt it to be their duty, especially if they were the eldest son. This, in turn, was both understood and appreciated by siblings and other kin. In the process, family ties may be strengthened.

While the notion of breakdown is linked with normative perceptions of the nuclear family, rural families in the West African savannah consist of interconnected households in one or more places. These households can be large or small, but very often children have several classificatory parents and grandparents whom they can call on whether or not their birth parents are present (Alber 2004; Vischer 1997). Family networks may be galvanized to ensure children's welfare, suggesting that in the case of orphans, as with the mobility of children in general, the processes of migration and their impacts will be very different for the economically secure households compared to those that are seriously poor. While family breakdown may be a factor in some children's migration, we cannot automatically make causal links between losing a parent, deep poverty and a rupture in family relations, but need to understand local norms of parent–child relationships and of who is considered family.

Children's migration and inter-generational conflict

Sometimes children's movement is an outcome of conflicts within the family or the household. Often such conflicts are related to the nature of the inter- and especially intra-household interdependencies we discussed in Chapter 2. In the West African context, as well as in other kin-based societies, corporate kin groups are especially important for long-term social reproduction, as they 'are a means of "locking up" access to labour and other resources, "embedding" them in political extensions of reproductive relations and specifying who can get labour or food or land or equipment from whom' (Robertson 1991: 42). In this instance, 'women work for men, juniors work for seniors, the poor work for the rich, and all these relationships are inserted into a web of social relations woven largely, in the case of small agrarian communities, through kinship, residence and patronage' (Moore 1988: 58). What is important in such households is access to labour, which crucially relates to how successful the household head is in managing the balance between the various kinds of economic activity of household members, as well as the negotiations and tensions surrounding these (Whitehead 1981, 1996).

Detailed ethnographic research on children's work for their households as well as indigenous conceptualizations of childhood illustrates how the way in which the balance between household members' various activities is managed lies at the heart of the conflicts between seniors and juniors. This research found that conflicts about work are the outcome of two separate issues. On the one hand, there are the day-to-day negotiations involved in gradually encouraging a child to assume some responsibility for contributing to their household, which children may try to avoid or resist. On the other hand, as children become older and emerge into a more differentiated world of work, where their interests became more separate from those of their parents, there is conflict not about not doing work, but about for whom that work is done (Hashim 2004: 89).

Seniors' inability or failure to provide children with opportunities could also result in children running away, as made explicit by what one teenaged girl said about her younger sister's move south: 'Children run because if they have nothing to do here and they see their parents are not supporting them they will run to find work.' The way in which a neighbour, Ama, spoke about her sixteen-year-old son, who had run away from home, also illustrates this well.

> The father says the boy's sister stole him; but I say he has gone for work. His sister wanted to send him [with her when she came for a visit] but we were not in agreement and so she left but three days later he dodged and followed her. She had found him work for a woman who owned a poultry farm, so I believe that's where he's gone. [...] He went in the dry season last year. We heard of him once. Someone from here was travelling there and saw him. We don't know when he will come home.

Changes in the composition of small households may result in children migrating to have more time for their own activities. In 2001, Ama's household consisted of an elderly household head, his second wife Ama, and an older teenaged boy, as well as Ama's son, who had subsequently run away. Another son in his mid-thirties had just returned from labour migration to the south of Ghana, and had not participated in any household farming that year, perhaps signalling the declining fortunes of the household, and the fairly difficult task of the household head to manage a balance between the household members' various economic activities. This son's two daughters also lived in the household but their mother did not as she had remarried out of the village. The last household member was the five-year-old son of one of the household head's daughters. In 2000/01, it was a poor but relatively secure household, which had some assets in the form of cattle and small livestock. By 2004, the household's circumstances had changed and the household had shrunk to consist only of the elderly couple, the girls and the young grandson. This was significant in terms of both why the household head had not wanted to lose the labour of Ama's son and also why the boy would be keen to leave, since the labour of only two males is likely to be insufficient for the household's subsistence and would certainly curtail any opportunities for the boy to farm for himself. The earlier research in Tempane Natinga threw up another relevant example, where a young teenager who, although living in his father's household with his paternal grandmother while his father was away in the cocoa-growing areas of Ghana, was frequently found in the company of a neighbour, an active trader and part of a secure and relatively wealthy household. The boy was clearly developing his neighbour, also a relative, as a potential patron, and the neighbour for his part was encouraging the relationship, getting the boy to participate in his trading activities and rewarding him with gifts of sandals and small livestock. These examples are reminiscent of Reynolds's findings in the Zambezi valley regarding how: '[c]hildren without the buffer of a secure set of kinsmen spend more time nurturing patron–client relations along kin lines' (Reynolds 1991: 128). What they show is that in complex family households, where relations are a mix of dependence, independence and interdependence, when seniors fail or are unable to support their juniors they risk them privileging the independent aspect of intra-household relations by seeking greater autonomy over their labour, either within the village or outside it, by tying themselves to alternative patrons. This underscores Schrauwers's point that there is a political economy of 'parenting', as economic inequalities constrain who may or may not attempt to bind a child to their household, and that in these processes of negotiating parentage (Schrauwers 1999: 312) children themselves are powerful agents.

The probability of this kind of conflict depends on the degree to which the head of their household and/or their seniors support children and provide them with the space in which to pursue their individual income-generating activities. If feeling too restricted, children of the age when most of their friends engage in individual income-generating activities may have an incentive to migrate, as long as they believe this will create space for them to benefit directly from their own labour by working for a wage or for an alternative patron. For girls, such as sixteen-year-old Fostina referred to earlier, who preferred to have a rice field of her own in the village rather than work for her aunt in a rural town, migration may not lead to benefiting directly from their labour. Unless they are permitted to do by-day labour, work for someone outside the family or farm their own small plot of land, as they would be able to in rural areas, it might actually be preferable to work under quite harsh conditions for a wage.

Heads of households need to ensure a balance between harnessing the labour of their dependants, both adults and children, while permitting them the time and resources to pursue their own private farming and/or income-generating activities. Household dependants, including children, for their part need to ensure that their obligations to their elders are fulfilled, not least because in doing so they make moral claims on household resources, including those necessary for the private enterprises through which they earn an independent income (Hashim 2004: 87; Thorsen 2005: 156–7). This goes some way to explaining why one father in north-eastern Ghana said that he had built a zinc-roofed room[5] for his teenaged son to persuade him not to migrate. It also accounts for why many adults qualified their explanations about their children's migration with comments such as this Ghanaian father's regarding his son's migration to Côte d'Ivoire: 'He went to search for money to marry. [...] It's not good for me, because I have to work alone; but I can't prevent him from going because I have nothing for him here!'

The way in which poverty is reiterated in adults' justifications of their children's migration is also common in Pays Bisa. However, Kanlou's description in January 2005 of what her teenaged daughters gain from working with a classificatory sister in a rural town some sixty miles away offers additional insights into parents' views on migration.

> Aïcha has worked for her [classificatory] sister during the dry season for some years. She works and then at the beginning of the rainy season her sister gives her a bit of money so she can buy clothes and the bowls she collects for her marriage. Not all fiancés have the means to give money to a girl to buy bowls, so if she has collected, she can bring them with her when she marries. It's better when Aïcha is in Bittou because there she can earn some money, here there is nothing. We don't have a market where she can try to sell a little bit, in Bittou it's better. When the children leave, they earn more. [...] I also think that when the children leave they become much more awakened, but if they stay with their mother they are not so open, but by leaving they start to develop. The girls develop through their friends because if they see that a friend is well behaved, she respects herself, she respects others, she dresses well, they will try to adopt the same behaviour as their friend. This is the reason for Aïcha's younger sister to go to Bittou this year; I hope she will develop nicely like her sister.

The focus on earning money is almost omnipresent, as is the talk about children's marriage, but it is clear that the practices surrounding marriage are also affected by the long-term economic circumstances. Another point emerging in relation to children migrating from Pays Bisa is the emphasis on awakening – 's'éveiller' – which both parents and children see as immensely positive. Its equivalent in the Kusasi vernacular was having one's 'eyes opened', which was also viewed very positively.

Negotiated moves: the gendered nature of children's migratory trajectories

In the Upper East Region and Pays Bisa, boys running away do not always overly perturb their seniors. Despite their 'dodging' or 'fleeing', parents expect boys to return, just as boys anticipate returning sooner or later. This is because of the nature of work and household organization in these contexts. Children belong to their father's lineage and, as most young married couples live in the household of the husband's father, boys know it is to their agnatic kin that they will need to look for support for land and inputs such as labour and seeds. Among the Kusasi, boys rely on seniors to provide them with the cattle for their bride-price. Boys' connection with a place therefore involves investing labour as a long-term resource strategy, both economic, such as in farming, and also social and cultural, in terms of building the relations necessary to ensure the ability to secure their own and their households' livelihoods, since securing livelihoods in this context requires cooperation among many. As noted in the previous section, their seniors, for their part, and particularly household heads, need to harness the labour of their juniors in order to secure the household's welfare, and consequently must provide them with the means to pursue individual endeavours. The effect on familial relations is that both a boy and his agnatic group have a stake in maintaining good relations (Hashim 2004: 91). This means that boys have to negotiate harder to migrate, if there is insufficient alternative labour in the household, but also that they can negotiate permission to migrate with promises of return. Parents in particular felt unable to refuse their children permission to migrate if they were unable to provide them with the resources to enable them to gain income-generating or educational opportunities. As we have seen, sometimes the conflict over the use of boys' labour may result in some boys running away.

In contrast, Kusasi parents acquiesce more readily in daughters' movements because their attachment to the family and kin group is of a different order than is boys'. On marriage, girls move away to their husband's community and become the responsibility of their husband's patrilineal groups, although ties to girls' own family and kin groups remain relatively strong. This means that as girls begin to reach puberty there is less commitment to keeping them in the household than for boys, who are the core labour force and the core future members of patrilineal households and lineages. This lack of attachment to the girls means that parents more readily agree to them moving to relatives in the south. As one Ghanaian father of an older teenaged migrant girl put it: 'I approved because she is a girl and so has to leave.' Although girls are significant labour assets for their mothers, the way in which decisions about marriage are discussed shows that as they enter their late teens, they may begin to withhold their labour to some degree, and it is expected that girls in their later teens should start to disassociate themselves from their own households. This gradual withdrawal is seen as an indicator that young women are ready to move on to their next house (Hashim 2004: 93). The transitional nature of girls' attitudes to work is clear in the following statement: 'When she is a child she will learn from her mother, but as she reaches the age of marriage she will start to show that she is able to do her own thing to demonstrate that she has learnt well and that she is ready for marriage.' It is even more overt in this next comment: 'A girl will reach the age of marriage when her attitude changes, as she knows this is no longer her house.' This, in conjunction with the changes referred to in the preceding chapter regarding the delaying of marriage in north-eastern Ghana, probably accounts for the relative ease with which girls were able to migrate. This does not mean that girls do not need to negotiate to move as well. As illustrated in an interview in May 2004 with Atembe – whose twelve-year-old daughter has become a migrant – concerns about their children's welfare, safety and morality are significant factors in parents' calculations about their movements; consequently among the Kusasi they often moved with and/or to kin.

I don't want her to stay too long because it's not good because I've seen other people's children and they stay there too long and there they spoil. [...] they can follow men there and when they come home they continue these same practices and then they fall pregnant. [...] Girls have travelled and their fathers don't know where they are and they sell cows to find them and when they find them they have delivered up to three and they don't even know who the fathers are.

The increasing pressure on Kusasi girls to bring something to their marriage in the form of both trousseaux items and some training with which to earn an income appears to be having the effect of large numbers of girls migrating – to the extent that a survey of the households in Tempane Natinga showed that even more girls than boys had moved out of the village, forty-one girls being absent as compared to thirty-six boys. Girls like seventeen-year-old Emina, whom we interviewed in Kumasi City in June 2004, used stark arguments with their relatives to get permission to migrate.

Me and my mother decided that I should come because there is a lot of poverty there. Although some of my family agreed for me to come here my senior uncle didn't agree because some girls come south and find work and when they get money they don't go back. [...] My senior uncle didn't agree but I told him that if I don't go I will suffer. [I said] 'You can't get it for me, my mother can't get it for me, so I have to go; otherwise when I marry I will have nothing.' In the end, he agreed.

Emina is arguing that her relatives are unable to provide her with a foundation for adulthood, and appealing to the idea of what a child can expect from guardians and parents. The clinching argument is a reference to providing for the basis of her future marriage. The reference to 'suffering' is the phrase commonly used in the context to refer to deprivation that justifies independence.

The ability of boys and girls to migrate and remain migrants for some time reveals just how different practices can be, despite the many similarities between the Upper East Region and Pays Bisa. Among the Bisa, boys readily migrate and, although their organization of farming is comparable with that of the Kusasi, their investment in social relations is not tied to the ancestral land but to the descendants of their ancestors, who live in many different locations. Consolidating the relationships with kin of various degrees of proximity is not something children mention as a reason for migrating (or for not migrating), but they find much inspiration from the ways in which established migrants embody being successful through clothing, gift-giving and commodities such as bicycles, radios and, of more recent date, mobile phones. The value of these commodities, then, is not just linked to materiality and their practical function, it is also symbolic and may enable a child to position him- or herself differently within the household or in the wider community.

The connection between migration and marriage is different too. Cattle do not figure in bride-wealth payments, although they do occur in lifelong obligations to offer a cow at funeral ceremonies. Much more important is the bride service, where the groom and his friends work for the bride's father and mother and a little for her too. At the consummation of the marriage gifts to the woman's kin group ideally include a ram, a cock, kola nuts and items of clothing and food for the visitors. In destitute families the sons may contribute to meeting these expenses, but it is rarely the motivation for their migration. Quite the contrary – fathers sometimes court a girl in their son's name and call him home to marry, even if this is against the boy's wishes (Thorsen 2005: 84–7). Marriage does not figure large in boys' motivations for migrating, but it does in their fathers' efforts to tie them into the household.

Although Bisa girls, as indicated above in Kanlou's account of her daughter's use of the money earned during dry-season migration, buy things for their trousseau and argue that it will eventually strengthen their position in the marital household, they are not allowed to migrate to nearly the same extent as Kusasi girls. Taboos around girls giving birth in their fathers' compounds (the feared outcome of migrant girls falling pregnant outside marriage) dramatically curtails girls' independent movement compared to boys'. Hence, when girls migrate they do so with relatives. Yet, in interviews, Bisa girls expressed their aspiration to become migrants, and their vivid accounts of what they could gain and how they would distribute their earnings mirrored the way in which boys spoke of these issues (Thorsen 2007a, 2010).

Conclusion

This chapter has explored why children may wish or be encouraged to move. The stories already beginning to emerge bear witness to the part children themselves play in influencing their life courses and in negotiating the often difficult circumstances of their home communities. The discourse on poverty and lack of opportunity to earn money in rural communities dominates the justification for migration. However, the mentions of also wanting to be familiar with the city or other places, to buy a bicycle, to help family members in other places and so on, reveal the many layers of motivation underneath the poverty discourse. The long histories of migration from areas of origin mean that children do know of alternative labour markets where they can earn an income. Children may also entertain a variety of educational aspirations that encourage them to move to access formal, non-formal and informal learning opportunities. Parents' and children's respective expectations and obligations to one another are significant factors in the negotiations about children's movements. Parents may encourage such movements or children may have to negotiate hard with their seniors to allow them to move. As an extreme measure, they may run away to pursue alternative patronage relations or to further their autonomy over their labour, especially when faced with the inability or failure of their seniors to provide them with the means to do so. Children's gender and age are crucial factors in the ability to migrate, and even within our very similar areas of origin, the different gender regimes influence both the motivations girls and boys have to move and the negotiations surrounding these. They also have an impact on how children make their journeys, an issue to which we shall now turn.

4 | Journeys and arrivals: introductions to new social worlds

'We met 18-year-old Amadou in January 2008 when he was working in the huge area covered by small hand-irrigated vegetable gardens lining Abidjan's airport, where most of the growers are Burkinabé and Malian. We had started coming to the gardens the previous year but this year we were lucky to meet a young man who mediated the contact with some 50 children and youth working there, so we spent many days doing interviews in a makeshift shelter in the midst of the gardens. Amadou was a skilled narrator and recounted the following story.

'"After my father died of a snake bite four years ago,[1] I had to drop out of CE2 [fourth grade]. I'm the oldest of my mother's and father's four children but the fifth son in the large family. As my mother was all alone and we had no money, I decided to join my older brother here in Abidjan. He agreed to my coming but couldn't send money for the ticket because no one would agree that a junior like me should receive money from him. Hence, I went to Bittou for five months and the following dry season to Tenkodogo for six months to earn money for my bus fare.

'"When I was 14 years old, I left for Abidjan with 10,000 CFA francs [£10] in my pocket and got stuck on the way [as a ticket all the way cost 25,000–28,000 CFA francs, equivalent to £26–29]. I got to Abengorou, where I stayed for ten months. At first, I worked on the cocoa farm of a Mossi[2] I met on the road and explained that I'd arrived from Burkina and didn't know anybody in this area. He told me to come with him and I did, even though I didn't know if he was going to kill me or what. He promised to find work for me where I'd earn 50,000 CFA francs [£53] in one year. I said, 'If it's like that, it's proper!' Meanwhile I worked on his farm. After two months, I asked about the job that he was going to find for me, but he wanted me to stay with him for another three months. I couldn't stay with him that long; he always insulted me and wanted me to work harder. He wanted me to stay on, so in the end I fled without having had a penny for my work!

'"I then started walking. For three days I walked, then I met a kind woman, a Boussanga [Bisa] from Bawku, who gave me some food and water, and even a pair of sandals. I worked in her groundnut field for three months and was paid 5,000 CFA francs [£5]. She really didn't want me to leave but I didn't have any relatives there; that's why I wanted to leave. If I died there, who would know? So I sneaked off but once I got to Abidjan, I phoned her to tell that I'd finally arrived.

'"First, I stopped in Aboisso for five months to earn money for the last leg of my journey. My father has a farm there – well, it's an uncle from my extended family – but I worked with him. After a while, I wanted to continue to Abidjan and he gave me a little money to get by. He couldn't give me more because he is also poor but I made my way to my brother."'

The nature of journeys and the circumstances at destinations impact on the vulnerabilities children might face. Open discussions about their wish to migrate may facilitate finding travelling companions, economic support for tickets and relatives prepared to put up or employ newly arrived child migrants, while journeys undertaken in secrecy may carry the risk of being cheated, lured into dangerous places or ending up without support at the destination. While there is a certain truth in this distinction between safe and risky journeys, this chapter takes a closer look at who may be involved in planning the journey and how concrete journeys unfold in order to examine whether it is a prerequisite for child migrants' security that their parents or guardians are involved in the decision-making.

Both applied and academic research has focused on independent child migrants in a short-term kind of way by foregrounding their immediate experiences. While this is important when trying to get a sense of children as a social category – children's being – it renders invisible the process of becoming and being a migrant, and of children's changing ideas over time and with experience – children's becoming. In this and the following chapters we aim therefore to bring to the fore the progressive nature of children's migration by distinguishing between early and later experiences and by looking at how migration changes the way in which children perceive themselves and construct particular identities in different situations. This chapter focuses on journeys and arrivals at new destinations, and explores how migrant networks may facilitate and shape children's experience of migration, be it through premeditated arrangements that ease the arrival, impromptu arrangements to help young migrants arriving without contacts, or leaving them to find their own ways.

Social networks, kin and relatedness

Even though advocacy and policy institutions have broadened their work from a narrow focus on risky journeys and trafficking to looking at household strategies for risk minimization and to acknowledging children's economic roles, their conceptualization of adolescents' active participation, and even self-determination, in migration decisions remain unexplored. This is linked with a tendency to shroud African families, and especially rural African families, in a lot of myth-making concerning the strength of rigid kinship systems, their unchangeable nature, and thus as something that breaks down rather than

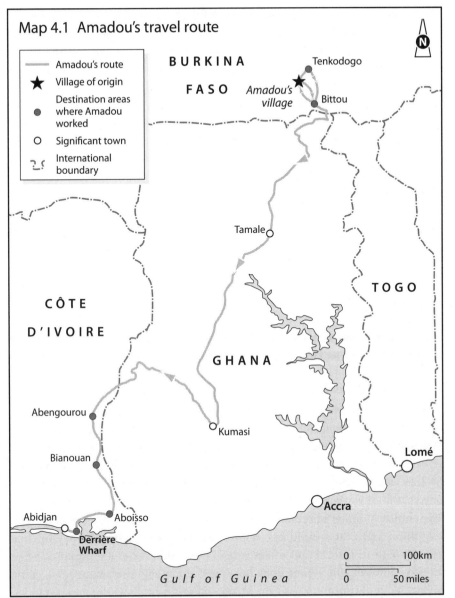

Map 4.1 Amadou's travel route

transforms. However, anthropologists have long argued that kinship systems provide a flexible language for forging social ties both inside and across descent groups (O'Laughlin 1995: 71), but the focus has been on adults primarily or, where children were involved, on inter-generational relationships shaped by adults' preferences and decisions.

One precondition for beginning to unpack how children use kinship relations is to understand how broadly kinship terms are applied, even within the official kinship terminology[3] that is rooted in the social structure. Among the Bisa, for example, 'brothers' and 'sisters' may be borne by the same mother or have the same father but have different mothers or share paternal grandparents, or belong to the same patrilineage, clan or ethnic group. All are categorized as older brother/sister or younger brother/sister in Bisa vernacular. Children, nevertheless, do make subtle distinctions between these siblings based on social and affectionate closeness and the context in which the relationship is invoked. Consequently, kinship categories, such as 'brother', 'sister', 'aunt', 'father' and 'mother', are not clearly defined in practical terms. Another issue that needs to be taken into consideration is the strategic use of kinship terms by both children and adults to conjure up particular kinds of relationships. Calling someone a brother or sister, a father, father's sister or mother's brother invokes the idea that a bundle of obligations and rights tie the two persons together, but it also invokes affectionate ties that may be linked as much with day-to-day relationships within a household as with blood ties. In short, there is a choice involved as to when friends, siblings, kin or others of the parental generation are called upon. That older children can be part of broader social networks in their own right is rarely considered in the literature on child migration (Thorsen 2009b). In the following, we add new dimensions to child-centred analyses and understandings by looking at children's social ties *within* and *across* generations.

Peer networks facilitating adolescents' migration

Terre des Hommes' study of rural girls who migrate from north-western Burkina Faso to Ouagadougou to work as domestics shows that this type of migration is an old practice that has changed over the years. Where in the past girls around the age of fourteen were accompanied by their future husband or a brother when leaving their village to look for urban work to earn their trousseau one year prior to their marriage, they now leave in groups of eight to ten girls. The empirical material reveals that parents generally agree to their daughters' migration and that around one quarter of them pay or help to pay for bus tickets, both to protect and to encourage the child (Terre des Hommes 2003: 12–17). However, the report does not touch upon why this change has come about, its implication for girls or, of key interest here, how the girls establish connections with one another to travel in large groups; only that new child migrants obtained information from their older sisters. Thus, it becomes easy to fall into the trap of moral panic and simply explain girls' increasing mobility as an outcome of their unruliness and the breakdown of family structures, despite the girls' parents often agreeing to their migration. Refraining from examining the underlying dynamics of changes also denies girls an active social role in their community, and their peer networks are ignored. Similar explanations are used to describe changes in boys' migration.

A study on male children's and youth's rural–rural migration to the cotton farms in northern Benin carried out by Plan WARO, Terre des Hommes and Lasdel-Bénin[4] hints at young people's social networks when discussing how child migrant workers are recruited. In the research report, a distinction is made between 'professional intermediaries' who make money by bringing young migrants to potential employers and 'socially related intermediaries' who usually facilitate placements of new migrants to attain symbolic status rather than material gains. The latter category of intermediaries, it is argued, are becoming younger, as is the pool of migrant workers willing to look for low-paid employment in the declining cotton sector (Imorou 2008: 25). Along the same lines, an IREWOC study in Burkina Faso of migrant boys aged ten to seventeen who work in the cotton fields in eastern Burkina Faso or north-eastern Benin adds information about 'socially related intermediaries'. They are young return migrants bringing new migrants along on their next journey, providing names of good employers or facilitating contact between children and farmers coming to their village to recruit migrant workers (de Lange 2004, 2007). How the contact between young 'socially related intermediaries' and future child migrants occurs remains an unresearched field, as do the reasons why children and youth journey with age-mates.

Recent academic studies document the ways in which children combine work, play and playful socializing with their peers when carrying out household tasks, and work alongside parents or independently (Dyson 2008; Katz 2004; Punch 2001a; Robson 2004a). While these studies draw attention to the porous boundaries between various tasks, they also highlight children's abilities to make space for social activities with their peers in their everyday lives. Katz describes how Sudanese boys in their early teens meet up with other boys shepherding in the grazing areas outside their village to play, eat and chat together while tending the animals (Katz 2004: 6). Similarly, Dyson illustrates adolescent girls' frivolous bantering among themselves while they collect lichen at wintertime in the forest in the Indian Himalayas (Dyson 2008: 169–72). Along the same lines, young male migrants in Ouagadougou and Abidjan explained their perpetual friendships across destinations despite long-term separation through having herded small-stock together in childhood. Comparable bonds of friendship and solidarity are developed among girls in the West African savannah when they giggle and gossip while working together during rotational work parties, collecting firewood or locust bean pods in the bush, or walking to nearby village markets. These types of social relations emerging from shared childhood experiences have been given little attention in relation to children's independent migration. Talata, a seventeen-year-old boy interviewed in the Central Region of Ghana in June 2004, described how a schoolmate was key in facilitating his migration.

> I will have been here two years in September. At home, there is no work and [...] all of us are sitting there. It's meaningless so I decided I would try to find work

to get myself something and also something to send home. I was even attending school but because of the lack of support, I stopped and came here. [...] One of my classmates directed me. I wanted to come [to find work] and he first came here and advised me, so I followed him later. My classmate helped me small [with the fare] and I added and came. [...] My classmate comes during the school vacations, works and then goes back. I'm staying with his sister's husband but I'm only helping with his farm on Fridays. I'm doing my own work [farming] carrots and sweet pepper and onions [...] If I want to go anyplace I have to tell [my classmate's brother-in-law] because if you travel and stay with someone that person is now your father, so it means that if there is any problem they have to take care of you.

Similar examples of the significance of peer networks are evident among Burkinabé children and youth. In a conversation in early 2005 with four itinerant shoeshiners in the age group fourteen to eighteen, it became clear that the two oldest had come to Ouagadougou every dry season in the past five years, during which time they had been in different types of jobs. Shoeshining was a tide-over occupation before finding employment and between jobs. That year, the older boys brought along two younger brothers – one from the same household and one whose mother came from their household – and they spent the first couple of days introducing the newcomers to the secrets of shoeshining, in particular where to find customers and how to behave when awaiting payment. These examples suggest that friendship and relations among siblings are interwoven and peer groups are essential for information flows. The care with which young migrants presented themselves on return to their village plays an important role in spurring both girls' and boys' wish to migrate. Frequently bonds of friendship come into operation here. Our studies show that even if young migrants boosted their status through conspicuous consumption of clothing, consumer goods or being generous to friends on market days because they had cash at hand, migration was often a double-sided experience. While children's positive and negative migration experiences will be dealt with in more detail later in this chapter and in the next, here we focus explicitly on the implication of young returnees' production of a migrant identity through activities oriented towards their peers and how that facilitates other children's migration. Can young return migrants, in fact, refuse or ignore friends and junior brothers who ask to accompany them on the next journey?

Our studies suggest that young returnees get caught up in asserting themselves as successful. On the one hand, they enjoy the material and social outcome back home when they have succeeded in saving up some money, and they may be keen to help their friends on to the same path and thereby gain social recognition, as suggested by Imorou (2008). On the other hand, they may wish to shield their friends and juniors from the hardships of migrant life that they have experienced themselves. However, de Lange (2004) notes that young non-migrants tend to think about such warnings as migrants' egoistic schemes to safeguard their own fortune by excluding others from gaining access to the same commodities. Such accusations would corrode returnees' status among their peers, reducing their ability to decline taking other juniors along on the next journey. The practices of child and youth migrants disclose another issue that minimizes the number of rejections of friends' appeals for help in migrating: the companionship does not cost young experienced migrants anything. This is because the children who would like to migrate with their peers are rarely young children but are in their mid or late teens. As this age group increasingly engage in independent activities to earn an income for buying clothes and other necessities and for multiplying their activities, these first-time migrants are able to pay for their own transportation. Hence, peer-mediated migration is mostly internal or over short distances of 100–125 miles for which the costs of transportation are low and thus affordable for children and youth (Thorsen 2009b). However, it is important to remember, as noted earlier, that some also receive money from one or more parents in the rural household to support their trip and encourage them to keep in contact with the rural family (Castle and Diarra 2003; Hashim 2005; Thorsen 2006).

Finally, among the Bisa, migration within peer networks is not based on labour needs; these slightly older friends and siblings are in precarious economic circumstances themselves and cannot easily find work for junior migrants, let alone employ them in their own enterprises. The relationships are therefore based on wanting to give friends and siblings of a similar age the same opportunities (Thorsen 2009b). The companionship of friends and siblings of a similar age is characterized by short-term circular mobility, which enhances the chance of parental approval since the young migrants can easily return to work on the family farm if need be.

Although the preceding case study involving Talata shows similar strategies in operation among the child migrants in the Ghanaian research, senior kin networks appeared far more significant in children's mobility. This might be because of the younger age at which children in this research migrated, as well as the gender profiles of these children, where boys and girls were interviewed in equal numbers.

An interesting and somewhat unusual example here, though, is that of a nineteen-year-old girl we happened upon when we visited a Kusasi chief in a rural town in the Ashanti Region to see whether he could direct us to any child in the vicinity who had migrated from the Upper East Region. Gifty was living in his household but had lived in a couple of other places, before ending up there seeking help. She had initially migrated with another girlfriend from the Bawku East district of Ghana's Upper East Region. She hailed originally from Bawku, the district capital, and thus would have been more confident and competent in navigating travel and more city savvy. She told me that four years earlier her friend had decided they would come, and when I asked her why she had come too, she explained.

> Because we always moved together. I didn't discuss it with my father [who lives in another town] but I talked to my mother who wasn't in agreement so I dodged. I had written my [JSS] exams and asked my mother if she was able to support me [through senior secondary school] and her response made me think that I should forget about education. [So] I took some of my things and I sold them to pay the lorry fare. [...] One of my friend's brothers was staying in the police station here so we stayed with him. One man had said they were looking for children to work cooking rice for a woman who was selling it but the pay wasn't good; just ¢3,000 [£0.19] per day, so I left after a few months. Then I came here as one man told me there was a Kusasi chief here. [...] My friend moved to a cousin in Sunyani and then I heard she moved back to Bolga [where she is originally from] [...] Here, I was making *kenke* [a local, corn-based food] and sell- ing it at the local school but it was not selling so I stopped and now I am looking for something. [...] I made a call to my mother. She asked me where I am staying but I didn't direct them because if I tell her she will come and collect me and the money that I mean to make before I return home I won't be able to. [...] If I go home, I will send the creams that [you] use on your hair and I will [...] learn how to be a hairdresser.

Getting in touch with established migrants

Children's movements in the African contexts have, in the anthropological and sociological literature, been associated with fostering practices and kin rela- tions without necessarily being linked with migration. Summing up the points we have made in the previous chapters: grandparents, classificatory parents and older sisters and brothers recruit children to carry out age-specific work that they do not have children for themselves, for company or to induce a childless woman's fertility.[5] Alternatively, they take charge of a child whose family is in a difficult situation, owing usually to illness or death, and they may take charge of children's school education. In many of these studies, children's relocation to live in the house of kin is presumed to be a matter primarily of adult decisions. In this book we challenge such presumptions and advocate the importance of examining children's own role in mobility related to what is conventionally labelled fostering. We argue that it is important to shed light on children's interests in being a 'foster child' and on the claims children make on senior kin.

For children originating in the Upper East Region, senior kin networks were far more significant in children's mobility than peer networks, which was also the case for girls from Pays Bisa, whereas Bisa boys were as likely to journey with siblings and friends of a similar age as with senior relatives. Children aspiring to migrate in Pays Bisa chat with visiting migrants to obtain information about various destinations and to strike up a relationship that will facilitate their migration.

> Ousman explained how, at the age of 19, he had come across a migrant visiting from Côte d'Ivoire while selling water in a town on the border between Burkina Faso, Ghana and Togo. 'During our chat, I told him that I'd like to go to Côte d'Ivoire to work but didn't have enough money for the ticket. He explained the wage system on his cocoa farm: if he gained 150,000 CFA francs [£158], another youth and I would gain 50,000 CFA francs [£53] to share.[6] He supplemented my savings with 10,000 CFA francs [£11] for the bus ticket and then deducted the money from my pay once I'd begun to work.'
>
> Paul described how he, at the age of 15 or 16, negotiated his departure. 'I made friends with this older migrant who was visiting our village and by the end of his stay, he agreed to bring me along to Ouagadougou to work on his brick-making site.'

In the two cases of befriending established migrants, the young migrants foregrounded their own resourcefulness in making the contact, and only in subsequent conversations did it become clear that they were related in intricate ways to the older migrants. In Ousman's case, the link was distant and related to marriage between the two extended families, while in Paul's case the owner of the brick-making site was perceived as an older brother because the young migrant was the son of his mother's sister. This additional perspective on the stories highlights that young people too have strategic interests and a desire to convey a particular image of themselves when recounting their story – in these cases the image of being assertive social actors who took the initiative to create an opportunity to migrate was important. However, their stories also provide a window on their understanding and translation of the social context, which lie beneath divergent perceptions of the relationship between junior and senior migrants that may surface at later moments. While adolescents seek to create themselves as autonomous individuals, established migrants may see them as family members and as young dependants. We shall come back to this point below, and just point out here that such divergences of perception may underlie established migrants' decision regarding whether or not to meet a young person's desire to accompany them.

The choice made by adolescents between approaching age-mates of a similar economic and social standing as themselves and senior migrants who would become their employer raises the question of why they make this choice and how it impacts on their early migration experience.

Adolescent boys from Pays Bisa occasionally travelled to Côte d'Ivoire on their own or with age-mates, but the higher costs of transportation entailed more planning. Amadou's story opening this chapter, for example, showed that he worked in rural towns during the dry season for two years before being able to set off on the journey that would eventually bring him to his older brother in Abidjan, and his journey had many unforeseen legs. The higher costs of transportation reduced children's ability to travel independently unless they, like Ousman and Paul, made arrangements with relatives or an employer to pay for their ticket, often on the basis of later reimbursement. This limitation was partially offset by the fact that children were not fussy about the kind of work they would do, which in turn meant that they could approach all visiting migrants to try their luck.

An important point to reiterate here is the broad notion of relatedness, which in the West African context of extensive mobility means that hopeful adolescents may approach a range of close and distant kin to enhance the likelihood of finding someone willing to pay for their journey. However, the age gap means that children's opinions are not important in determining older migrants' social standing and they may easily ignore the subtle requests put forward by hopeful children. Migration with older established migrants, therefore, is characterized by inequality. Established migrants agree to take youngsters along if they need extra hands on their farm, in their business or at home, but sometimes also when they do not need additional labour power (Thorsen 2009b). This is in part because of the poverty and marginalization of rural areas, which provide few opportunities for children and youth to make a living, and both rural parents and established migrants may wish to help them overcome this limitation (Whitehead et al. 2007). It is also because of the importance of social relations and networks in African economies (Morice 1987) and the migrants' links with the youngsters' parents. The motivation of established migrants to bring children and youth with them, therefore, is any combination of labour requirements, wishing to help juniors to do well in their own right and to help their families. This may be to the benefit of the child wishing to migrate but it may also result in children and/or adults acquiescing in a child's relocation, despite their better judgement. Moreover, the relationship could also work the other way. The presence of one young migrant boy of about eight or nine from the Upper East Region was explained by an adult in the house to which he had been moved as being due to his father wishing to cement a distant relationship with this household, which was of significant social standing and power. Children, then, may move to other households to reinforce ties between adults (Hashim 2004: 107). As we shall discuss later, the nature of these relationships and motivations for agreeing to take on a migrant child may have implications for the extent to which youngsters' migratory experiences are primarily positive or negative.

The way in which children use social networks to facilitate their independent migration by finding travel companions who can show them the route and in some cases help finance the trip follows the logic of chain migration. This concept has mostly been used in the context of migration into North America, from the 1990s onwards, especially from Mexico (Wilson 1994), while the focus in the African context has been the interlinking of rural and urban communities. The presence of a migrant community at the destination lowers the costs and risks of movement and thereby promotes the migration of a broader set of people (Massey et al. 1993). Children's journeys are thus a product of many earlier journeys by older migrants. The notion of chain migration brings to the fore the question of how independent child migrants are. While this question would not be raised for adults, who are theorized as individuals and complete persons, children are conceptualized in much of the policy literature as persons-in-the-becoming and dependants per se. This is why child migrants are so often seen as victims or as passive elements in adult strategies.

Children's and youth's journeys

Despite the focus on trafficking and measures to intercept child migrants on the move, most studies underpinning international and national policies are silent about how journeys are undertaken concretely. It is presumed that by targeting drivers of long-distance buses and minibuses, as well as police officers working at border posts, through information campaigns and control, children's movements can be contained. Awareness-raising at this level is perceived as more efficient since rural parents are often seen as part of the problem; owing either to their ignorance of the dangers to which child migrants are subjected or to their reliance on children's income. Again, children's own ideas are overlooked, as is the context from which they start their journey.

The first journey

As discussed in Chapter 3, when children leave in secrecy it is frequently seen by outsiders as a conflict creating or being the outcome of a rupture in the relationship with their parents. To assume that this is always the case, however, is to assume rather normative ideas of how families function and of inter-generational relationships. As noted in the previous chapter, there may be a variety of reasons why children leave without parental permission. In this chapter we want to explore further what light secret departures shed on decision-making within a household. Moreover, we examine what the implications of running away are – or not – for children's actual journeys.

Sitting at the edge of his vegetable garden near Abidjan's airport early in January 2008, twenty-seven-year-old Gambile looked back at his first migration to Ouagadougou. He had worked in a cafeteria where we had been regular visitors since 2005. At first he said he had left home in secret, but then went on to describe his departure for Ouagadougou when he was sixteen or seventeen years old, after he had had to drop out of secondary school because his father did not have money for the school fees.

> I'd prepared all my clothes, packed my bag and chosen the day I'd travel, but
> I hadn't said anything to my father. My mother had a hunch because she'd

washed my clothes. The day of my departure, I rose at four o'clock in the morning while everyone still slept, I woke an older brother who knew about my plans, and he asked if I was ready. When I said yes, he wished me a safe journey. Then I woke my younger brother who also knew my plans and he got up, carried the bicycle outside our courtyard without waking our father and then pedalled me to town to see me off at the bus station. Once my father found out, what could he say? From that point, he would just wish me the best of luck!

Gambile's story illustrates how various family members apart from the household head were aware of his plans to migrate. In so doing it challenges the image of the family and the household as a utilitarian entity where all actions are in the mutual interests of the family, but rather demonstrates that household members may have diverging interests. Power hierarchies within the household may imply that other members become quiet accomplices in children and youth's strategies. Alternatively adults can assert their preferences by asking for a child, recruiting a child without the household head's and/or other adults' knowledge, or by declining to bring a child along on migration. Finally, both the head and other family members may forgo their immediate labour needs for the sake of longer-term interests in terms of children's sustained incorporation in the family (Hashim 2004: 109–10).

Second, the emphasis on inter-generational conflict and rupture does not sit well with the importance of social relations and of children as social security for ageing parents. No doubt conflicts do occur, some so serious that little contact is maintained between a young migrant and his/her rural family, but in most cases secret departures relate more to adults' and children's diverging judgement of a child's ability to withstand hardship at the migration destination. As children can rarely tell a senior openly that they disagree with her or his views because it would be considered disrespectful, they either bring up other reasons for wanting to migrate without countering the senior, or they choose to 'flee' home without the household head's approval (Thorsen 2006). Parents often empathize with children's decision to 'flee' (Pays Bisa) or to 'dodge' (the Upper East Region). They admit that this has been a common practice for a long time, and they may indeed have 'fled' or 'dodged' themselves in their youth. Moreover, they are acutely aware of the limited possibilities in the villages of earning a comfortable living as a farmer or of finding alternative employment. The outcome of leaving secretly is that parents worry about their children's well-being until they hear where they are and how they are doing, and that children may miss out on help in paying for the ticket.

Safety mechanisms, trafficking and opportunistic journeys

Commissioned research to document different aspects of children's migration for policy purposes has exposed that parents may help their children to leave. Around one quarter of the respondents in studies of independent child migration in Mali (Castle and Diarra 2003) and Burkina Faso (Terre des Hommes 2003) were given money by parents to cover fully or partially the costs of transportation and the early stay at the destination. This is primarily a means of protecting the child. According to one mother, she supplemented her daughter's savings 'because I couldn't see my child travel without giving her something' (ibid.: 16). Another mother in south-eastern Burkina Faso, whose husband had allowed their sixteen-year-old son to migrate, gave the proceeds from brewing beer to her son to pay for the bus fare, though without her husband's knowledge, as he might otherwise accuse her of having sent away his son if the boy remained too long in Ouagadougou (Thorsen 2006: 102). It is important also to note that fathers are equally interested in their children travelling safely and they subsidize both daughters' and sons' journeys (Castle and Diarra 2003: 68). While in some cases peer-mediated migration involves children running away from home, the above findings make clear that this is far from always the case.

The effects of anti-trafficking measures such as regional vigilante and surveillance committees aiming to increase public awareness of the dangers awaiting mobile children and to intercept children on the move are slowly emerging in research findings. Castle and Diarra's research with Malian child migrants, for example, documents how older children repatriated in the spirit of child protection often had a very different view on the effects of these well-intended protective measures, as had their parents:

18-year-old male migrant: [My older brother] said he had heard on the radio that we had been repatriated. I went to greet my mother and my father. My mother was in tears saying that we didn't listen to people and we had gone all that way for nothing. [...] [Our peers] laughed at us because we had been repatriated – we couldn't even set foot outside of our families (for fear of being teased).

18-year-old female migrant: Our friends teased us because we didn't obtain anything because we had been repatriated. [...] [My parents] said that it was because we did not ask permission to go to Abidjan that we were repatriated [...] Our peers say that we didn't earn anything and that we didn't even have our bus tickets reimbursed when we were repatriated. We told them that it was because of the intermediaries that we were repatriated and for no other reason. (Castle and Diarra 2003: 118–19)

These accounts suggest that children and adults had similar views on migration and what it takes to be a successful migrant, but that they viewed the lack of success through different prisms. The peer group focused squarely on the lack of visible material outcomes, while the older generation scolded the young repatriated migrants for having been too independent, indicating that success could be achieved only by seeking their seniors' advice and involvement. Peer and/or family pressure encouraged repatriated children and youth to embark on a second journey shortly after their return. So the assumed protection, in reality, introduced an extra cost inasmuch as they had to pay the bus fare twice and possibly also bribes, since the introduction of checks on young migrants' identity cards and other documents might be exploited as a basis for bribery by the police (ibid.: 120).

While these measures seem to have done little to decrease children's migration, they have sparked off adaptations in travel practices. In Mali – and in other contexts where anti-trafficking measures have been promoted insistently – they have had the effect of making journeys more clandestine and dangerous because honest drivers and intermediaries, who have often acted as children's advocates and protectors, fear being branded as traffickers. Children may thus be forced into the hands of potentially unscrupulous drivers or intermediaries (ibid.). In northern Benin, vigilante committees have had interesting effects. On the one hand, they have led to diffused and covert journeys where children travel in pairs or on their own and often break the journey into shorter legs to avoid interference. Furthermore, they have resulted in some parents bringing their children to the destination. On the other hand, parents and children also use the committees. Some parents interact with professional intermediaries to send off their children, then notify the local anti-trafficking committee, which stops the intermediaries and extracts money from them, whereas some children use anti-trafficking committees to claim their payment from employers who default (Imorou 2008).

In spite of the significant advocacy and intervention programmes launched by the ILO-IPEC and the LUTRENA programme, the impact of vigilante and surveillance committees and anti-trafficking measures varies tremendously from one region to another. In both our study areas, the impact has been negligible: none of the children or youth interviewed had been intercepted and the theme of trafficking rarely came up in conversations. Ibrahim's account below reveals that some of the migrants came into contact with malevolent intermediaries whom they labelled (border) 'crossers'. We have known Ibrahim and his family for about ten years and have followed his migration from his village to a rural town, to Ouagadougou and, in 2007, when he was twenty-three or twenty-four years old, to Côte d'Ivoire. By the time he travelled to Côte d'Ivoire he was street wise, but he nevertheless experienced difficulties.

> The manner in which they tired us on the border, really it wasn't for children! I travelled to Côte d'Ivoire with a friend from my village. After having spent about five years in Ouagadougou I know city life pretty well, he didn't but he'd been at school. We went via Ghana and crossed into Côte d'Ivoire at Noe. That was the difficult part!
>
> These bandits – one of them a Burkinabé, a Mossi, who approached us in the bus station – told us that we would have to pay 10,000 CFA francs [£10] to cross

the border unless we went with them. I didn't trust them, especially because they would take us one by one, so I refused to budge without my brother. I didn't want to get myself killed in the bush or let them kill my brother. We started arguing and in the end, the police interfered and brought my friend and me into a small house. They asked us to pay 5,000 CFA francs [£5] each but the bandits had already taken my 5,000 CFA francs to get us over the border, all I'd left was 2,000 [£2] something and my friend had 5,000 something. Now the bandits turned up and began to negotiate with the police, they added 2,000 CFA francs from my friend to the 5,000 CFA francs I'd already given them and paid the police. Then they walked away from the border post with us, immediately asking how much we had left. When we answered that we had nothing left, they searched our pockets and took every single coin. After that, they tried to place us with a cocoa farmer who would pay us 100,000 CFA francs [£105] at the end of the year but I refused to work there. Then they wanted to place my friend alone but I told them that we had come together and were going to stay together. They threatened to bring my friend back to the Ghanaian side of the border but this time he refused to budge. Ha! They stood there and I thought, 'this is it'. But they only said that we would have to phone our brothers to come and pick us up because they would no longer try to help us.

Before they left, they phoned my friend's uncle but he just said that since his nephew hadn't phoned ahead to tell him about the journey, he knew nothing about this story, so his nephew would have to find work where he was and then return to Burkina. 'Well, if it's like that', I said, 'I'll try to phone my uncle in Abidjan.' He was a bit more positive but told us to stay put for two days since he had a naming ceremony for his newborn son the next day, after that he would come and pick us up. I'd kind of hoped for better news. I also have a brother who has a cocoa farm in Sassandra and I was sure that he would want someone to work on his farm. When we called him, he told us that if he travelled all the way from Sassandra to Noe to pick us up, it would almost be as far as going to Burkina! There we were, we didn't have anything to eat and we slept outdoors! We had to beg to eat!

We felt really, really miserable then. We had counted on our relatives [...] but then it was our own fault as well because we hadn't phoned to confirm that we were coming. That was the problem, you see, life here is not like in our village. We knew that, but if we'd called they would have told us not to come, therefore we were obliged to come without saying anything. Even if your relative is disappointed when you turn up, he can't tell you to return home, well, some do but most choose just to take you in.

Together with Amadou's story opening the chapter, this detailed account of a trip from the young migrants' village of origin to Abidjan reveals a lot about the optimism with which children and youth set off from home, the hazards they encounter on the way and their strategies to make claims on kin at the destination.

While travel costs on short journeys are usually fixed, it can be difficult to estimate the amount of money needed for a longer journey involving several buses, border crossings and the invariable roadblocks located on busy roads. Under the guise of security, they are points of extortion of money from passengers, especially from those who do not have all the required documents or are of foreign origin. Castle and Diarra (2003) note how Malian travellers of all ages cross the border to Côte d'Ivoire on foot or motorcycle taxi on the back roads to avoid the border police, who will ask money irrespective of whether the travellers have the right documents or not. After the eruption of the civil war in Côte d'Ivoire in 2002 and the subsequent partition of the country into the rebel-controlled north and the government-controlled south, the number of roadblocks increased drastically and many Burkinabé migrants began to travel via Ghana to avoid them. However, underestimating the travel costs is not always the reason for getting stuck. As Amadou's story shows, adolescents and youth know the approximate costs but still head out with much less money than required in their pocket. They expect to find work along the way and are not worried about working on plantations for a while, even if some of them have aspirations of urban work. Some work in plantations for a few years before continuing or heading home to visit the family. Others are lucky to encounter a friendly driver who brings them to Abidjan for free, or a stranger who helps them with a bit of money (ibid.: 71–2).

Young migrants may not be anxious about getting stuck at some point in their journey since they rarely have a job lined up at their destination and a delay does not matter. Their main objective is to earn money; whether they work in rural or urban areas may not make much of a difference. However, different payment schemes may appear more or less risky. The boys and youth from Pays Bisa in Côte d'Ivoire worried more about being cheated of their wages than about having to work for an employer they happened upon along the route. Although many were remunerated on an annual basis, others preferred undertaking casual contracts, whereby they would see the fruits of their labour more quickly and have more flexibility to continue their journey. In contrast, children and youth from the Upper East Region often stated a preference for annual payment as they felt they were less likely to squander the money than if they were paid monthly (Hashim 2005: 20). Second, young migrants emphasized the dangers they encountered, stressing that they could have been killed, as illustrated in the opening story and the account of meeting border 'crossers'. The story recounted by twelve-year-old Djamilla in Kumasi City in June 2004 highlights the fact that hazards can also be of a more subtle but sustained character, where the danger is not only of being killed but of suffering abuse and being exploited because of a child's social position.

When I first came here [south] I was staying at a village and they were punishing me so I ran away. [...] [I was in the village of] Sakora-Mapong [with] a Kusasi, but not a relative. [...] He saw me in my village and said that I was suffering so he brought me here. I wasn't getting food and I couldn't get clothing to wear because my parents aren't there [i.e. deceased] [...] but the suffering [in Sakora-Mapong] was worse. [...] I would go early in the morning to fetch firewood, then I would fetch water and prepare food, but I wouldn't get enough to eat and I haven't seen him buy me anything for all this suffering.

I stayed one year and one month. [...] The woman I am staying with now used to come to the village to buy cassava and I was carrying the cassava for her and crying, and she asked me why I was crying so I told her the whole story and asked her if she could find me someone to work for. I just followed her straight away; I didn't know whether she would find me work or kill me.

Thus, children may recognize the potential dangers of travel, emphasizing their courage and possibly exaggerating the dangers somewhat in the traditions of storytelling. Finally, those adolescents and youth travelling with peers, and thus not subjecting themselves to the inequalities of inter-generational kinship relations and to waiting for an established migrant to take them along, strategically avoid making arrangements prior to their journey. If a relative at their destination has discouraged them from travelling, it would be considered very disrespectful to turn up asking for help, whereas getting there unexpectedly may elicit assistance, as discussed above, although they also are aware that they risk being disappointed, should their relative be unable to find them work. This way of journeying is not just an outcome of youthful sanguinity and risk-taking. Older migrants heading for Gabon and Equatorial Guinea journey in a similar way and either work or rely on having money wired from relatives when they get stuck in Nigeria or Cameroon. It also mirrors the way in which transnational migrants travel from West Africa to Europe (Collyer 2007; Fall 2007).

Arriving in new spaces

Far from home or in a foreign country, trafficked children – disoriented, without papers, and excluded from any protective environment – can be forced to endure prostitution, domestic servitude, early and involuntary marriage, or hazardous and punishing labour. (UNICEF 2003: 7)

The strong focus on trafficking and the worst forms of child labour in child rights advocacy has framed the debates about independent child migration, and many in-depth studies have centred on decision-making processes at home and/or on working conditions and potential hazards at the destination, with the aim of deepening our understanding of migrating and working children. The representation of trafficked children in Africa in the quote above is in stark contrast to the courage and resilience children and youth recounted to us in their accounts of independent journeys. This may be the result of differences between the profiles of trafficked children and children migrating voluntarily. Nevertheless, we think it is important to explore a stage in children's migration process that we know little about – namely, children's experiences of arrival in new places.

The way in which children undertake a journey is often decisive in terms of where they will live on first arrival. The literature focusing on fostering arrangements frequently assumes that children travelling with established migrants will stay with and work for their senior travel companion. Our studies suggest that such assumptions often hold true, but equally may only do so at the beginning. Importantly, however, we aim to draw attention to the many children journeying with peers, siblings of their own age or on their own. Some of them set off without prior arrangements with kin at the destination, while others are expected and collected from the bus station. It is important to examine in each context the outcome for such children in terms of the risks and difficulties they face.

In their study in north-western Burkina Faso, Terre des Hommes found that rural girls journeying with peers frequently stayed with a '*tuteur*' or '*tutrice*' – a male or female guardian – from their village when they first arrived in Ouagadougou. People interested in recruiting a domestic worker came to their households to meet the newly arrived girls and only the older and more experienced female migrants looked for work themselves by going from door to door. Once they were employed, most girls moved to the employer's house. From the girls' perspective, these guardians were an extra source of security because they could mediate if conflicts arose with the employer, and most of them thanked the guardians by bringing them gifts (Terre des Hommes 2003: 17–18).

The boys from Pays Bisa arrived in Ouagadougou in smaller groups or on their own and, even if they rarely had one or two migrants from their village who would accommodate all newcomers, they also found '*tuteurs*'.

Hamidou came to Ouagadougou in 1997 at the age of twelve. He was on his own but knew the name of the neighbourhood where his father's sister (*pugudba*) lived. Although he started asking around while on the bus to establish the precise location of her house, he ended up searching for her for almost two weeks while staying in the house of a Bisa migrant he had met by chance. Eventually after a lot of asking around, he found his *pugudba* and moved to her household.

Shortly after his arrival at his *pugudba*'s house, he overheard her complain to her children that he did not *want* to work. As he said, 'I worked as a domestic for a week but had quit because my employer didn't treat her children well. She'd taken charge of many children from her village and although she was kind to me, she always shouted at those children and I was afraid that she would eventually be malicious to me too. My *pugudba* didn't understand that and now she was telling her children that I was lazy and that if I didn't want to work, I could go back to the village.' His *pugudba* did not know that Hamidou had overheard the conversation, but it pushed him to find another job in order to leave her house as quickly as possible.

What is particularly interesting in this account are the claims children and youth implicitly make on kin senior to them by boldly arriving prepared for work without thinking of their own security. Their stories show that kin – in the broadest sense – pick up these young boys and offer them food and accommodation temporarily or in the longer term. Such claims need not be articulated; they go without saying since they are part of a shared habitus (Thorsen 2009b). Amadou's description of his journey also offers evidence of this practice but shows that children who are given a roof over their head and food may be treated as free family labour (the Mossi cocoa planter) or that remunerated labour may be treated like a family member (the Boussanga groundnut farmer). Likewise, Ibrahim and his friend, who got stuck on the border between Ghana and Côte d'Ivoire, counted on being assisted and accommodated by kin. His story illuminates the strength of juniors' claims on membership in households headed by matrilineal or patrilineal kin once they are at the destination, but shows that they may be thwarted if they try to arrange accommodation prior to arrival, but less easily so if already en route.

Equally interesting are the ways in which kin encourage or oblige children to work by either acting as intermediaries in finding employment, or by disapproving of their choices, such as in the example of Hamidou's aunt. The pressure under which kin put rural juniors to find work or accept the employment presented to them is in part because of the fear that idle youth will become delinquent and eventually end up in prison. It is also because they want to help children along the path of eventually becoming successful migrants with good earnings.

Conclusion: journeying as part of extensive migrant networks

Very few children travel alone when going to destinations beyond the rural towns in their region, and even then they usually travel in pairs or in groups to make it an amicable social event. The contemporary practices in the Upper East Region and Pays Bisa reflect former practices of children travelling with kin in a variety of fosterage arrangements, and of young men travelling with their friends to cocoa-growing areas or the large market towns and cities such as Kumasi, Accra and Abidjan. Many children travel with kin for whom they will work in farming, the domestic sphere or in informal businesses. While some of them replace school-going children in carrying out a range of tasks for their relatives, this is not the only reason for their migration. The high population density in many rural areas and the rate of urbanization in recent years mean that labour could be recruited locally. Bringing children from rural communities is a manifestation of the expansion of the social space from their rural community to the community of migrants from their region in which adult migrants also generate social status.

What appears to have changed in recent years is that a number of children in their early to mid teens are able to bypass fosterage arrangements or coming under the patronage of an established migrant by travelling with peers. As a result, they are not obliged to continue working within the institution of the family for the household head and/or the person who has brought them into the household, but can take up waged work. However, the ability to travel with peers is highly context specific; in Pays Bisa it is primarily boys who have the option, in the Upper East Region children of both genders tend to travel with or to kin, whereas girls from the Sourou province in Burkina Faso set off to Ouagadougou with their friends. The interesting point about children's ability to migrate with age-mates is not so much that there is a market for their labour but, first, that those who have migrated once or twice can begin to establish their social status and network through acting as intermediaries and as sources of information. A second interesting point is that older migrants at the destination support peer-facilitated migration by taking upon themselves the role of seniors providing accommodation and, sometimes, the mediating of employment without necessarily benefiting from the children's labour. This suggests that they take their status as parents or older siblings seriously, but also that transformations in the organization of extended families mean they are not necessarily interested in having access to more children's labour. Unable to keep the children away, since they do not advertise their intention of coming, established migrants may try to send them to work in their own right. This dynamic facilitates children's and youth's migration by keeping the risks of suffering to a low level and therefore offers some latitude in deciding at which point in their life they become migrants.

5 | Navigating migrant life: processes of constructing identities

'Sitting in the shade of a wall outside the bar where shoe-shiners from two neighbouring villages in Pays Bisa met every day to have a brief rest at midday, we learned a lot about their struggles to earn a living and cope with misfortunes and about their hopes for the near future. But their stories also revealed some of the aspects that life in Ouagadougou added to their understanding of themselves and their relationships with others. Usually we stopped to greet the boys when meeting them elsewhere in the city, but since March 2005, we have come to the bar to do interviews in order not to hinder their work.

'On this day, 19-year-old Rasmane, who first came to Ouagadougou when he was 17, talked about what he had learned. At first, he had been a shoe-shiner but now worked at a barbecue outside the bar. "As I'm not with my parents, I must do everything to get by on my own, to have something to eat every day [...] but if you stay in the village, the only option is to farm and it will take ages to develop your ideas because you awaken once you see things. Next time I visit [my family], I'll show my older brothers respect as if they were my father [his father had died] and I'll definitely show my mother much more respect. If you stay in the village, you often lack respect for your seniors, but here in Ouaga, I've learned how to show respect to those bigger [older and/or wealthier] than me and I've seen that it's really important. Before, if my mother asked me to run an errand, I would just say 'no' without getting into trouble. But now I miss her, so whatever she asks of me the next time I see her, I'll do for her.

'"I've also found out that it is best to manage on your own. I have some brothers here in Ouaga but if they are no good and if they aren't honest, it's difficult. For example, if you work and you give your money to a brother for safekeeping, and the day you wish to leave you discover that he has eaten [spent] your money, you can't do a thing. When I first came to Ouaga two years ago, I worked in a small restaurant and spent my wage buying some enamel food containers but I also saved 7,500 CFA francs [£8] that I gave to my friend for safekeeping. When I was ready to leave, I asked for my money but he didn't know where it had gone, all 7,500 CFA francs! That's why I prefer to keep my savings myself."

'We were taken to the house of a Kusasi chief in Kumasi town who we were told, with his wife, was actively trying to locate vulnerable children brought from the north and place them in Kusasi households as foster children. We met three children whom they'd placed like this. One child we spoke with was a slip of a girl of about 11 years of age, who had been orphaned some years earlier.

'"My parents are dead and I asked my brother [kinsman] who is staying in this place [Kumasi] if I could find work here. He said yes. In the house, I was getting no food to eat and [my grandfather's wife] was always shouting at me, so I didn't tell anyone; I just escaped. I followed a woman from my place and she brought me here but left me on the roadside. I was working for three months as a head-porter and sleeping in the market sheds, and then I met the chief's wife and I was very happy. I asked her if I could follow her home so she could find me work. She placed me in this man's house. [...] I am not doing any work, I'm just staying with him and helping in the house [washing bowls, fetching water, sweeping, and looking after his children]. [...] They are treating me well, except that when they prepare food they don't prepare enough, so I don't eat and satisfy. [...] I can't leave because I don't know the way. I want to stay small before I go home, so I can get my things to send home. If I go home, I have no one to care for me. If I knew I had someone there to care for me, I would prefer to go home. [...] Now, I want to learn work. If they bought me a sewing machine I will do that, if they put me in hairdressing, I will do that."'

This chapter is concerned with child migrants' lives at their destinations. The different motivations leading children to become migrants in the first place, as well as the justifications placing their journeys within local perceptions of mobility, shape children's expectations of what they can gain through migration. These expectations, in turn, translate into their practices and embodiment of being migrants and make clear to us that children's independent migration is not just about earning money or pursuing formal education or vocational training, although these issues are central to children's narratives. Migration is also a process of social learning through which the young migrants enact different forms of self-realization and occupy multiple positions (de Boeck and Honwana 2005: 3), as workers, students, junior kin, migrants and peers, to mention but a few.

Much of the applied research documenting children's work in the late 1990s and early 2000s stresses their vulnerability, arising from what is perceived as a too early introduction into working life or the risk of exploitation and maltreatment as workers because of their young age. However, children's independent migration inevitably involves work; because their journey is motivated by the desire to earn money, established migrants agree to their coming because they need the help of a girl or a boy, or they move to relatives with the hope of continuing formal education or entering an apprenticeship at the destination. For children, being part of a relative's household implies carrying out certain types of work associated with their gender and age, not just because they are living with people other than their birth parents but because that is what household membership entails. In the documentation of child migrants', and, in particular, girl child migrants', unpaid domestic work in the household of a relative, the analyses frequently are synchronic and narrowly focused on the vulnerabilities the migrants face (Anti-Slavery International 2001; Erulkar and Mekbib 2007; ILO 2004; Riisøen et al. 2004). The paths that these children and youth follow in the course of their migration tend to vanish from view, thereby curtailing our understanding of child migrants' negotiations of work and, perhaps more importantly, of selfhood.

This chapter documents a range of vulnerabilities young migrants from the Upper East Region in Ghana and Pays Bisa in Burkina Faso are exposed to, and shows that chronological age and even a certain level of street savviness do not eliminate their exposure to deceit. However, our view of these child and youth migrants as competent social beings pushes us to explore how they act upon deception, how they apprehend their situation and what they do to fulfil their ideas of what it means to be a migrant. The aim of the chapter, thus, is to shed light on the interconnections between migration, vulnerability and children's and youth's identity construction, to understand nuances in boys' and girls' navigation of the social and economic contexts at their migration destinations.

Getting into migrant work at rural and urban destinations

It often is assumed that children migrating with relatives inevitably become unpaid family labour. However, the following accounts by child migrants in central Ghana indicate that gender and age differences may exist with regard to working for relatives or taking on paid work. Akuka was eighteen when he was interviewed in a village in the Ashanti Region of Ghana. Both his parents were alive, and living and farming in their home village in the Upper East Region. He had never attended school and had been a migrant since the age of fourteen, working always in rural areas in farming. He explained his migration as being the result of the deep poverty in his home village and his wish to help his parents, and he described how he had travelled with his brother, who also paid his bus fare.

> Before coming, I didn't know what work I'd be doing but after one week at my brother's house, he asked me to work [for] an Ashanti man in a nearby village. I stayed for one year and farmed maize, tomato and cocoa with him. He treated me well, I had no problem with food or the place where I was staying and after one year when my contract ended he paid me ₵250,000 [£16]. Since then I have been working with my brother farming maize and tomatoes, I've also done onions but didn't get the money [to hire land] to do that this year. My brother sometimes gives me ₵150,000 [£9] [...] You can say that the work with my brother is for us but I sometimes go by-day for me and get paid ₵10,000 [£0.63] per day.

Hawa had been somewhat younger when she migrated from the Upper East Region to the Brong Ahafo Region of Ghana; aged seven, she had come to live with her brother. Her account of the motivation behind this decision included her birth parents' deep poverty, the idea that her brother would send her to school and her brother's request that she come and take care of his wife's child. It was not clear from the account she gave aged fifteen whether the idea that her brother would send her to school was wishful thinking.

> I was helping my brother's wife while she was farming. After three years of being here they sent me to an Ashanti lady. I was sitting with a woman from this village selling vegetables by the roadside and the Ashanti woman stopped and asked her, won't you give your sister to me. [...] The woman used to come and buy from our village [...] I didn't just go like that. At the time my brother wasn't there, but his wife agreed that I should go. I was staying with the Ashanti woman in Kumasi selling soap, milo and that type of small thing from a table. After working for her for four years, I decided myself to stop and she brought me back here. [...] When I left she bought me a sewing machine. [...] Now I've entered into apprenticeship work but I occasionally help my brother farming and I also help his wife fetching water and cooking. I sometimes go by-day and collect my ¢10,000 [£0.63] but I'm only free on Saturdays and Sundays. I haven't paid any apprenticeship fees yet but I'm hoping my brother will help me.

Akuka's and Hawa's stories show that children migrating with relatives do not necessarily remain unpaid family labour but may be allowed or encouraged to engage in work for others that will earn them money and also increase their skills. Aged fourteen, Akuka was considered old enough to work for a stranger, and he was indeed pleased to earn an income. Although the amount he earns is a pittance, this needs to be put into some context. In 2001 in the Upper East Region of Ghana, one bag of staple crop would cost between ¢100,000 and ¢120,000 (£6.25–£7.50) depending on the time of year, and seven bags of maize or millet are sufficient for a year for a family of ten. Prices had gone up by 2004, but not significantly. Second, Akuka, like most rural workers,[1] gets his meals as part of his work within a household, along with his accommodation. Finally, the work that Akuka did would be similar to what he would be doing in his own village, for his own household and for which he would not be remunerated. As he himself put it, 'In my life I have never seen ¢250,000 [£15.60]!' His brother's mediation of employment may well have been linked with wanting to accommodate Akuka's desire for an income, or with his own farm being too small to require Akuka's labour.

Other motivations for encouraging children to work for non-related individuals could be related to a perceived need for disciplining young workers. As Rasmane's story at the beginning of the chapter suggests, children and youth who have only just left home and are used to working in a close familial setting may refuse to do certain tasks, something that is considered as lacking respect or laziness. This is a complex issue and relates to the conflicts between seniors and juniors in terms of getting children to work to begin with, and then getting them to work for others when they may prefer to work for themselves, as discussed in Chapter 3. In the Upper East Region, for example, parents' role is to get very young children 'used to work'. Accusations of *kba'ya* or laziness and a parent 'not liking' them appear to be the extent of any sanctions. As children become older, they are taught about the importance of work, since this is 'food', and either food is withheld from them if they have not pulled their weight in its production by 'escaping to play in the bush', or in extreme cases they may be beaten. However, around the age of fourteen children's interests become more separated from those of their parents, and conflicts arise as to whom they work for, as they discover the growing possibilities of alternative sources of support or income (Hashim 2004: 89). When children refuse work, therefore, this may be related to wishing to work for themselves. In Ghana, this is especially the case for boys, whose work is more highly valued and more 'economically productive', and thus more likely to bring them financial reward. For girls, it is almost expected that they should start to disassociate from their households, and their gradual withdrawal is seen as an indicator that young women are ready to move on to their next house (ibid.: 93).

Many of the boys migrating to rural areas travelled with siblings and peers of a similar age who already knew of employment possibilities on smallholder farms and bigger plantations and simply entered into the same type of employment (de Lange 2006; Imorou 2008). However, not all chose such a secure path; Castle and Diarra's study of children migrating independently from two rural regions in Mali indicated that boys migrating to rural areas of Côte d'Ivoire were likely to be in a similar situation to Amadou, whose interrupted journey from Pays Bisa to Abidjan we followed at the beginning of the previous chapter. They arrived in cocoa-growing areas with only a vague idea of how to find work and frequently ended up working for people whom they did not know prior to their arrival, although many were originally from Mali (Castle and Diarra 2003). Allegations have been made about child migrants working as slaves and being locked up on cocoa farms in Côte d'Ivoire (Riisøen et al. 2004: 31–3). None of the young Malian migrants interviewed by Castle and Diarra, the young Bisa migrants who had worked in plantations before coming to Abidjan or the return migrants in Burkina Faso and Ghana, however, provided evidence of this type of maltreatment.

Although girls also help in farming and, by their mid-teens, may do by-day labour to earn an independent income, like Hawa, not all girls get into paid employment. Interviewed by two child researchers from her village,[2] a girl from Pays Bisa in Burkina Faso rationalized the work she had done helping to farm maize and cassava during a four-year stay in Côte d'Ivoire as a result of not finding paid work and, ultimately, of not having been to school. However, as most employment in rural areas is in farming and urban work in domestic service and small-scale trade, which do not require literacy, this kind of discourse is more informative about child migrants' production of identity than of their lived realities at the migration destinations. It is clear that this girl felt that working on a family farm raising crops with the ambiguous quality of being both food and a commercial commodity was not prestigious. In terms of girls engaging in migrant work outside the family, Hawa's story appears to be an example of a typical trajectory in contemporary West Africa, where female work is oriented towards domestic work and trade and therefore tends to direct girls to rural towns and urban areas. This tendency of girls moving towards urban work is confirmed by Castle and Diarra's study, which showed that most Malian girls travelled to Bamako or neighbouring Côte d'Ivoire where established migrants – usually their relatives – helped them find employment in domestic service, street trade or small restaurants. Only one out of fifteen girls who had been in Côte d'Ivoire had worked in agriculture (Castle and Diarra 2003: 49). Young migrants from the Département de l'Atakora in north-western Benin also followed gendered routes, with a large number of boys going to the cotton fields in north-eastern Benin and girls to rural towns and cities (Imorou 2008).

However, it may be that this typical trajectory is not so typical after all but rather the outcome of either a methodological bias focusing on urban-based migrants or a difference between the communities from which child migrants originate. For example, the research in Ghana focused on rural-based children, and among the children in this study, Hawa was more of an exception that the rule, in her movement between urban and rural, and kin and non-kin households. In addition, in contrast to those who migrate from the Pays Bisa, the adults who migrate from the Upper East Region frequently move primarily to farm in the cocoa-growing areas of Ghana. Consequently, this is the children's frame of reference in terms of both their motivations for migrating and of where they can move to, since many move with or to kin.

Another factor in where children go and what they end up doing at their migration destination, and in what their aspirations are in migrating, is what and where they come from to begin with, as the following interview extract from sixteen-year-old Magid illustrates. Magid was originally from Garu in the Upper East Region, which although only a village too was on an important route for the export of produce and livestock, as well as having electricity, meaning that it was rapidly urbanizing and transforming into a rural town. Magid was also unusual in that he was a Mossi and not a Kusasi; and this may account for the fact that he did not farm himself, only helped his father occasionally on his farm, his main occupation being loading the trucks, buses, minibuses and taxis, collectively known as cars, that passed through Garu. We found him working in the bus station of Kumasi town, doing similar work.

In Garu, I was loading the cars to Bawku. I have a friend who is a driver and I told him I wanted to come [south] and he said to enter [the car] free. I was in

Ghana Station in Adoboné but there was a confusion there so they brought us here. The confusion was that I was working with a friend's brother and he always grew angry with us and he said he would tell the elders to sack us so we packed and came back to Garu after two weeks, because I anyway was sick, and then I came here. When I came here, I have [classificatory] brothers staying with the leader [at the transport park] and he told me I could enter this work. There are about 22 who work here in groups and they give the money to the first employed and he divides it among us according to our rank. My friend takes it and he divides it between us. If he takes ₵40,000, I will take ₵20,000. It can be ₵20,000 [£1.26] or it can be ₵3,000 [£0.21] in a day [...] I want to know the place so my eyes will be open. If not this, the work has no money at all. Sometimes food problems worry me; and even today, I had a problem. We brought some people from the roadside [to load] but there was a fight with some of the other loaders [for not waiting their turn to load] and one boy was beaten, so the people dropped us and we didn't get paid. If our cars come, we sleep in them but if not we sleep on the benches. [...] I want to go home but there is no money so I decided to stay and work small to get money. Then I will just tell the leader and he will allow me to board a car free. [...] If I get my money I will take some and buy my room furniture, because I have a room but no furniture now, and I will buy my clothing. [...] When I go home I will be a loading boy or will push the [goods transport] cart my brother has.

This also shows how the ways in which child migrants find employment outside the family when arriving at urban destinations depend on the situation at that particular destination. Children from the Upper East Region in Ghana primarily found work through kin or other social networks, including their peers, whereas children from the Pays Bisa in Burkina Faso also found work by going from door to door in Ouagadougou. Jacquemin (2009: 63) draws attention to a new practice in Abidjan of placement agencies for domestic workers, which have grown in popularity since the late 1980s, especially for girls over fourteen years of age. However, for newly arrived migrants from Burkina Faso, the increased distrust of migrants after the beginning of the civil war meant that they were completely dependent on their social network to mediate employment in Abidjan (Thorsen 2009a).

Rural children and youth who have come to the city to work cannot afford to be idle. Not only do they need money for food and accommodation, earning money is also the principal motivation behind their migration. They are also obliged to work even if they live with kin in order not to be labelled as lazy and sent home (Chauveau 1998). The range of possible jobs may seem immense at first glance, but the young migrants quickly discover the different types of constraints they face. Often they enter occupational niches through friends and relatives and, thereby, join scores of child migrants in a similar situation to themselves. In Ouagadougou, this mechanism has given rise to the stereotype that all shoeshiners come from Pays Bisa, in Accra and Kumasi that girls working as head porters – *kayayei* – are from the Northern Region, and in Abidjan that boys collecting metal for recycling on small carts are from Mali. Another pigeonhole into which girl migrants are placed is that of domestic service, if they are young, and prostitution if they are slightly older. In fact, occupational opportunities for child and youth migrants are much more wide-ranging.

Fourteen-year-old Yacou, who left home with a friend in 2005 without his parents' knowledge, described how children migrating independently could find work on their own account in Ouagadougou. He was a good storyteller, and during an interview in the courtyard behind the cafeteria where he worked five months into his migration, he stressed his ingenious choices rather than the hardships he had experienced, which had led him to change jobs six times during his first five months.

> When we arrived, we knew that a distant relative was selling bread at the bus station. He bought us food and took us to his house where we could sleep. My friend and I walked around the streets together, like we were joined at the hip, in search of work and when someone wanted to employ my friend but not me, I thought, 'Oh no, I don't know Ouagadougou, I'll get lost' and I said to those choosing my friend that they should not take him because he was a thief. I pushed my own case because they wanted to employ my friend but thought I was too little, and my friend would have stayed there selling cakes. My friend doesn't understand French so I chatted with them in French and I didn't say directly that he was a thief [...] but afterwards he was a bit angry with me and only cooled down after I had promised to give him 700 CFA francs [£0.74] and a bicycle.
>
> We then met a woman who took us on to sell tamarind juice for her. In the morning we picked up the juice and then walked around in the streets to sell and when we came back she only would give us 75 CFA francs [£0.08] to eat with. After a while, an older brother summoned us and said he would help us find work because we were suffering. My friend was anxious and didn't know how to quit the job, but I said, 'Leave it to me, I can do it!' The next morning I picked up the juice and went off with the ice box, found a tree, lay down and drank a lot of tamarind juice. If someone came to buy, I said, 'No, don't buy this, it's warm!' Someone came by, opened the ice box himself and picked a bag of juice for 50 CFA francs [£0.05], this was the only money I brought back to the woman and I told her, 'Really, it hasn't worked today!' Then she chased us away.

Many of the boys arriving in Ouagadougou from Pays Bisa, especially the younger ones, began their labour migration as street vendors of cold drinks as Yacou and his friend did. This was a common, but highly seasonal, occupation in rural towns and cities in Burkina Faso, where women and a few men needed boys and girls to sell their home-fabricated juices or snacks from trays carried on the head or in iceboxes on a small two-wheeled cart, known as a '*pousse-pousse*'. Usually, the young street vendors worked on a contractual basis; in Ouagadougou they earned a 20 per cent commission of their actual sale and in rural towns between 15 and 20 per cent. Once the rains began and temperatures cooled, the trade became unprofitable, and if the employer did not switch off her or his freezer, the child vendors earned too little and looked for other employment. Indeed, employers often switched off their equipment unless their selling location was near a hospital, bus station or a police barrier with a constant level of sale. If the children could not find a job, they became itinerant shoeshiners; otherwise they primarily worked as dishwashers, kitchen hands and waiters in small informal restaurants, or made bricks or collected sand for brick-making. Children migrating independently from the Upper East Region in Ghana found employment through networks of kin and friends to work minding a small store, street-vending food items and water, selling kola nuts, moulding concrete bricks, processing chickens and other food items, selling vegetables, working in a bar, shining shoes, helping to brew millet beer and herding, and as head porters.

Street vending is usually presented in the literature as an example of self-employment or micro-enterprise, where traders may draw on the labour of their own children. However, as Schildkrout (2002 [1978]) illustrated in her study of children's work and gender relations in Muslim households in Kano, northern Nigeria, urban children's increased enrolment in school has led to a shift in the division of labour. In Kano, women often keep purdah[3] and can only sustain income-generating activities such as street vending, which requires interaction with people of both genders, if they are able to foster or employ children to do the work (ibid.: 352). Women's reliance on the labour of children other than their own is not only an issue for women in purdah but for all women whose businesses have a small profit margin, whose income-generating activities decrease the time available for domestic work or whose children attend formal education (Jacquemin 2007; Boursin 2002 and Kobiané 1999, cited in Pilon 2003: 22).

With the rise of informal economies, an increased stratification has taken place, and new forms of employment have emerged outside the formal structures of a regulated labour market which are far from being typified by self-employment and small businesses run by unpaid family labour. Frequently, such forms of employment are ambiguously defined because employers seek to cast doubt on the legal nature of the relationship, on the existence of an employment relationship and on the respective terms of reference for the employer and the employees (Chen 2004: 22). According to Roy and Wheeler (2006: 454) more than 80 per cent of all enterprises in West Africa in the early 2000s operated informally, and they provided jobs for around 50 per cent of all workers. Most children find work in the informal labour market, where regulatory labour laws are rarely observed (Bourdillon 2006: 155). In the advocacy literature addressing the exploitation of children or the low enrolment rates of girls in formal education, women's reliance on children's labour has primarily been linked with girls' domestic work, often without reflecting on the recruitment process. As a result, women's recruitment of boys and girls to do different types of work has been overlooked, as has the relationship between employers and employees in the informal economy, which is located anywhere on a continuum between a child worker being an integrated part of a relative's household and being employed and paid an agreed wage.

Work like shoeshining and being a head porter involves only a minimal investment, such as buying a little wooden stool, a shoe horn and some shoe cream, buying or hiring a large basin in which goods can be carried, or hiring a cart. The low entry costs enable children to set up as marginal independent actors in the informal economy (Awumbila and Ardayfio-Schandorf 2008; Kwankye et al. 2007; Ofosu-Kusi and Mizen 2005). While this type of lowly paid work may not be their first choice, children are often obliged to earn an income to manage on their own, as Rasmane's account at the beginning of the chapter shows. One sixteen-year-old boy, who had spent seven years in Accra, for example, complained that 'sometimes the market women refuse to let us carry their loads because they claim we are too small to carry the load. On a bad day, I will make no money, and that means no food. I sometimes go to bed with no food and I cry' (Boakye-Boaten 2008: 82). Younger children who have only just arrived experience particular difficulty because they have not yet established relationships with regular customers (Kwankye et al. 2007) or with shop owners who will allow them to carry goods for their customers (Payne 2004). This illustrates how norms in a specific location regarding what constitutes appropriate work for children of a certain age and build may protect children from very hard physical or harmful work but render them vulnerable in another sense, by not allowing them to earn money to buy food and other necessities. These norms may not conform to those set by international standards and, as is the case with other social norms, variations exist in the way people interpret them and in the degree to which people adhere to them. Middle-class urban dwellers and poor rural farmers, for example, may differ in the way they think about children's work for the family, as well as in the way they think about children other than their own living in their household, and about how children living in relatives' households should be treated. Children and youth, on the other hand, also have different ideas about their position in the household in which they live and about their capacity and need to work. These ideas reflect the economic status of the household, their family and at what age they are expected to provide some of their own necessities, and perhaps also assist their family. In settings where the enforcement of labour market and child protection legislation is ineffective, it is particularly important to explore how social norms regarding children's work are negotiated and transformed through adults' activities *and* through children's and youth's activities.

Striving for autonomy

Whether children migrating to relatives at rural or urban destinations become unpaid family labour or are encouraged to become wage labourers or independent actors in the informal economy can be an arena of negotiation and outright disagreement. Boureima, whose trajectory in Ouagadougou we have followed between 2005 and 2008, provides an example of how children negotiate in a social context where they are considered disrespectful if speaking up to a senior. His story also shows the scurrilous remarks and vulnerabilities children experience when insisting on navigating their own path. Boureima is an orphan; his mother died when he was only eight months old and his father when he was around ten. When we first met him at a brick-making site on the outskirts of Ouagadougou in March 2005, he was fifteen years old, skinny and, on that particular day, really disheartened because he had just found out that he had been cheated of 15,000 CFA francs (£16). He had come to Ouagadougou in 2004 with his mother's younger sister (*na puure* – literally 'little mother') but left her house over a disagreement about his remuneration.

> I walked around the neighbourhood selling iced water and also helped her sell water and cakes in front of the hospital. Her children are still too small to work, so I was the one who worked while her children went to school. At one point, I asked her to pay me; not much, just buy me some clothes, but she said she had no money for clothes, so for that reason I left. I'd come to Ouagadougou to work! I went to the Sankariaré market but the only work I could find was to sell water. I got 100 CFA francs [£0.11] when I had sold for 500 CFA francs [£0.53] and they gave me food and I slept in their house. I could make more than 3,000 CFA francs [£3] per month because sometimes I sold for 2,000 CFA francs [£2] in one day and that gives 400 CFA francs [£0.12]. I did this job for less than a month, then my brother told me that I could find a job where I would dig up sand, load it on a donkey cart and make bricks and I could earn 6,000 CFA francs [£6] per month.
>
> What is difficult about this job is that my boss asks me to dig enough sand to fill four carts per day and I find it really difficult and tiring. Also, I had earned 25,000 CFA francs [£26], taken out 10,000 CFA francs [£11] to buy a pair of trousers and left the rest with my boss. As me and my brother had decided to go back to our village to work, I wanted to collect my money but because the brick market doesn't work at the moment, my boss had spent my 15,000 CFA francs [£16] and told me to wait until the market took off again and he would give me my money and whatever I earned in the meanwhile. My brother left for the village yesterday, while I'm waiting for my money and it isn't sure that I'll be going.

Boureima's account brings to the fore how different individuals involved in the relationship may have diverging ideas about the status of the work relationship and the way in which deep social relations shape the informal labour market. Where Boureima's understanding of the relationship with his *na puure* hinged on the idea of an employer and an employee, although he did not care much whether he was paid in kind or in cash, in her view, the fourteen-year-old boy could, and should, be incorporated into her household as a son on whose help she could count. It was a clash over the labelling of Boureima as a dependent child or as a youth who could provide some of his personal necessities himself because he was working, relating to the different conflicts around work between juniors and seniors discussed earlier in the chapter. However, the conflict was also over his being an independent-minded boy with a yearning to experience life in Ouagadougou. From people around Boureima in Ouagadougou and in his mother's village we learned that he had worked for a number of brick-makers and had changed jobs frequently. His brother had mediated the first employment with a brick-maker who, owing to Boureima's slight build, let him drive the donkey cart without having to dig and load sand, and who provided housing and invited Boureima to come to his house in the evenings to watch television. Mostly, Boureima wandered off, buying a cold yogurt drink with fermented millet called *dèggè*, and went to the video clubs to watch films, much to the regret of his older brother and the brick-maker, who both talked about the boy's squandering of money despite their attempts to inculcate in him the need to save.

Boys, and in some localities also girls, who assert themselves as capable of coping on their own and as wanting to discover for themselves what it means to be a migrant make themselves more likely to be constantly criticized by the adults around them for doing the wrong thing, as well as more vulnerable to harmful work and exploitation. On the one hand, this is part of their enactment of self. Through proving to others that they have the resilience of youth to endure hardship and the capacity to earn an income, or through resisting being treated like children, they negotiate their social position. As such, their activities and behaviour represent their interpretation of what it takes to be a youth in the social context (Thorsen 2006). In other words, they draw on the discourses about youth and migrants, as well as youth's and migrants' practices, in their village in their initial positioning and gradually add new elements to this interpretation as they absorb impressions and ideas in the localities where they live. On the other hand, their practices demonstrate that children's and youth's actions are neither oriented towards adults all the time nor always towards some form of life-course transition. Sometimes their activities are primarily a manifestation of being children or being youth, and the peer group is as important as, if not more important than, adults in shaping youth's social and cultural practices (Bucholtz 2002). Boureima's evening wanders, for example, were not an outcome of the attraction of bright city lights; his village had two video clubs drawing electricity from car batteries, and young and old women earned an income from selling snacks. For Boureima and many other young migrants, leisure activities outside the scrutiny of adult relatives or employers were about the liberty to experience and observe, and thus about – as they said – 'opening their minds' to other practices and possibilities than those of their village, and thereby 'becoming civilized'. However, through leisure and work they also became familiar with the other side of the coin; that is, with practices of exclusion and marginalization, when being exploited by employers, treated condescendingly in the streets because they were young and poorly dressed, barred from certain localities, and unable to afford all pastimes.

Although eighteen-year-old Adiara, who worked in her older brother's café in Ouagadougou, enjoyed the social life around the café and constantly joked with the young men hanging out in the café when they were between jobs or had a day off, she complained that her brother never gave her any gifts. 'My brother will buy a new pair of shoes for his wife or a dress without ever buying anything for me, despite my working in the café every day and never having any time off. For a short while I worked as a domestic elsewhere but then my brother's wife fell ill and he called me back.' Unlike Boureima, who just walked off, Adiara felt obliged to help her brother, even if it meant putting aside her own wish to earn an income. They were full siblings and he was her only brother, so in the long term he would be the one to support her and support her case in the patrilineage. In fact, he had already travelled back to the village to find out why she had come to Ouagadougou, and had refrained from sending her back, despite the fact that the head of the family constantly demanded that she return to marry. We regularly chatted with Adiara at her brother's café between 2005 and 2008, when she finally went back to her village. Every year she complained about not being remunerated for her work and said she would soon return home. Nevertheless, she stayed for around three years, at the end of which her brother bought her several pieces of cloth, which were to be sewn into beautiful sets of clothes, possibly just before she married.

Reynolds's research on children's work in the Zambezi river valley found too that girls performed more work than boys and frequently worked for their brothers. She suggests that girls work for their brothers not only because they are obliged to, but also because this suits their strategies for securing care and protection, since girls recognize that in adulthood brothers are a means of support (Reynolds 1991: 124–5). These sorts of relations thus continue in the places to which children migrate, as Adiara's example shows. Thus the extent to which children dispense with their aspirations to earn an income as migrants and to gain autonomy is rooted in the cultural discourses and practices surrounding their gendered identities and their migration. Girls like Adiara, who come from a region where few girls migrate independently, have fewer peers to look to for inspiration to resist being family labour without a regular wage that they can control. Moreover, they are less likely to have the encouragement of other relatives to take a position as a wage earner, as, for example, Boureima had in his brother's mediation of employment outside his *na puure*'s household. Girls from the Upper East Region in Ghana, on the other hand, are afforded a relatively more autonomous position at the migration destination, as Hawa's account above shows. Relatives mediate employment for girls as well as boys, though girls' remuneration is often in kind rather than in cash. Nevertheless, even though girls from the Upper East Region may aspire to earning an independent income, they are more likely to work for related households. This is partly because their roles and identities are tied up with caring for others. Another pertinent point is that as education is more highly valued in the south, girls may end up substituting for the domestic labour of their relatives' own children, who are being sent to school while they are not (Hashim 2007). The relative wealth of the households to which they move, compared to the poverty of their villages (and the lack of opportunity to earn an income from farming, in contrast to girls in Pays Bisa), means that they are more able to move, but more likely to move to related households in the hope that they will be rewarded for their 'help'. Thus, migration practices are an outcome of children's and their relatives' perception of age-appropriate behaviour outlining when children of either gender should have more autonomy and earn an income to meet some of their personal needs and – as must be reiterated – are an arena of negotiation. Relatives may evaluate a child's readiness to take on certain types of work differently from the outset (Thorsen 2006), but it is also important to remember that children's self-perception changes in the course of their migration. Being subjected to a broader range of cultural discourses and practices through meeting other people, gaining social resources and having to deal with new situations inevitably shapes how young migrants perceive themselves and determines their behaviour. For children, migration is in itself a form of learning, and they develop a new sense of themselves and their capacities through their experiences at the destination.

> Persons develop more or less conscious conceptions of themselves as actors in socially and culturally constructed worlds, and these senses of themselves, these identities, to the degree that they are conscious and objectified, permit these persons [...] at least a modicum of agency or control over their own behaviour. (Holland et al. 1998: 40)

Of course, children who are not migrants also pick up different conceptions of themselves in their encounters with various people and situations but, as Rasmane's account opening the chapter suggests, migration adds new dimensions to this process. Jacquemin's study of girl domestic workers in Abidjan illustrates well that girls migrating from rural areas to the city not only learn urban domestic work but also to negotiate with the sisters, aunts and strangers who mediate their work placements. Through a case study presenting the trajectory of a domestic worker named Assana, we learn that the girl was brought to Abidjan by an older sister to help and learn the domestic work of urban households. Once she knew the basics of the work, but refused to do some of the tasks her sister assigned to her, she was placed with her sister's friend 'to learn to work properly'. After some time, an aunt made claims on her labour temporarily because she needed a conscientious girl to look after her young children while she was away on a journey. Then Assana again joined her sister before being placed as a domestic in the household of an acquaintance of her sister. Finally, she found a job through the mediation of a friend of a similar age, where she received her wage directly. The case study offers valuable insights into the way in which Assana increasingly had a say in these moves, and even travelled back to her village to involve her mother in important decisions to secure a mediator if conflicts arose with her sister or aunts (Jacquemin 2007: 274–81).

Two important points underpin young migrants' striving to be autonomous, whether they are boys or girls. First, they do not remain in the same position throughout their migration; the negotiation of the social positions of being a child, youth or any other social category that a child seeks to claim impacts on how they see themselves, as well as on what the people around them think are appropriate activities for them. Second, young migrants' performance of migrant practices and their self-understanding is embedded in social relations. The multiplicity of relatives and other adults who may have different ideas of what a child or youth can and should do creates an uneven field of power and authority, which, in turn, allows girls and boys to shape their own trajectories to some degree by turning to those who are likely to support their own aspirations.

Mobility at the destination

The continuum of informal employment relationships – from feeling part of a household without equating this with being of the same standing as the employer's children to being paid an agreed wage or a fixed commission – shapes children's migration experiences and enables or circumscribes their ability to realize their dreams. Children's recruitment into various jobs is often less about their skills than about their introduction by a mediator or their comportment when approaching a potential employer or their age if an employer requests a child, as was the case when Hawa went to work for the Ashanti woman in Kumasi.[4] Understanding where on the continuum a child places his or her employment relationship will allow us to better apprehend their perception of being exploited and the events that bring about actions of acceptance or resistance.

Madi, who did not know his exact age but had lived in the rural compound of an Islamic master for around seven years and, probably, was fifteen or sixteen years old, had come upon different types of employment relationships during his first three months in Ouagadougou. When we interviewed him in May 2005, he worked as a dishwasher in the same cafeteria as Yacou, and we talked with him during a quiet moment of the day.

> First I sold iced water from a *pousse-pousse* but as the trade no longer worked after the rains began, I left and looked for another employment. At first, I had worked for a woman in Dapoya [a neighbourhood in central Ouagadougou]. I lived in her household and usually started work at 7 am, after having had break-fast and finished around 9 pm, when I had dinner. When the temperature began to cool, after the first rains, I sometimes only sold for 350 CFA francs [£0.37] in a day and when I sat down to eat she wouldn't serve any food. Also, she talked a lot [argued]. Afterwards, I sold iced water for a man in the same neighbourhood for about a month. I moved to his house when I changed job and I ate my meals there but I couldn't make enough money to save anything. A few weeks ago, I came to this cafeteria, where I will be paid a monthly wage. I don't know how much yet – my older sister is married to my boss's younger brother so I didn't like to ask how much he would pay. I now live in a house in the non-titled neigh-bourhood[5] with three other boys employed here; two of them are here today and the last one is tending to the sheep and cattle belonging to our boss.

Madi perceived all his jobs as employment relationships, as did his employers, despite the fact that he lived in the employer's household and food was part of the pay. Indeed, one of the reasons for his first change of job was the dwin-dling pay resulting from declining sales, further exacerbated by his employer's intermittent withdrawal of food. It is impossible to know whether the woman thought he was not working hard enough and, thus, was reducing her profits by his laziness or whether she tried to make him leave without directly telling him to do so. Madi was certainly not the only one to experience a decrease in the income he expected. In Ouagadougou, it was common practice for employers to pick on the slightest mistake to cut wages to cover imagined or real losses, and delays in payment of up to several months were frequent. This aspect of informal employment is most discouraging for children and youth who are prepared to work hard, but also an indication of the negotiations surrounding what exactly is perceived as hard work. Furthermore, it is an indication of the actual exploitation in contemporary West African economies of the low-skilled labour force, which to a large degree consists of children and youth. Although most children migrating independently are at the bottom of the economic and social hierarchy when they first arrive at a destination, they quickly learn how the informal labour market operates through trial and error and the tales shared among friends and family, and they move within this social field.

When Madi wanted more security, for example, he made use of his social network; the fact that he was connected distantly with his new boss through ethnicity, area of origin and marital ties was an important asset in a setting where deep social relations *are* the fabric of society. Moreover, Madi had friends working in the cafeteria and he probably had a good idea of the level of wage his boss was likely to offer and the regularity with which he paid his employees. He is also likely to have known about his boss's bad temper, which added to the complaints the ten employees made about a range of issues, from cuts in their wages when they broke crockery to their workload. Many of them had worked as street vendors or shoeshiners before coming to the cafeteria, and they found it hard to work from 7/7.30 a.m. until 10 p.m. every day without breaks. An important point here is that although long working hours are frequently used as a measure of exploitation, child migrants do not always perceive them as such. Madi had worked just as long hours when selling iced water, but being on the streets was as much an opportunity for the children to meet and chat with their friends, to see different parts of the city and participate in cultural events, as it was about work. In this sense, the circumstances of street working children resemble those of rural children, for whom play and work are frequently intertwined (Katz 2004: 60). For the workers in small food places in Ouagadougou, the feeling of working too hard was linked with the manner in which their everyday mobility was curbed owing to their long working day. Between peak hours, it was common to see kitchen hands and waiters asleep behind the counter or chatting among themselves or with friends passing by, but the fact that they had to be present even if there was no work to be carried out frustrated them. One employee pointed out that the worst thing about working such long hours was that they had no time for themselves. This was not because they wanted to use all their spare time to explore the city, hang out with friends or partake in sport or cultural activities, but because they wanted to supplement their meagre income by diversifying their income-generating activities. Such economic strategies have mainly been described as adult migrants' strategies (Hart 1973), but with the recent focus on urban youth in Africa, evidence is emerging of the flexible ways in which they seek to secure an income – for example, in Accra by picking up trade items in one part of the city and selling them in another (Langevang 2008), or by trading fruit and food items that sell well at that particular moment (Payne 2004).

A burdensome workload may result in children changing job, as may a bad-tempered employer, but the most frequent justification given in interviews was of a financial nature; either children sought better-paid jobs or independent trade and service activities which they thought would produce a higher income, or they had been deceived by their employers. This justification for changing jobs – sometimes very frequently, as revealed in Yacou's trajectory of six occupations within five months – reflected the importance of material wealth in the construction of success, as well as poor youth's real desires for clothing, radios and bicycles. In 2006, nineteen-year-old David[6] worked at a barbecue for a non-related employer. When we met him the previous year he had been a shoeshiner and had also briefly held a job in a bar. Although his paternal uncle and his older brother lived in Ouagadougou, he moved to his employer's household because it was too far to walk from his relatives' house every day and the cost of shared taxis would make inroads into his wage. His boss had offered a wage almost double the amount that Yacou and Madi earned, but whereas they ate at the cafeteria, money was deducted from David's wages for food; except the employer rarely paid David his full wage.

> Apart from the first month, my boss never paid the 15,000 CFA francs [£16] that he'd promised me per month. At least, I convinced him that if he didn't have enough money at the end of the month, it was better to give me 500 CFA francs [£0.53] per day and subtract 200 CFA francs [£0.21] for food. I bought a little notebook and asked a friend who knows how to write to help me keep my records because my boss frequently ran out of money before the end of the day. [...] His wife was very kind to me. At a time when he hadn't paid me for a while, she advised me to run away with the revenues of one day.[7] I hadn't thought about this option and, in fact, I thought about it for a long time before following her advice. What finally made me do it was a phone call from home to let me know that my father had fallen ill. When I told my boss that I'd like to go home to help farm, he asked me to wait a little, as he didn't have money right now. At the end of that day, I took the revenues – 25,000 CFA francs [£26] – and I gave 5,000 CFA francs [£5] to his wife before leaving. My boss owed me 35,000 CFA francs [£37].

Employers took advantage of children and youth being used to interdependencies within their rural households. Hence, when the young employees asked for their wage or savings, employers were able to draw on their understanding of the need to collect larger sums of money from several sources or to delay the payment for other reasons. Sometimes, as in Boureima's case above, they waited in vain, even when their relatives interfered and put pressure on employers to pay their arrears. Others, like Rahid, who had worked as a domestic for a man from Pays Bisa with whom he was not related, were paid eventually. Rahid explained that he had worked for five months without receiving any pay and finally in the sixth month was paid 25,000 CFA frances (£26). Even though the money did not cover what he felt he was owed given his workload, Rahid chose to leave the employment, not to be cheated further. It was indeed rare that the young migrants took the extreme measure of emptying the cash drawer, though several were accused – rightly or not – of stealing small amounts of money.

Stereotypical representations of male youth as delinquent and entangled in illegal activities have further light shed on them when we consider David's story from his perspective. We first heard of his 'theft' from his infuriated employer in April 2006; additional information was provided by his paternal uncle and finally the details were filled in by David in November 2006. We are not promoting a romantic notion of the innocent child here, merely stressing the structural inequalities that lead to children and youth being labelled as criminals when they react to deception. Employers exploit the high demand for work among youth, the informality of employment relationships and the inability of youth effectively to oppose exploitation, except by changing job or becoming an independent actor in the informal economy. A group of youth from Pays Bisa taking a break from itinerant street work in Ouagadougou pointed out that it was not worthwhile to take cases of non-payment to the police. The costs of making a claim – paying stamps, slipping a few extra notes into the file to persuade the police officer to open a case and forgoing income for several days when pursuing the case – would outweigh the amount of money owed to them. Additionally, they were afraid the boss might know someone at the police station, who would be more likely to believe him than a poor youth from a village if he turned the complaint around and accused the youth of having stolen (Thorsen 2009c: 17). Structural inequalities therefore exacerbate the exploitation of children and youth in several ways, and undermine their opportunities to earn the income that is crucial for success as a migrant.

The dynamics at rural destinations are similar, except payment usually happens on an annual basis, reflecting the payment of farmers by cocoa traders and the large cotton companies some time after the harvest. As a consequence, children and youth may work for a full year before finding out whether their employer has the intention of paying them or not. Although two migrants in Ghana had reported problems with this system, most preferred it as 'that way it stays', meaning children would not be tempted to squander the money. For young migrants from Pays Bisa working on cocoa farms in central Côte d'Ivoire, non-payment led to a change of employment after one or two years, and sometimes to engaging in by-piece contracts to earn money for a ticket home or onwards to other rural areas or to Abidjan. A study of children and youth working on the cotton farms of north-eastern Benin reveals that they counter this type of exploitation by increasingly rejecting annual contracts to work on shorter contracts to secure their payment. Another security measure for young workers is to join employers with a good reputation and, thus, to find work through intermediaries (Imorou 2008).

Educational dreams and dilemmas

The provision of education is very often identified as among those measures necessary to abolish child labour[8] (Hashim 2004: 21). Programmes targeting working children, consequently, tend to promote schooling and/or vocational training, and especially the placing of street-working children in non-formal apprenticeships (Diouf et al. 2001; cf. Beauchemin 1999). The importance ascribed to different forms of education is mirrored in the frequent references to youth unemployment in Africa as being an outcome of skills deficiency or youth

having the wrong skills (UNOWA 2006). Although opportunities for school education and vocational training may be present in some rural settings, children's
migration is often motivated by desire to access better schools and training
facilities for non-farm occupations, and/or to acquire money to cover their costs.
Empirical findings, however, suggest that different categories of children and
youth have different aspirations and expectations. Lachaud (1994), for example,
notes how youth with no formal education are rarely unemployed because they
orientate themselves towards non-formal apprenticeships or begin to work in
the informal sector. In contrast, those who have completed secondary education
often have higher expectations when it comes to wages and working conditions
(Chauveau 1998: 28). Studies from Ghana suggest that children from among
the poorest areas of the country are the least interested in formal schooling
(GSS and World Bank 1998: 26) and the most likely to be interested in pursuing
vocational training of some kind (GSS 2003: 43). Ethnographic research, though,
suggests that those children from families with a historical accumulation of
human capital based on formal education appear more likely both to pursue
this strategy and to succeed in its pursuit (Hashim forthcoming). Thus, it is
not merely that different categories of children and youth of both genders have
different aspirations, but that adults and children evaluate how the benefits
of formal and non-formal education compare with informal learning through
working. Moreover, they look at the extent to which these forms of education
will guarantee a viable livelihood for a child in the future (Moore 2001: 8; Punch
2002a: 126). Moreover, how we consider different activities that children undertake may contrast with the manner in which they themselves view them. In other
words, the very dichotomy between learning and work that is evident in the
Western model, where the former is seen as an age-appropriate behaviour and
the latter not, may inform the ways in which we look at children's activities. In
contexts such as those in which we work, education is not implicated in childhood in the same way. Rather, it may be seen as a new form of recruitment to
work, representing, as it does, *possibilities* for alternative livelihoods (Hashim
2004: 170). This accounts for why many of the children in the Ghanaian study
referred to their apprenticeships as 'entering work'. Whether or not they are paid
as apprentices is irrelevant to their description of it as work, and it is important
to highlight this, as work is very much part of children's identities and others'
perceptions of them as a 'good child' (ibid.: 82–3). While such considerations
may lie beneath the decisions leading to a child's migration in the first place,
they do not end with the journey. Part of children's construction of self reflects
their impressions and experiences at the destination and may form their views
on education and learning once they discover other possibilities and obstacles.

Some of the children in our studies had migrated to acquire money for their
school fees, either through older siblings or from paid work. The discourses
on formal education locally in their villages and nationally determined the

significance of this motivation as a justification for children's migration. Even though migration did not guarantee that they could pursue their educational aspirations, the accounts of children who migrated from the Upper East Region in Ghana showed that in some cases formal education was an important element in their construction of identity, and their migration was often synchronized with the school year (Hashim 2007). That children's return to their village may be timed to fit in with the school year was also found by Kwankye et al. (2008: 19), who, in a survey of around three hundred return migrants aged fifteen to thirty in the Northern Region of Ghana, found that 26.6 per cent of the interviewed boys and 40.8 per cent of the girls had migrated and subsequently returned to their village to continue education. Children migrating from Pays Bisa in Burkina Faso more often justified their migration by the fact that they had dropped out of school, and those who tried to earn enough for their secondary school fees by working in small restaurants while doing evening classes were reticent about stressing their schooling. For them, having to combine classes and struggling to pay their fees with a constant threat of being barred from school without having achieved was not part of the image of being success-ful, and was therefore something they did not volunteer in conversation. Their perception of what constituted achievement mirrored the current structure of the labour market in Burkina Faso; statistics show that the difference in job opportunities in 2003 was insignificant for those who had completed primary education compared with those without any formal education. More than 97 per cent found employment in a private business or started their own micro-business, as did 67.9 per cent of the women and 69.3 per cent of the men who had completed secondary education (Bourdet et al. 2006). Continued education at secondary level increased youth's employment prospects only marginally. Canagarajah and Pörtner's analysis of the Ghana Living Standards Survey, for example, suggests that 'the effect from having some middle school education is not that large' (Canagarajah and Pörtner 2002: 59).

Although a minority, some of the children from Pays Bisa who had never attended school entered the formal education system through evening classes in Ouagadougou, as did children who had to drop out of school because their parents could not pay the fees. Seventeen-year-old shoeshiner Jean-Paul was one of them, and he explained that the difficulties he experienced were an out-come of not having been to school. In his view, his parents had not understood the importance of school education, but to resolve the problem he enrolled in evening school in 2004 to learn to write and paid 8,500 CFA francs (£9) in two instalments. In 2005, he progressed to CP2 (second year) but had to leave school and Ouagadougou because a brother returning from Côte d'Ivoire called upon his help to build a house for their parents. In Burkina Faso, the possibility of entering formal education exists only in larger cities. Since the 1970s, when evening classes of two hours' duration were set up in Ouagadougou and Bobo-

Dioulasso to help poor students complete secondary school, the scheme has spread to most larger rural towns (Pilon 2002), as well as to primary education, where it enables a range of poor people – from the most vulnerable children to adults – to attain basic literacy (Konkobo 2008). Many children from Pays Bisa believed that they would have more job opportunities if they were literate, and in that sense formal education was a means of ameliorating their economic situation. In contrast, most of the rural children from the Upper East Region in Ghana did not value literacy as much as having the skills necessary to pursue a vocation or a trade; either in addition to farming or instead of farming.

Lamissi was about eighteen years old when interviewed in her home village in May 2004. She had had a variety of migrant experiences, moving south first when she was a young child of about four with her parents. On her parents' return to the north a couple of years later, she stayed on with her brother and embarked on a number of different experiences which can be described as formal, informal and non-formal training, although Lamissi herself did not put it in those terms.

> I stayed with my brother to attend school but when he stopped supporting me in the second year of primary school, I dropped out. I lived with the brother for some time and found [bread-making] work interesting so I asked him [whether] I could enter work. I then went to live and work for a [non-related] woman selling beaufruit [a pastry snack] as I wanted to earn money in order to learn the work. After one year, I had earned sufficient money and left the woman, despite liking the work and being treated well, but I wanted to learn to bake bread. Once I'd learnt I sold bread for one year before I returned home. I can't work here though, as the travel to the nearest town where there are ovens would cost more than I would be able to make selling the bread. I'm hoping to enter a weaving apprenticeship at a centre in Garu, but I have no money for the fees. [...] Life here is not interesting because there is nothing to do [meaning no work by which to earn any money] so I might go to the south again to find money.

It is clear from Lamisi's account that learning work was an important part of her childhood and of her mobility. In her discourse, learning the skills to make and sell snacks by working with a female trader was just the start of a trajectory of different attempts at 'learning work'. For many girls and boys across West Africa, the engagement in small-scale trade gradually informally teaches them to become traders in their own right in a progression from the status of free or lowly paid labourers to eventually having their own goods (Fréchette and Aduayi-Diop 2005; Ly 1985). In Ghana, however, the discourses and practices concerning education are both gendered and geographically located. In the Upper East Region apprenticeships were seen as a more suitable form of learning for girls than secondary schooling, and girls who had their own income-generating activity, such as being a seamstress, could expect to make better marriages, as well as secure some independent income and respect (Hashim 2004: 135, 2005). Although poverty probably played a determining role in shaping Lamissi's trajectory, entering an apprenticeship was also a way to position herself as someone who had diverse capacities to earn an income, even if not in her village. Furthermore, her account reinforces the fact that the opportunities for learning a trade are far more numerous in the southern areas of Ghana than in the rural villages of the north, which encourages migrant children to aspire to achieve some form of training for a livelihood.

Across West Africa, opportunities for non-formal apprenticeships have proliferated, in part because states fail to provide more formal structures to accommodate the demand for technical training. The cost of attending technical college, in addition to their lack of a primary education, means that many poorer children and youth are excluded from pursuing formal training (Chauveau 1998; Diouf et al. 2001; Kielland and Tovo 2006). In their book *Children at Work*, Kielland and Tovo suggest that children's entry into an apprenticeship is first and foremost a parental decision based on a simple cost–benefit analysis. Here the costs consist of the indirect or direct costs arising from forgoing the income from the child's labour and the investment when paying a mentor's fee. The benefits in the longer term, according to Kielland and Tovo, are rooted in risk-averse behaviour, in that parents spread income potentials by sending their children into different forms of education and reduce expenses by having skilled juniors on whose services they can call for free (ibid.: 75–7). This representation of decision-making within a family underplays the possibility that parents may forgo their own interests to enable their children to explore new experiences (Hashim 2006: 29). It also does not take into account the fact that children make strategic life choices, including about education, and negotiate with adults to do so.

The importance of social networks in entering an apprenticeship in the Sahelian countries is a significant difference from the situation in the coastal countries, where it is common to pay a substantial fee to the mentor (Chauveau 1998; Guichaoua 2006; Riisøen et al. 2004). In both cases, however, it is difficult for children migrating independently to negotiate an apprenticeship on their own. Diouf et al. (2001) raise the question of whether youth's entry into this type of non-formal training is a 'forced' choice and discuss both youth's and their parents' views on apprenticeships. Drawing from a study in Senegal, they point out that most parents claim that they decided to enlist their children in skills training, while 42 per cent of youth claimed to have made the decision themselves, though 39 per cent of them acknowledged their parents' influence. That only 3 per cent of youth decided to become apprentices without their parents' or siblings' intervention gives an indication of just how difficult it is for children to find an apprenticeship on their own. They nevertheless do find alternative ways of influencing the skills they learn, for example by moving on to another job that allows them to acquire skills informally, or by approaching older relatives who may mediate an apprenticeship.

After working as a shoeshiner in Ouagadougou for three years, twenty-year-old Adama finally entered into an apprenticeship. We have known Adama and his rural family since early 2005, when he had just run away from home to become a shoeshiner in Ouagadougou. His father is deceased but he comes from a well-off and well-functioning family, where his father's younger brother (*baba puure* – literally 'little father') has taken responsibility for him, together with his mother. In fact, his *baba puure* had encouraged him to start the apprenticeship to improve his future possibilities and had made contact with a friend of his who was a tile-layer. Adama's account in March 2008 did not include this piece of information; his aim was to establish his ability to make wise and forward-looking choices.

> I began this apprenticeship in tiling when I came back from the village four months ago and saw that I no longer earned enough as a shoe-shiner. I'd returned to visit my family and help farming but came back to Ouagadougou after ridging the millet. With the little rain we've had this year, there was no point in staying for the harvest. It's good to visit your family who brought you into this world, but it's difficult to stay in the village. Unless it's market day, there is nothing to do. Here it's better and my boss treats me as an employee, giving me 1,000–1,500 CFA francs [£1.20–1.80] per day. Nevertheless, I'd like to find another job because he makes us work too hard. Several of my friends have gone to Côte d'Ivoire, one even left yesterday. [...] If I earn a bit extra, I might go abroad. I'll do whatever job. As long as I earn some money, I can apply myself to the work but I don't know what kind of work I can find. It depends. [...] Someone can be in Côte d'Ivoire and find it interesting and when you finally get there yourself, you might find it interesting too but you might also find it very difficult.

Adama's desire to go to Côte d'Ivoire indicates that he was perhaps not seeking an apprenticeship actively and on his own account but rather to please his parents until something better came up. Adama's and other independent child migrants' trajectories show that children from Pays Bisa often stuck with lowly paid work for a few years in spite of their parents' encouragement to think ahead. The parents overlooked their sons' wish for immediate incomes to buy clothes and small commodities, and only when the boys at the age of nineteen or twenty years had satisfied some of their yearning for money were they ready to pursue strategies that would equip them better in the longer term. Delaying vocational training can, however, also be linked with difficulties finding a mentor or, in contexts where fees are paid, finding the required money. In other words, social and economic inequalities impact in different ways on child migrants' choices and on their ability to choose.

These trajectories introduce a new dimension to the discussion of non-formal education; as training is rarely available in small villages, many children depend on urban relatives or linkages between rural parents and urban artisans to enter apprenticeships with or without fees (Morice 1982). Second, Adama's account reveals that apprentices may desert their placement, a fact that may add to the difficulties for young migrants in finding a mentor without an intermediary acting as guarantor. The decision to abandon their training may be the outcome of not seeing the value of the skills, of not learning enough or of being impatient to have an income, but it may also relate to the way in which the non-formal apprenticeship system works. When relatives find a placement for a child, they rarely consider what the child finds interesting but either choose a trade they hope will bring the child most opportunities and income security in the future or a trade in which they have friends willing to mentor the child. Hence, when apprentices choose to end a learning relationship, they need to consider their other options as well as the intermediary's reaction, but if the transfer of skills is negligible, their choice may be deemed sensible.

Navigating identities and social contexts as migrants

At the observable level, following the prominence children and youth ascribe to earning money immediately through working or in the future through pursuing formal education or vocational training, their identity as migrants is rooted in return migrants' degree of success in their village and circumscribed by structural inequalities. These inequalities make it difficult for them to obtain the wealth necessary to radiate success through conspicuous clothing, the purchase of a bicycle or bringing home gifts, as was the case in Pays Bisa of Burkina Faso, or obtaining those items associated with their progression into adulthood in the Upper East Region of Ghana. In both areas, it was difficult for child migrants to be able to support the older generation. Moreover, these inequalities impede young migrants' ability to fully participate in life at their destination – for example, by partaking in youth and street cultures – because they are obliged to work long hours, they are barred from certain public places and they are poor. However, looking at their pride in broadening their horizons through living away from home, schooling and apprenticeships, and the way they link this with understanding how to cope with misfortunes, how to manage economically and socially, and how to deal with hierarchical relations, suggests that the construction of success is also an inner process of apprehending social values. Depending on their degree of success, their length of stay and their gender, the process can profoundly change their self-perception and, thus, the way they position themselves vis-à-vis relatives, friends, employers, clients and others in a reiterative process of constructing their identity and being assessed by others.

Following the lead of the contributors to Werbner's (2002) *Postcolonial Subjectivities in Africa* and Honwana and de Boeck's (2005) *Makers and Breakers*, a key element in theorizing youth's actions and strategies is to scrutinize how young people's identities are shaped by a number of factors. These include others' perceptions of them, their resistance to or acknowledgement of such perceptions and the concrete constraints they experience owing to marginalization and exclusion. Children and youth migrating independently are construed, and construe themselves, as 'children' irrespective of whether they are indeed classificatory children or have a kin-like relationship with the household head or a senior household member (Robertson 1984; Bledsoe 1990). Sometimes this construction contradicts the fact that they left home to prove that they were old enough to gain more autonomy and, at some point, they inevitably strived to pursue what they considered important attributes of being youth, and preferably successful youth. For youngsters wanting more autonomy to pursue their ideas about urban youth identities and to indulge in leisure activities, moving away from kin does not necessarily solve the problem. Employers often manipulate the employer–employee relationship to get around the issue of payment. At other times, children's movements may not be about achieving more autonomy but about fulfilling seniors' expectations of them, merely in a different spatial locality, and thus rather than being in contradiction their actions are in conformity with their role as 'good' children. For example, as we saw in Adiara's case, compliance is more likely to secure current and future well-being, as well as the well-being of those with whom she has an affective relationship. Irrespective of whether their movement is about conformity or about an assertion of their autonomy, their choices must be considered from the perspective of the different subject positions available to them – as dependants or independents – which may carry more or less social reward than others, while some may be more or less negatively sanctioned (Moore 1994: 65; Kabeer 1999: 457–8). In the concluding chapter of this book, we will explore these different subject positions to return to our discussion of children's agency in their movement and thus to understand better their choices in migration.

In line with Miles's discussion of how adolescent girls in Ecuador gradually discover the constraints imposed on their ability to pursue professional careers promoted in the national school curriculum and the media by everyday practices of local gender models and class-based inequalities (Miles 2000), we argue that children settling in as migrants progressively come to an understanding of their possibilities and constraints. Focusing on young rural migrants in the city, Ly (1985) argued that the city played a profound role in their socialization by teaching them to adapt to constantly changing situations and introducing them to a social system based on competition, initiative and 'la débrouillardise' – the necessity of being astute and resourceful. Although rural destinations may have other dynamics, children learn, in our view, similar social skills of adaptation, ingenuity and perspicacity. The knowledge and skills acquired through migration may transform children's ideas of what being a good child or a successful migrant means, and they may shape their ideas about how they can possibly attain their objectives.

6 | Moving on

Until recently, most of the engagement with the subject of children who move without their parents has been at the level of policy and/or advocacy on behalf of children. Much of this literature has perceived child migration, at worst, as an example of child trafficking and at best as fostering, although this has also often been apprehended from a negative perspective and seen to be the outcome of familial poverty and the inability of parents to properly care for their children. We have argued that at the heart of these types of explanations is a particular conceptualization of childhood. As we shall come to a little later in the chapter, this is the case even where children's movement is viewed in the more positive sense as a 'rite of passage'.

In contrast to these understandings of children's movement without their parents, in this book we have illustrated how for children in the West African savannah, the motivations, negotiations and decision-making surrounding their independent migration are far more complex and are frequently an outgrowth of economic and social processes in children's home areas, as well as at their destinations. In this final chapter, we explore in more detail what our empirical work can contribute to explaining children's migration in a more nuanced way that includes both negative and positive elements in the mobility of which their migration is part. This in turn will lead us to the key question of how we conceptualize children's agency. Much of the time children's lack of agency is foregrounded in universalized approaches to childhood. However, we cannot help be struck by how at odds to the reality this is. Through their many activities, within the framework of the family and outside it, children, as well as youth, 'seek to become a part of the given social structures, either formal or informal' (Diouf 2005: 229). While societal arrangements concerning age frequently mean that young people's agency is curtailed, it is not necessarily curtailed in the same way and to the same extent in all areas of their lives. Moreover, as Foucault famously wrote, 'Where there is power, there is resistance' (Foucault 1978: 95–6). As any parent is acutely aware, children, even small ones, can be very effective at exercising their agency, at resisting parents or at negotiating. Children can make key decisions and can have a wide range of responsibilities, such as helping to support younger siblings and heading households (Leinaweaver 2007; Lund 2007). Why are we then constantly confronted with images of children as vulnerable victims in need of adults' protection? That children exercise choice – or assert their own agency – appears to be a particularly challenging issue for many adults.

Clearly, notions of children's agencylessness are tied to ideas about childhood as a period of dependence, growth and nurturance; in other words to universalized ideals of childhood, where adults are assumed to know best and children's position in society is related to their being perceived as immature physiologically, physically and mentally. Nevertheless, and somewhat ironically, adults are instrumental in creating degrees of powerlessness for children, with the result that some of children's vulnerabilities relate not to their various ways of being young persons, but to the restriction of freedoms associated with adult paternalism. Therefore, the language of child protection itself, the very idea that children need protection, opens the door to vulnerability (Nieuwenhuys 1996). For example, ideologies of children's dependency and vulnerability contribute to the subordinated position of children in the labour market (Elson 1982), while child labour laws circumvent children's abilities to organize or negotiate with employers. Even rights enshrined within international conventions that aim to empower children can be instrumental in this. Article 12(1) of the Convention on the Rights of the Child (CRC), for example, guarantees children the right to express their views and to have them be given due consideration in accordance with the age and maturity of the child (UN 1989). However, it is adults who determine whether children are sufficiently mature, and thus to what extent their views will be followed; especially since Article 3 declares that 'the best interests of the child shall be a primary consideration' (ibid.), rather, therefore, than the child's own views (Pupavac 2003: 4).

The reason we foreground these issues here is related to a feature we referred to at the very beginning of this book; namely, that when presenting the findings of our research, we often invoke very strong responses from our audiences. These responses relate to the challenging issues we deal with in two senses. First in how strongly held ideas about childhood are, ideas which our material often challenges, by demonstrating, for example, how some children initiate their own migration, pay for their own schooling and/or change jobs with, or without, the mediation of someone in their social network. Second is the fact that we do encounter young people who are paid minuscule wages, are cheated or treated badly in other ways, and thus the material, in some senses, reinforces the idea of child migrants as vulnerable and victims. The challenge to us has been how we address both aspects; that the children with whom we work are constrained in many respects but that they also do not conform to the universalized model of childhood as vulnerable and dependent.

We are fortunate in that the different groups of children we each have worked with bring to the fore these opposing aspects. In Ghana, for example, the research was 50 per cent with girls, and involved some work with quite young children (some as young as nine); indeed, the whole cohort was slightly younger at the time of migration than were the Burkinabé children taking part in the research. These children, thus, were constrained in different ways by gender and age hierarchies, and their experience of these constraints sometimes emerged in interviews as a negative assessment of their migration. Also significant was that much of the research in Ghana was with rural-based children, and thus children who remained within the more hierarchical household-based relations. In contrast, the research with Bisa children in both Burkina Faso and Côte d'Ivoire mainly included boys, as very few girls in Pays Bisa were allowed to migrate independently, unless to kin, and this was limited owing to the conflict in Côte d'Ivoire, where the majority of adult migrants from that region live. This research therefore included some girls in rural towns, but principally was with urban-based boys and male youth. Household-based relations also confine them, especially if living with and working for kin, but, by virtue of being male, they were less constrained in their movements owing to fears for their personal safety. Another factor in allowing Bisa boys more freedom to explore the city was that they frequently shared a small house with siblings and friends of a similar age. The fact that labour markets traditionally provide more opportunities for employment for males than for females may also be significant, since boys may be more confident that they can find work at their destinations, albeit poorly paid and insecure work. The research with these young people was also conducted over a longer time period; consequently, it captured changing aspirations and young people's responses to being cheated or treated harshly, sometimes recounted by the young people themselves and sometimes by their parents, siblings or friends. By its nature, therefore, the research portrayed a longer-term perspective, including children's tactics and strategizing in the face of the many constraints under which they operate. This was in contrast to the more snapshot view of the lives of children in the Ghanaian research, which, although it sought information regarding past events and experiences, tended to foreground more immediate negative experiences. Also relevant was that on the relatively rare occasions (four) where children in Ghana were traced following interviews with birth parents or other significant adults, we found that children were much more critical of their treatment than were the adults involved, as did Notermans's examination of children's accounts of their movement between households in East Cameroon (Notermans 2008). Thus, both our methodology and the profiles of the children we worked with were relevant to which aspect of experience we tended to privilege, and this was mirrored in the conversations and debates we had during the process of writing the book.

In this final chapter, therefore, we take up the theme of children's agency in their migration in order to challenge representations of child migrants as passive victims of exploitation, lacking an active role in decision-making and migration processes. However, we also caution against taking this position too far, as we do not want to represent children as completely autonomous agents. Instead we stress the need to understand that their choices are an outcome of numerous and changing aspirations and opportunities, and that they are made within a variety of constraints and limitations. These larger questions concern the degree to which children can make choices, the nature of children's agency and how that agency has a bearing on other people's practices; themes that until now have been under-researched (Bluebond-Langner and Korbin 2007: 242).

Although charting children's agency is notoriously complicated because of their subaltern status, their role in moving between different houses and places offers a unique insight. This is because considering matters of residence where children are actively making decisions or articulating preferences regarding whether they move and to where enables an investigation of children's decision-making capabilities, the constraints under which they operate, and how much room there is for them to strategize or negotiate (Leinaweaver 2007: 376–7). Our empirical findings include further insights owing to the additional focus on mobilities at home and at migration destinations. This allowed us to extend the investigation into more complex aspects of decision-making processes and power hierarchies in multiple locations, as well as the influences of children's changing self-perception and aspirations due to their experience of new social worlds. Before we come to the question of choice and agency, however, we wish to explore the notion of children's movement as a transition to adulthood, as this example serves to illustrate further the implications that universal ideals of childhood have for understanding childhood in other places.

Revisiting the universalized ideals

At the beginning of this book, we noted how universalizing ideals regarding what childhood should properly consist of frequently inform approaches to children in other places, despite the fact that childhood is lived and experienced contextually. An emerging critique of these approaches in the West African context has presented children's and youth's independent migration as a rite of passage (Castle and Diarra 2003) or as a practice perceived as a means for boys to become adult men, either in place of initiation ceremonies or by exerting some control over the timing of initiation or marriage through meeting indispensable expenses themselves (Boutillier et al. 1985; Piot 1999). For girls, on the other hand, migration is perceived as a means to delay marriage, resist patriarchal norms or, eventually, boost their status within marriage (Casely-Hayford 1999; Castle and Diarra 2003; Lambert 2007; Lesclingand 2004). Although these explanations have served as a starting point for conceptualizing West African children and youth as social actors, little attention has been paid to how transition metaphors are frequently used differently for boys and girls. A more detailed interrogation of these metaphors reveals how such explanations may be underpinned by universalized ideals of childhood.

The linking of migration with the transition to adulthood and thus as a rite of passage is premised on two tendencies within many contemporary approaches to childhood, which we began to unpick in Chapter 1: the internationally dominant model of childhood and its inherent notion of universality, and the sedentarism underpinning much social analysis. The notion that childhood has a universal cut-off age of eighteen is premised on the idea of life cycles and, as pointed out by Johnson-Hanks, assumes that everyone in all societies goes through the same coherent life stages in an ordered sequence of becoming. This assumption precludes the possibility of reverting to an earlier stage, as well as of transitions happening in some spheres of life and not in others (Johnson-Hanks 2002: 866). In the analysis of West African migration practices, transition metaphors frequently and implicitly are equated with a non-gendered (boy) child's transition to adulthood. When linked with youth, this is seen as positive and a sign of their capacity to take some control over their life, but when linked with young boys, their independent migration is presented as premature and damaging to them because they are perceived as becoming adults too early. However, as argued in Chapter 1, different forms of transitions marking a variety of social categories and statuses intersect with one another and blur the boundaries of any model of childhood. The resulting multiplicity of possible transitions induced us to explore the aspirations that motivate children to do particular things, as well as the constraints and enabling factors that have an effect on their ability to actually do what they intend to do.

When migration is presented as a rite-of-passage metaphor, van Gennep's proposition comes to mind – that every rite of passage is constituted by three stages; separation, liminality and incorporation (van Gennep 1960). The first stage of separation, then, would be consistent with child migrants' leaving home and possibly seeing this as a rupture in family relations. The second stage of liminality would be presented as children being uprooted because they were away from their family. Additionally, their liminal position would imply that they were in the process of becoming while living at the migration destination. Finally, the third stage of incorporation would be linked with children's and youth's reintegration into the rural community upon return. In this model, the family is seen as a sedentary unit, which migrants leave and to which they return. Seeing migration as a rite of passage in this light ignores two important aspects of West African children's migration. First, the stretching of families and homes to multiple locations and the fact that many adults have, or take, some sort of parental role in child migrants' lives imply that they are actually not outside the family. Second, an overemphasis on liminality and becoming tends to overshadow the fact that children are 'social actors in the present, with a marked role and presence in the very heart of the social context' (de Boeck 2005: 199). These aspects of children's being prompted us to explore how migration affects different spheres of boys' and girls' lives, and how they themselves influence the making and breaking of family and family-like relationships.

The institution of the family is the one shaping children's lives most significantly, and the one we are compelled to reconceptualize because the word 'parents' tends to invoke a strong image of a birth mother and father in a nuclear family, which is inadequate for understanding children's involvement in decision-making in West Africa. Although the household is a site of hierarchical relations that place children at the bottom of the pecking order, it is also a site of diverse interests where several family members within and outside the rural household may interfere in decisions and advocate their preferences in direct or indirect ways (Guyer 1988; Whitehead 1994, 1998). The important point is that decision-making is not an issue narrowly between children and their birth parents but between a range of family members living in the rural household and elsewhere. Consequently, when making decisions, attempts are made to accommodate a plethora of individuals with whom children have a social relationship, of whom some are of a similar age, some are older and some are younger. What children, and adults, choose to do, therefore, must be seen in light of such considerations, a point we shall turn to next.

Evaluating children's choices

In Chapter 3, where we talked about the motivations behind decisions for children to move, we discussed those children who moved 'to help' relatives. We referred to the fact that, among these mainly younger and/or female children, there appeared to be a picture developing of them as pawns in relation to the various requirements adults have for their labour or for wider social needs. We suggested, though, that these issues are context specific and that the degree of compulsion to move needs to be established, not assumed. We also noted that it is only by accessing the views of children themselves that it is possible to assess this, and that the vast majority of child migrants we worked with viewed their mobility as their own choice. In this section, we explore in more depth the question of children's choices, as this issue is intrinsic to how interventions aimed at supporting children can end up creating vulnerabilities or exacerbate children's difficult circumstances, as Castle and Diarra's (2003) study, discussed in Chapter 4, illustrated. At the heart of these issues is a question we are often confronted with, both when analysing our data and when presenting it. This question fundamentally relates to how one evaluates a child's choice when it results in an action that on the face of it appears not to be in her or his best interest.

Useful to such an inquiry is feminist theorists' work, which has explored the choices women make that appear detrimental to women's health and welfare, or which accommodate forms of gender inequality, such as bearing children beyond one's capacity or aborting female fetuses. However, 'if these choices are likely to give women greater respect within their communities for conforming to its norms, or to penalize them if they do not, their own values and behaviour are likely to reflect those of the wider community and to reproduce its injustices' (Kabeer 1999: 457–8). In other words, the context in which individuals are living shapes their interests, so that how people define their goals and what they value will reflect their social positioning (ibid.: 461). When evaluating what action an individual chooses to make, therefore, it is necessary to examine the extent to which action itself is framed by this. This is because the 'rules of the game' implicit in different systems of kinship, inheritance, and so on, inform both rational choices and the less conscious aspects of subjectivities, predisposing individuals to favour differing strategies in different contexts (Kandiyoti 1988, 1998). In other words, when trying to explore individuals' choices, attention needs to be paid to the conditions in which choice is presumed to have been exercised, which includes not only an assessment of individuals' material conditions but their subject position.

Considering this from the perspective of a child, if a subject position, such as being a 'good child', carries much more reward than others, and some are negatively sanctioned, then clearly that is relevant to any assessment of choice. Consequently, the children with whom we work may choose to migrate because they wish to help their parents. Given the manner in which childhood is constructed in the local context as involving work as an age-appropriate behaviour for children, and the impoverishment of communities, this makes a great deal of sense. At the ideological level, it is a choice that reflects the value attached to work in this context and the value attached to a child's adoption of a work ethic. At the material level, it reflects the necessity of a child's contribution to their households, the ability of a child to pursue his or her own livelihood activities, so he or she can buy things, and the potential rewards for such behaviour. Moreover, these issues are not inseparable, as is clearly alluded to by a young Kusasi boy, who said of the sanctions imposed if he refused to do work that 'then, if they are eating you cannot go near them', referring to both aspects of reward for work.

To explore the implications of this in more detail it is useful to consider the issue of children's formal education. This is because one of the problematic aspects of children's migration frequently raised in the literature is that it is detrimental to children's education as children drop out of school in order to migrate for work. It is on this basis that many interventions aimed at preventing children from migrating are justified, in addition to the assumed inherent dangers associated with children's movement away from their immediate families. We should point out at this stage that children rarely dropped out of school to migrate in the contexts in which we work (only three children in the Ghanaian study and none in the Burkinabé study), and, as we have shown, migration may also be positively implicated in children's learning (see Hashim 2007). Nevertheless, this example serves well to explore the issue of children's best interest because of the persuasive evidence suggesting that educational levels are an important determinant of longer-term life prospects (Kabeer 2000: 464). The effect of making a choice to give up schooling to migrate can thus be seen as potentially detrimental to a child's long-term welfare. The question then becomes: is a child's individual choice to give up school to 'help' a relative the extent of one's assessment of the matter, or should the fact that these choices both stem from and serve to reinforce juniors' subordinate status be a cause for concern? In other words, because childhood is subject to strong context-specific *doxa*, or those aspects of culture or tradition that are so normalized or naturalized that they are not a subject for negotiation (Bourdieu 1977), one has to question whether a child's choice to drop out of school can be taken at face value. Do they indeed know what is in their best interest? As both Fierlbeck (1994) and Jackson (1997) warn, there are significant dangers associated with placing emphasis on consent or cultural norms instead of the achievement of more objective and concrete standards, since these can be utilized to validate and to entrench the status quo. Utilitarian arguments that a choice has been voiced and that is sufficient may not be valid if one is to adopt a moral stance (Glover 1995: 123), and these types of arguments are frequently invoked by child welfare activists when we present them with evidence that children are choosing to migrate.

In evaluating choices, however, if, as has been discussed, choice reflects individuals' subjective interests, as well as objective ones, then 'the political force of consent, based as it is upon choosing one particular alternative rather than any other within a range of choice [...] requires a "situated" account of values' (Fierlbeck 1997: 40). In other words, it is very difficult to prescribe whether or not a choice is a 'good one', since any assessment of individuals' choices necessarily entails bringing in an alternative normative standpoint, a set of values other than the child's. A key question, then, is to what extent does this normative standpoint express values that are relevant to the reality it seeks to evaluate (Kabeer 1999: 458)?

As a result, from a normative standpoint, the choice to give up schooling might be perceived as detrimental to a child's welfare. However, it is difficult to claim this, not only because not giving up schooling might mean not having sufficient funds to cover a household member's medical bill or to pay for food during the hungry season, but because it would be damaging to children's sense of themselves as a 'good child'. These considerations in any case are interrelated since it is not individual autonomy and self-realization which is valued in these contexts, but relatedness and relationality (Hashim 2004: 185–9). Any separation of the material conditions of individuals' existence from the influence of such factors in the shaping of their beliefs and behaviour ends up being not only artificial but also analytically constraining. The implication of this is that if we wish to go beyond simple assertions that children are not passive victims in their migration or alternatively that they are fully self-determining individuals able to choose from a range of real choices, we need to explore how children exercise agency within particular sets of social relations. In the final part of this chapter, we shall consider some examples of this both in children's originating villages and at destination, in order to consider some of the strategies and tactics children adopt in negotiating their social worlds.

Strategies in moving and the multiplicity of possible transitions

The decisions made by children, parents, siblings or other relatives before and during a child's migration are layered and not all are equally important. Decisions about bigger events such as the first journey or subsequent ones to other destinations or back to the village, changes to employment, schooling, non-formal education and so forth, are subject to interference by more people concerned about a child's welfare, prospects for the future and/or benefiting from this child's migration materially or symbolically. Johnson-Hank's notion of vital conjunctures is useful for thinking about these fundamentally strategic decisions from a child's point of view. Following de Certeau, strategies refer to an individual's ability to reinforce his or her power by combining social positions of power, by using the social orders and their dominant discourses to his or her own end and by drawing on material resources to do so (de Certeau 1984: 37–8). In decision-making, strategic choices depend on having the power to carry them out (Cornwall 2007: 28). Vital conjunctures, for their part, refer to influential moments of change in a person's life when expectations structured by the local context blend with hopes for the future, despite its uncertainty (Johnson-Hanks 2002: 868–9). For children and youth in West Africa, changing jobs or entering and ending school or an apprenticeship are vital conjunctures, as are having children, marriage, constructing a house for a parent, and the death of the father or mother, to mention but a few. Children's migratory journeys can also be such a vital conjuncture. The multiplicity of conjunctures highlights the fact that life transitions are non-synchronous and that growing up is not a uniform process, but rather one that involves multiple and variable paths (ibid.). The relevance of thinking about migratory experiences from this perspective lies in the refocusing of attention from specific life stages and transitions (to adulthood) or an event (migration) to the variety of alternatives that children can imagine, hope and strive for – their aspirations. As we have noted, these aspirations in turn are framed by the terms or the rules of the already existing social construct or social institutions, such as the different systems of kinship or household organization, and so on. The object of analysis thus becomes focused on variations in life experience and the choices enabled or constrained by these social institutions and norms, rather than the differences in expected life stages and or associated behaviours, which subsequently become perceived as deviant (ibid.: 878).

The way in which children (and adults) speak about the reasons underlying children's migration reveals much about the deep-felt poverty and the emotional work invested in the incorporation of children into the extended family. Such work aims to get children to consider the interdependencies within the domestic economy, and balance the need for their labour and help at home with their desire to play, have adventures, pursue formal education or earn money. In other words, they are encouraged to balance the collective interests of the household with their individual desires in a manner that reflects the increasing expectations of them, as they grow older, but also their changing desires (Hashim 2004: 82–9; Hashim 2006: 6–7). However, this work may also have a longer-term perspective of incorporating both boys and girls into the web of kin to ameliorate the future possibilities for the children and to ensure their eventual support of their parents and other significant adults (Thorsen 2005: 145–51). In Pays Bisa, for example, many married migrant women send small gifts to their parents, in particular to their mother, which have huge symbolic value. Additionally, the link between married daughters and a household is sustained through the kinship structure, which attributes importance to a child's *donno ko* – the mother's place – but requires emotional work to turn it into practical kinship relations. Women also are key figures in care work and may spend several years in their natal household to care for an elderly parent. Similarly, in the Bawku East district, girls rarely move very far away from their natal villages when they marry and often continue to farm the land that they have farmed privately before marriage, relying on the support of kin in their home village to do so. Women also rely on their families for support at times of crisis, and might even return home permanently. It is also common for young women to come home for a few weeks after the birth of their first child, returning to help their mothers with their farming and provide other forms of support. Marriage, then, does not sever women's ties with their natal household but transforms them, and the ways in which children (both old and young) are linked with their households is relevant to how decisions are made regarding their migration.

If we return to the example of wanting to be a 'good child' and how that may be linked with the vital conjuncture of the very first journey as a migrant, temporality comes into the picture. One child's choice may be linked to the immediate reward of being considered a 'good child' there and then, while another child's choice may be associated with the hope of eventually being deemed a 'good child' some time in the future. A child joining the household of a relative as part of an arrangement principally agreed by adults is an example of the former. In reality, very few children are uninterested in migrating as mobility is so engrained in their society that living in multiple locations is the rule rather than the exception. Hence, the practice of migration is as normal for the children in our studies as farming, trading and, for some, going to school, and yet it is not an everyday activity. For boys and girls alike migration is part of the social fabric of their lives because so many adult members of their families and/or communities are migrants, and because the prospect of moving to live with a relative or, depending on the practices surrounding migration in their particular context, migrating independently is always present. If children of either gender diverge from this common practice of privileging migration, they are rarely forced to leave or sent away against their will but instead are enticed by promises of formal or non-formal education, paid work and so on, which may or may not be met. This may make them feel obliged to leave, but children may also behave strategically in ways that convince the adults around them that they are not old or sensible enough to move anywhere or to do what would be required of them (cf. Johnson-Hanks 2002: 868; Valentine 2003: 38). When such behaviour falls within the common conceptualization of age- and gender-appropriate behaviour, children can influence decisions about their own lives without the perception of them as 'good children' changing; there is thus some scope for navigating within the social context of the family. This issue of negotiating to which social categories a young person belongs is one we discuss in detail below.

In the cases where a child is concerned about being a 'good child' some day in the future, the underlying motivations are often intertwined with what children feel is expected of them and how they believe it best to justify their migration to get the approval of parents and other significant adults before migrating or *ex post* when having left secretly. Thus, the motivations which young migrants mention when asked about them in interviews are along the lines of being a 'good child' who returns to the village at the beginning of every rainy season to work on the household head's farm. This, for example, was very common among the itinerant shoeshiners in Ouagadougou, but subsequent interviews in the following years and visits to their families revealed that few went home if their labour was not needed and their families generally agreed to, and were even involved in, this decision. In contrast, the children in the Ghanaian research who had been living away from their originating communities for some years rarely reported returning home. The fact that children decided and/or were en-couraged to continue working where they were is perhaps not surprising. Being a 'good child' incorporates within it aspects of independence and degrees of self-reliance, which their migratory experiences enabled them to perform. Thus, children could fulfil their aspirations for an independent income or pursue an apprenticeship, i.e. not return home, while also not challenging notions of them as a 'good child'. Alternatively young migrants alluded to being a 'successful migrant', where a 'good (male) child' constructs a new house for his father and one for his mother and a 'good (female) child' prepares for her marriage but also brings home gifts for her mother and siblings. These longer-term perspectives are thus associated with a series of vital conjunctures, of journeying, changing occupation, constructing houses and marrying, which are circumscribed by the opportunities available to young migrants at their destination, but which also reinforce how the trajectories of being and of becoming are multiple and varied.

Achieving the aspirations associated with some conjunctures, however, is determined as much by income levels as decisions that are necessarily within the child's capacities or capabilities. One such example is that of constructing a house for a parent and thus being able to give a highly symbolic gift that shows every passer-by that this senior person has a successful child and is well looked after, as, for example, Bisa boys aspired to do. Children earning minuscule wages, as do most of the children in our studies, are not in a position to buy all the wood, corrugated iron sheets and possibly windows and a door, in addition to paying a mason and remunerating additional labour power to build a new house. Although Bisa boys frequently spoke of their wish to construct a house, and Bisa girls occasionally did, their parents did not expect them to do so in the early years of their migration. What was important to parents was the expression of consideration and affection. In Pays Bisa, some of the boys in Ouagadougou and Abidjan contributed to constructing a house by pooling resources with older brothers, but more often their contribution was in returning to the village to provide labour power. Among the Kasena, who originate in the Upper East Region of Ghana, it also is common for male migrants to construct a room in their father's household to physically and symbolically assert their belonging, and thus their place in the inter-generational hierarchy (Cassiman 2009: 31). In contrast, among the Kusasi, who were the majority ethnic group we worked with in the Upper East Region of Ghana, the building of rooms was of a different nature. The arrangement of living space within compounds is culturally significant, and while there is a wide variation in household size and composition, the arrangement of rooms and yards within each compound is highly conventional and reflects the relationship between household members (Whitehead 1996: 91). Children share their mothers' room, until boys are considered too old, when they move into a general room shared by all unmarried male household members. It is usually not until they are married that males will have their own room, and these are built during the dry season using the labour of household members and neighbours. Thus, building their room did represent a transition into a particular social category – adult – but did not usually require a migratory journey to earn the income to achieve this. However, getting the income to furnish a room did because 'a woman will not agree to marry unless you have your furniture – a good bed and living room furniture'.

These practices focus on young male migrants and suggest that it is a gendered conjuncture, especially in societies where girls move to their husband's household upon marriage. This, however, is not necessarily the case; residential practices upon marriage did not deter the desire of young married Bisa women in their late teens and twenties to contribute to their parents', and especially their mother's, physical and symbolic well-being. However, they were impeded in doing so by their income levels, resulting from constraints imposed by their husbands on their taking up employment (Thorsen 2010). Kusasi women were also concerned with their mothers' welfare (as well as siblings', especially females), but were not so much constrained by their husbands as by the lack of opportunities to earn an income. Although constructing a house or buying furniture for a room is vital to being perceived as a successful migrant, and thus represents one vital conjuncture, it is clear that for child migrants it is a future possibility and something that figures in the aspirations shaping their strategic decisions, but also in their justifications for migrating. Thus, by considering these vital conjunctures, our focus is drawn not to specific events but to the variety of imagined alternatives shaping children's choices, among which migration may be one.

Negotiating social statuses

The aspirations that motivate children to take up a variety of subject positions are closely linked with their imaginings of self and, thus, to the way in which their identities develop in and through participating in social, economic and political activities (de Boeck and Honwana 2005: 1; Holland et al. 1998: 5). The young migrants in our studies were not just focusing on their status within their family; they were just as interested in positioning themselves vis-à-vis their peers and in creating and re-creating their identities as migrants, children, youth, boys, girls, and so on; among others, through visible markers such as clothing, hairstyles and behaviour. The variety of subject positions available has the effect of making social categories, such as children and youth, heterogeneous. Moreover, as Johnson-Hanks's (2002) notion of vital conjunctures underscores, these social categories are also elastic, because there is no single trajectory to 'adulthood'; rather, transitions are non-synchronous and reversible. The time at which children go through different vital conjunctures varies, as does the number of times they go through them. Although passing through them is subject to a child's capacities and competence in navigating her or his social contexts and in positioning her- or himself in these contexts, it is also contingent upon other people's actions and activities. In other words, as young people experience obligations and restrictions in their daily lives but also actively define and produce these lives (Robson et al. 2007: 135), they are both acted upon and acting in the spaces they occupy. One aspect of the heterogeneity of social categories, such as child or youth, derives from the negotiation of what these entail at the collective and individual levels, and another aspect from the variety in children's experiences that shape what they want of life and what they expect of others.

Both aspects have an impact on children's migration, as becomes clear if we consider the strategic decisions surrounding children's first and subsequent journeys, important to which is the evaluation of a child's ability to endure the hardships that adults assume they may face because they themselves have been migrants in the past. This issue is of lesser importance when children migrate with or to adults who are expected to take on the parental role of providing food, care and other necessities for the children and guide them on to a path that will increase their possibilities in the future. Negotiations become important when children's and adults' views differ, as we alluded to above in the example of children being coaxed into relocating by promises of education or paid work. The adult perception of children being too young to migrate without, or at least to, another parent figure is not just an extension of universalized ideals of childhood and their insistence on children's proper place being within the bosom of the family. It can relate to the necessity of their labour in their home village. Alternatively, it may underlie the request from anxious parents and relatives in West Africa that a child should wait a year or two before migrating, based on evaluations of an individual child's capacity to cope with migrant life. It may also mirror how the child's everyday activities are perceived as the doings of a small child, an older child, a conscientious child, a rogue and a range of other possible subject positions, and how parents and other significant adults think about the child's best interests. Moreover, evaluations reflect material and emotional relationships between the child and the adult and the balance they each strike between their own and the other's needs and desires. In short, a mixture of concerns and considerations shapes how the wish of a child to migrate is assessed.

At the general level, negotiations aim at characterizing children and youth as social categories; they shape and are shaped by the discourses surrounding who fits in and who does not, as well as what is appropriate behaviour for smaller and bigger children and for boys and girls. Although everyone brings into play the same discourses, the fact that they are constantly moulded by outside influences and people's actions means that the norms to which children and adults may point when justifying actions and opinions are ambiguous. Another important aspect of the broad negotiations, of which evaluations are part, is that they are not between two persons, or between a child and her or his parents who act as one. Rather they involve a host of persons who play, or would like to play, a role in the child's life, and who have different views of what is best for the child, the family or the household. Accordingly, evaluations, whether they concern individuals or general social categories, are rarely identical because they do not necessarily focus on the same aspects of how self is constructed and practised and, thus, of children's positioning within the given context. Not all adults necessarily come to the same conclusion, and children are not always focused on becoming but just as often on being children or being youth. Evaluations are an essential part of negotiations over meaning, practices and individual strategies (Thorsen 2006: 90–94). This means that while children encounter constraints when opposing some seniors in their family, they may have the backing of others. As our studies and a number of other studies show, many children in West Africa migrate independently with the approval and support of their parents. However, when a child sets off from home without informing those members of the family who have the power to hinder the journey, the child challenges how he or she *imagines* these adults will evaluate his or her capacities and competence. This is because, had the child discussed the issue of migration openly and been told to wait, he or she would have shown lack of respect if leaving in spite of advice. The same strategy is used when a child seeks to decrease the likelihood of being told not to come by not phoning a relative at destination to announce his or her plans. Yet the other side of the coin, which is often forgotten because adults – and parents in particular – are usually presented as authoritative figures vis-à-vis children, is that parents' request to wait is also part of the negotiation, and it challenges the child's self-perception of what they are capable of. Even though the notion of respect constrains children's ability to discuss and counter openly adults' views, the secret departures demonstrate that not all children are equally constrained.

Child migrants' tactical choices

When children and youth either acquiesce to a move at the behest of a relative or establish relationships with migrants to facilitate their migration, they place themselves in a hierarchical relationship where they are the juniors and frequently seen as children, which in turn has implications for how their work is thought about and rewarded. As these children become older they may begin to engage in the types of negotiations we considered earlier in their attempts to resist efforts to position them as unpaid family labour. In addition to the limitations placed on them by adults' evaluations of them as children, children encounter a number of constraints and vulnerabilities. These may be triggered, among other factors, by socially defined norms regarding gender roles, local practices in the labour market, stark competition with other children and youth in a similar situation, and other limiting factors. Children's experience in the informal labour market is one example of the vulnerabilities often pointed to in discussions of children's work and children's independent migration, and thus we shall focus on this here. However, it is only one among many limitations children experience, and our aim in looking at this is not to provide formulaic conceptualizations of vulnerability but to help us in exploring how children navigate their social worlds and challenge or conform to the constraints under which they operate.

The way in which the economy and the labour market function in West Africa was described as early as the 1970s by Hart, who coined the idea of an informal sector in a study of Frafra migrants' economic activities in Accra and the precariousness of their incomes, which necessitated them diversifying their income-generating activities (Hart 1973). In the 1980s, a number of studies in francophone Africa described the economic activities of poor people as '*la débrouillardise*' – the need to be astute, resourceful and flexible to get by (Ly 1985; Morice 1987). Today, the level of informalization is likely to be even higher, with only a small proportion of employment for those with little or no education being formal, and most small businesses operating without any form of registration. These sorts of practices and the norms arising from them, therefore, fundamentally regulate how the labour market for informal employment operates. Although the outcomes are primarily to the advantage of employers, young employees also interpret their social environment and adopt tactics to navigate it. In contrast to the strategies outlined by de Certeau, tactics are calculated actions which are only effective if taken at the right moment (de Certeau 1984: 37–8). Employers frequently demand that their employees work long hours or decrease their wages, if paying them at all. These practices inhibit children's accumulation of economic resources through work and the diversification of their sources of income, and in turn their ability to build up symbolic capital through gift-giving and investments in their village or at the destination, as well as their engagement in social and cultural activities with young people outside their immediate group of co-workers and friends. Young people negotiate and resist by testing the boundaries of what they can do without being chased away by their employer or by moving on to other jobs, occupations or destinations, on occasion helping themselves to compensation from the cash drawer. By employing tactics such as these, in which they simultaneously comply with hierarchical pecking orders or demands on them in the labour market and resist excessive ones by moving on to new jobs, or new destinations, or take their due when it is withheld, young migrants navigate their social contexts. Although children's tactical choices rarely affect an employer significantly, given the large number of children and youth willing to work should one employee leave without giving notice, they are examples of young people's active engagement with their social contexts and their attempts at overcoming institutional limitations, such as those created by the informal labour market.

Tactical choices aim primarily at meeting individual aspirations and do not amount to a collective transformative action. In fact, they may even support the informalization and fragmented nature of the economy because the best route out of susceptibility to bad employment conditions or deception by employers is to become an independent entrepreneur in the market. Nevertheless, the exercising of tactical choices, of acting upon opportunities when they arise, is part and parcel of the way in which the informal economy operates for those at the bottom, those who are subject to multiple forms of exclusions owing to their being young, poor, newcomers and so forth. Across francophone Africa, they summarize the aim of their manifold activities as *'Je me débrouille'* – I get by – which epitomizes their endeavours to be successful in attaining their objectives, their willingness to engage in new opportunities and their cultural repertoire in making their lives (Waage 2006). Although children who have not migrated may also use the terminology of *'se débrouiller'*, the migratory experience teaches children the ability and necessity of navigating the economic context at the destinations in a much more profound way, which is equally useful to a migrant as to a non-migrant. These constraints can thus serve to empower young migrants, providing them with a greater repertoire of strategies, tactics and coping mechanisms.

Several accounts given by child migrants from the Upper East Region and Pays Bisa showed that the complexity of households and the links to established migrants in other locations, who are still considered household members, give some scope for young people to create new relationships of the child–parent or sibling type in different places. While strategic decisions may have landed a child with particular kin, such an arrangement is almost always a temporary one, which may last many years or only a brief period of time, depending on the expectations the child has of kin and vice versa, as well as on other available alternatives. Some children actively pursue alternative parents or seek opportunities outside those offered by kin, if they think that it will place them in a better position to earn money, learn new skills or develop social relationships that will facilitate journeys to other destinations or create better learning and/or earning prospects. While the decision to move between different kin or to others is strategic, the opportunity actually to do so often rests on a tactical choice to move if the chance arises. Children's social position may inhibit them from planning ahead and in realizing all the things they would like to or can attain, but they do find room to make and enact choices within these limitations.

Postscript

As this book goes to press, we note that a new issue of a leading journal devoted to considering children's social relations and culture in global society has been published under the title of *Childhood and Migration: Mobilities, homes and belongings*. According to its editors, who point out how surprisingly little attention has been paid to childhoods that are characterized by migrancy and mobility, the purpose of the special edition is to illuminate different aspects of children's migrations and mobile lives (Ni Laoire et al. 2010: 156). We wholly endorse such attempts, and our objective has been to make a similar contribution. However, when first discussing this collaboration, our initial impetus was to respond to the ways in which powerful ideas about childhood have resulted in assumptions that children's migration represents deviance and danger, with children's parents frequently viewed as complicit. Spurring us on were the reactions to our work from policy-makers and children's advocates, whom we frequently had to convince of our genuine concern for the welfare of children. Throughout the course of writing the book, we have come to focus less on countering these representations of children. Indeed, it occurred to us that by simply reacting and responding to these adults, whom we do not doubt have children's best interests at heart, we were contributing to the construction of children as passive objects. Our focus, subsequently, has transformed into one that aims to contribute to the body of research that explores children's lived experiences, and how young persons are actively involved in their worlds; in shaping them, in negotiating them and in challenging them. We hope to have represented the most burning concerns of the children with whom we worked, about their role in the construction of their worlds in ways that others may learn from and utilize to best support and assist young migrants and those around them who have their best interests at heart.

Notes

I Introduction

1 We use the terms 'developing world', 'Third World', 'majority world' and 'global South' interchangeably, although we do recognize that none of these terms captures the diversity of cultures and economies encompassed by them and so use them purely as shorthand to refer to societies that share broadly similar socio-economic profiles. The same applies to the terms 'the West', 'the industrialized world' and/or 'the developed world'.

2 Children's cognitive development is theorized along the lines of two models; one formulated by Piaget and the other by Vygotsky. In Piaget's conceptualization, children progress through a universal set of stages, gradually increasing their ability to think analytically until they reach the completeness of the rational adult. As a contrast, in Vygotsky's model, children's learning is active and they become skilled at thinking analytically through contact with the people around them who are already adept. The context, therefore, is much more important than in Piaget's universal model, but the end result is perceived as the same: becoming a complete and rational adult (Ansell 2005: 16–17).

3 This is in contrast to the experiences of children in African societies, where even when legislation exists and prescribes certain elements of childhood, it is rarely enforced and therefore plays an insignificant role in defining children's lives.

4 For examples, see Samuelsen (1999) on the Bisa, Bonnet (1981) on the Mossi and Cartry (1982) on the Gourmantché in Burkina Faso, Piot (1999) on the Kabre in northern Togo, Gottlieb (1998) on the Beng in Côte d'Ivoire, Ferme (2001) on the Mende in Sierra Leone and Journet (1981) on the Dioula in Senegal.

5 Until recently, care-giving has not been on the research agenda for Africa but has become an issue with the AIDS pandemic and the increased need to provide care for terminally ill people, orphans and old people left without able-bodied producers (Kesby et al. 2006). The situation of orphans has been picked up in the emerging research on childhoods in Africa, and evidence of the inability of extended families to carry the burden of social security and the appearance of new concepts such as child-headed households have caused unintended moral panic about the breakdown of families and unprotected children (Evans 2010; Nyam-bedha and Aagaard-Hansen 2003). The strong focus on AIDS-related changes in eastern and southern Africa in particular has shifted attention away from the dynamics of care-giving in families that are not hit by the pandemic. In West Africa, the infection rate is much lower, and the pandemic has not had the same impact on social relations; thus it is important to explore practices and expectations related to care-giving.

6 We use the term 'education' in the broadest sense – that is, as learning; while 'schooling' or 'formal education' is used to refer to the institutionalization of learning, including vocational training. Apprenticeships are regarded as non-formal education, although it is important to note that those participating in our research did not always differentiate between formal vocational training provided by private or state institutions, and more informal apprenticeship opportunities. For a definition of the various terms associated with education, see Leach (2003).

7 The truth of the matter, of course, is that far from being a sanctuary, the home is the place where children are most likely

to be abused or harmed. For example, in the UK the vast majority of children who are killed are killed by a parent or close relative (Moore 2004: 739). This serves further to underscore how this model of childhood is an idealized version, and one that is far from the reality in much of the world.

8 See Van Hear (1984) for an exceptional early example of the inclusion of children in a study of migration.

2 Contexts of migration

1 Kusasi children dominated the research in Ghana; however, Mossi and Busanga (another ethnonym for Bisa) children were also interviewed.

2 Since both phases of research were carried out in Ghana, the Bawku East district has been divided into the districts of Bawku Municipal and Garu-Tempane.

3 Iman Hashim's work benefited greatly from having access to Ann Whitehead's 1975 and 1989 research and baseline data in the same village of Tempane Natinga, which showed remarkable stability in many aspects of household organization and community life.

4 The division of work and dependants' – wives, married sons and unmarried children of both genders – rights to engage in own-account farming, trade or other income-generating activities is highly institutionalized and reflected in Bisa vernacular. *Dɔcta hɔ,* which is the household head's farms, literally means morning activities, while *yile hɔ* literally means afternoon activities and encompasses all the things that children, youth and women do.

5 Owing to the nature of the kinship structure, anyone who has an agnatic link in previous generations may be thought of as being a household member. However, until they return one does not know which household they will return to, whether they will build a new household, or indeed whether they will in fact return. It is very difficult, therefore, to make claims regarding the exact numbers of migrants from a specific household (Whitehead 1996).

However, these numbers reflect individuals who heads considered to be part of their household and who, at the time of the survey, were living elsewhere.

6 These numbers derive from a questionnaire focusing on the household composition and reflect the whereabouts of village women's children and/or married women's absent husbands. Consequently, the numbers may not include long-term migrants whose mother or wife does not live in the household.

7 Although children exercised a great degree of autonomy over their income, this is not as straightforward as it would appear in the Ghanaian case as the landlord or household head, theoretically, owned any assets in his household. Consequently, if income is converted to livestock, in theory at least, the landlord has the ultimate say over its disposal, although he may choose not to exercise this control.

8 http://www.meba.gov.bf, especially the sector programme for developing the educational system at the level of primary education and alphabetization (PDDEB).

9 This refers to the number of children enrolled in primary school who are of official primary school age, expressed as a percentage of the total number of children of official primary school age.

10 This system of farm Koranic schools was described in the early 1980s by the anthropologist Mahir Ṣaul (1984).

3 Choosing to move

1 At the time of both periods of fieldwork, the education system in Ghana consisted of nine years of free, compulsory schooling – six years of primary school and three years of junior secondary school (JSS). Following this, students who qualify can proceed into senior secondary school (SSS). Students who pass the SSS Certificate Examination at the end of three years of SSS can then pursue a degree course at university, or a diploma course at some other tertiary institution (GME 2000). NB: The education system was again reformed in 2007.

2 At the time, 16,000 Ghanaian cedis (₵) were worth £1.

3 This is a generic term for the area surrounding Kumasi, so can be a rural area, not the urban capital of the Ashanti region.

4 In the same manner, Qvortrup (1985) notes how schooling is work but has been reframed as education, and is dealt with within non-work/labour frameworks.

5 As well as being more durable and labour efficient than the grass roofing more commonly used, these corrugated metal roofs serve as a sign of prestige and wealth.

4 Journeys and arrivals

1 The timeline in Amadou's story is not chronologically consistent, owing probably to his not knowing his exact age and to the fact that people in Pays Bisa ascribe little value to being exact about age and time. In Burkinabé lingo, the common way of delineating time is to speak of 'two days', which may mean anything from a couple of days to several months.

2 The Mossi is the largest ethnic group in Burkina Faso and, as the boundary between the Bisa region and communities of Mossi runs through Tenkodogo, many of the young Bisa who have worked in Tenkodogo during one or more dry seasons are familiar with Moré, the vernacular.

3 Bourdieu distinguishes between official and practical kinship; official descriptions of kinship relations represent the social structure embodied during ceremonies where people have particular roles because of their position in the lineage or in relation to the person(s) at the centre of the ceremony. Practical aspects of kin relationships are, on the other hand, 'something people *make*, and with which they *do* something' (Bourdieu 1977: 35). In day-to-day transactions blood ties are therefore not necessarily the most important (Bouquet 1993; cf. Holy 1996).

4 Both Plan International and Terre des Hommes are international NGOs working with child rights. Plan's West Africa Regional Office has commissioned research on children and youth's mobility in West Africa, in which the applied research institute Laboratoire d'Etudes et de Recherche sur les Dynamiques Sociales et le Développement Local (Lasdel) takes part.

5 There is a belief among the Bisa that caring for a child may enhance the chance of a woman conceiving; hence, after some years of trying to conceive and of undergoing indigenous treatment, a childless woman may demand, or be offered, the small child of one of her brothers, a co-wife or another woman in the marital household. If she subsequently becomes pregnant, the fostered child is perceived to have brought her luck. She has, in other words, proved her maternal capability, and this to a degree where ancestral spirits accept her as a host for their coming back in the form of a baby.

6 This system of remunerating labourers on a one-third share system is common on smallholder plantations throughout Côte d'Ivoire unless the labourers choose to work on a piecemeal contractual basis, in which case they are given a fixed sum for clearing, weeding or harvesting a piece of land. The system is similar to the *abusa* system on cocoa farms in southern Ghana (Amanor 2001). This farmer's innovation was to have two young employees who would share one third despite the fact that such an agreement would usually be between the farmer and *one* worker only.

5 Navigating migrant life

1 In 2004, the cost of a basic meal bought on the street in Ghana was about ₵1,000 (6 pence) and urban-based children normally got about ₵2,500 (16 pence) per day for street meals. In Burkina Faso, a meal of rice and sauce could be bought for 75 CFA francs (8 pence) on the streets of cities and rural towns in 2005. Most child migrants doing physical work, such as itinerant trading and shoeshining, spend 250–300 CFA francs (26–32 pence) on food per day, unless they are eating with an employer.

2 In Zéké village, we trained six girls and six boys to carry out interviews with their peer group to explore how children spoke about their migration aspirations and experiences. Although this material is a thin description of current practices, it provides valuable insights.

3 Purdah is a practice among some Muslims in which married women keep themselves secluded and therefore do not leave their houses and courtyards except to visit relatives or female friends, attend religious ceremonies on the occasion of births, marriages or funerals, visit the sick or seek healthcare for themselves or their children. Generally, married women in non-poor families comply with purdah while poor, widowed and divorced women are unable to do so because the restrictions on their mobility undermine their livelihoods (Schildkrout 2002 [1978]).

4 Requesting a child is not something that happens at random; usually such requests are made within social networks of kin, friends, trading partners, religious communities or other institutions connecting people. Children are not passive in such requests; they may have discussed the possibility of living with someone to work for them or to pursue education before an actual request is made, as may one or more parents or siblings. In other words, requests for children are embedded in local ideas of mobility.

5 Young migrants in Ouagadougou could access cheap housing on the margins of the city where temporary mud-brick houses constantly sprang up to make claims on plots as the urban titling process slowly progressed. They primarily found such houses in the neighbourhoods where many migrants from their region had settled. Alternatively, their employers put them up in one of the mud-brick houses they had constructed when bidding for several plots in the hope that at least one would become theirs.

6 David's paternal uncle, a salt trader at the Katré Yaar market in Ouagadougou, has since early 2005 mediated the contact between many youth and Thorsen. Several times, we have spent a Sunday in his household interviewing youth from Pays Bisa or having a meeting with the Association des Enfants et Jeunes Travailleurs to see whether the young migrants could benefit from membership. We followed David's migrant life closely between 2005 and 2008, bringing us into contact with several employers and also helping us to keep in touch with some of his friends, whom we interviewed in 2005.

7 In West Africa, wives and husbands usually have separate purses and discrete responsibilities within the household, while at the same time having a shared interest in the well-being of household members. In a case like this, several issues may have led the boss's wife to give advice to her husband's economic detriment. First, she may have felt that he was neglecting his moral responsibilities towards a young, hard-working and respectful household member. Second, she may have felt equally uncared for in her husband's economic dispositions and therefore had little stake in his economic gains.

8 The latest ILO Convention on child labour, the Worst Forms of Child Labour Convention, is just one among others that includes education among the measures stipulated to address child labour.

Bibliography

Abebe, T. (2007) 'Changing livelihoods, changing childhoods: patterns of children's work in rural southern Ethiopia', *Children's Geographies*, 5(1): 77–93.

Abu-Lughod, L. (1993) *Writing Women's Worlds. Bedouin Stories*, Berkeley: University of California Press.

Agarwal, S., M. Attah, N. Apt, M. Grieco, E. A. Kwakye and J. Turner (1997) 'Bearing the weight: the *Kayayoo*, Ghana's working girl child', *International Social Work*, 40(3): 425–63.

Aitken, S. C. (2007) 'Desarrollo integral y fronteras' [Integral development and border spaces], *Children's Geographies*, 5(1): 113–29.

Ajayi, A. O. and D. O. Torimiro (2004) 'Perspectives on child abuse and labour: global ethical ideals versus African cultural realities', *Early Child Development and Care*, 174(4): 183–91.

Akabayashi, H. and G. Psacharopoulos (1999) 'The trade-off between child labour and human capital formation: a Tanzanian case study', *Journal of Development Studies*, 35(5): 120–40.

Akresh, R. (2004a) 'Adjusting household structure: school enrolment impacts of child fostering in Burkina Faso', BREAD Working Paper 089, Bureau for Research in Economic Analysis of Development.

— (2004b) 'Risk, network quality, and family structure: child fostering decisions in Burkina Faso', BREAD Working Paper 065, Bureau for Research in Economic Analysis of Development.

Alber, E. (2004) 'Grandparents as foster parents: transformations in foster relations between grandparents and grandchildren in northern Benin', *Africa*, 74(1): 28–46.

Amanor, K. S. (2001) 'Land, labour and the family in southern Ghana. A critique of land policy under neo-liberalisation', Research Report 116, Uppsala: Nordic Africa Institute.

Anarfi, J., E. N. Appiah and K. Awusabo-Asare (1997) 'Livelihood and the risk of HIV/AIDS infection in Ghana: the case of female itinerant traders', *Health Transition Review*, supplement to vol. 7, pp. 225–42.

Anarfi, J. and S. Kwankye (2003) 'Migration from and to Ghana: a background paper', with O. Ababio and R. Tiemoko, Working Paper C4, Development Research Centre on Migration, Globalization and Poverty, University of Sussex.

Andvig, J. (2000) 'An essay on child labour in sub-Saharan Africa – a bargaining approach', Working Paper 613, Norwegian Institute of International Affairs.

Ansell, N. (2004) 'Secondary schooling and rural youth transitions in Lesotho and Zimbabwe', *Youth and Society*, 36(2): 183–202.

— (2005) *Children, Youth and Development*, London: Routledge.

Ansell, N. and L. Young (2002) *Young AIDS Migrants in Southern Africa*, London: Brunel University, DfID and ESCOR.

Anti-Slavery International (2001) 'Situation des enfants domestiques et le trafic des enfants au Burkina Faso', Research Report, Ouagadougou: GRADE-FRB for Anti-Slavery International and WAO-Afrique.

Ardener, E. (1977) 'Belief and the problem of women', in S. Ardener (ed.), *Perceiving Women*, London: J. M. Dent & Sons, pp. 1–17.

Aries, P. (1962) *Centuries of Childhood*, London: Cape.

AU (African Union) (1990) 'African Charter on the Rights and Welfare of the Child', OAU Doc. CAB/LEG/24.9/49 (1990), www.africa-union.org/root/au/documents/treaties/text, accessed 11 September 2006.

Awumbila, M. (1997) 'Women, environmental change and economic crisis in Ghana', in E. A. Gyasi and J. I. Uitto (eds),

Environment, Biodiversity and Agricultural Change in West Africa: Perspectives from Ghana, Tokyo, New York and Paris: United Nations University Press.

Awumbila, M. and E. Ardayfio-Schandorf (2008) 'Gendered poverty, migration and livelihood strategies of female porters in Accra, Ghana', *Norsk Geografisk Tidsskrift* [Norwegian Journal of Geography], 62(3): 171–9.

Bastia, T. (2005) 'Child trafficking or teenage migration? Bolivian migrants in Argentina', *International Migration*, 43(4): 58–89.

Beauchemin, E. (1999) 'The exodus: the growing migration of children from Ghana's rural areas to the urban centres', Accra: Catholic Action for Street Children (CAS) and UNICEF.

Benedict, R. (1938) 'Continuities and discontinuities in cultural conditioning', *Psychiatry*, 1, reprinted in R. A. LeVine and R. S. New (eds) (2008), *Anthropology and Child Development. A Cross-Cultural Reader*, Malden: Blackwell.

Bequele, A. and J. Boyden (eds) (1988) *Combating Child Labour*, Geneva: ILO.

Berthelette, J. (2001) *Survey Report on the Bissa Language*, SIL International.

Bey, M. (2003) 'The Mexican child: from work with the family to paid employment', *Childhood*, 10(3): 287–300.

Bledsoe, C. H. (1990) 'No success without struggle: social mobility and hardship for foster children in Sierra Leone', *Man*, 25(1): 70–88.

Bluebond-Langner, M. and J. E. Korbin (2007) 'Challenges and opportunities in the anthropology of childhoods: an introduction to "Children, Childhoods and Childhood Studies"', *American Anthropologist*, 109(2): 241–6.

Boakye-Boaten, A. (2008) 'Street children: experiences from the streets of Accra', *Research Journal of International Studies*, 8: 76–84.

Bøås, M and A. Hatløy (2008) 'Child labour in West Africa: different work – different vulnerabilities', *International Migration*, 46(3): 3–25.

Bonnet, D. (1981), 'Le Retour de l'ancêtre', *Journal des Africanistes*, 51: 133–47.

Bouquet, M. (1993) *Reclaiming English Kinship: Portuguese Refractions on British Kinship Theory*, Manchester: Manchester University Press.

Bourdet, Y., M. Koné and I. Persson (2006) 'Genre et economie au Burkina Faso – vers l'egalité des chances?', Country Economic Report 2006:7, Stockholm: ASDI/SIDA.

Bourdieu, P. (1977) *Outline of a Theory of Practice*, Cambridge: Cambridge University Press.

Bourdillon, M. F. C. (2005) 'Translating standards into practice: confronting local barriers', in B. H. Weston (ed.), *Child Labor and Human Rights*, Boulder, CO: Lynne Rienner, pp. 143–66.

— (2006) 'Violence against working children. A report on recent research relating to work that is harmful to children', Stockholm: Save the Children Sweden.

Boursin, F. (2002) 'Travail and trafficking des enfants *versus* scolarisation', Paper presented to the colloquium on *La recherche face aux défis de l'éducation au Burkina Faso*, Ouagadougou, 19–22 November.

Boutillier, J. L., A. Quesnel and J. Vaugelade (1985) 'La migration de la jeunesse du Burkina', *Cahiers de l'ORSTOM, Série Sciences Humaines*, 21(2/3): 243–9.

Boyden, J. (1997) 'Childhood and policy makers: a comparative perspective on the globalization of childhood', in A. James and A. Prout (eds), *Constructing and Reconstructing Childhood: Contemporary Issues in the Sociological Study of Childhood*, 2nd edn, Basingstoke: Falmer Press.

— (2001) 'Some reflections on scientific conceptualisations of childhood and youth', in S. Tremayne (ed.), *Managing Reproductive Life. Cross-Cultural Themes in Sexuality and Fertility*, New York and Oxford: Berghahn Books.

Bredeloup, S. (2003) 'La Côte d'Ivoire ou l'étrange destin de l'étranger', *Revue Européenne des Migrations Internationales*, 19(2): 85–113.

Breusers, M. (1998) 'On the move: mobility, land use and livelihood practices on the Central Plateau in Burkina Faso', PhD thesis, Department of Rural

Development Sociology, Wageningen Agricultural University.

Bucholtz, M. (2002) 'Youth and cultural practice', *Annual Review of Anthropology*, 31(1): 525–52.

Caldwell, J. C. (1969) *African Rural–Urban Migration: The Movements to Ghana's Towns*, London: Hurst & Co.

Camacho, A. Z. V. (1999) 'Child domestic workers in Metro Manila', *Childhood*, 6(1): 57–73.

Canagarajah, S. and H. Coulombe (1997) 'Child labor and schooling in Ghana', Policy Research Working Paper 1844, World Bank Human Development Technical Family African Region, Washington, DC: World Bank.

Canagarajah, S. and C. C. Pörtner (2002) 'Evolution of poverty and welfare in Ghana in the 1990s: achievements and challenges', Africa Region Working Paper Series no. 61, Washington, DC: World Bank.

Caouette, T. (2001) 'Small dreams beyond reach: the lives of migrant children and youth along the borders of China, Myanmar and Thailand', London: Save the Children.

Carsten, J. (2000) 'Introduction: cultures of relatedness', in J. Carsten (ed.), *Cultures of Relatedness. New Approaches to the Study of Kinship*, Cambridge: Cambridge University Press.

Cartry, M. (1982) 'From the village to the bush. An essay on the Gourmantché of Gobnangou (Upper Volta)', in M. Izard and P. Smith (eds), *Between Belief and Transgression: Structuralist Essays in Religion, History, and Myth*, Chicago, IL: University of Chicago Press.

Casely-Hayford, L. (1999) 'Education for all in Ghana: a cultural enquiry', Paper presented to the Education in Africa Conference, University of Edinburgh Department of African Studies, 10 May.

Cassiman, A. (2009) 'Home call: absence, presence and migration in rural northern Ghana', *African Identities*, 8(1): 21–40.

Castle, S. and A. Diarra (2003) 'The international migration of young Malians: tradition, necessity or rite of passage?', Research report, London: London School of Hygiene and Tropical Medicine.

Chauveau, F. (1998) 'Stratégies pour les jeunes défavorisés. Etat des lieux en Afrique Francophone sub-saharienne', L'Institut International de Planification de l'Education/UNESCO.

Chen, M. (2004) 'Rethinking the informal economy: linkages with the formal economy and the formal regulatory environment', Paper presented to the EGDI and UNU-WIDER Conference 'Unlocking human potential: linking the informal and formal sectors', Helsinki.

Cheney, K. E. (2007) *Pillars of the Nation. Child Citizens and Ugandan National Development*, Chicago, IL, and London: University of Chicago Press.

Clifford, J. (1992) 'Travelling cultures', in L. Grossberg, C. Nelson and P. Treichler (eds), *Cultural Studies*, New York and London: Routledge, pp. 96–116.

Collyer, M. (2007) 'In-between places: trans-Saharan transit migrants in Morocco and the fragmented journey to Europe', *Antipode*, 39(4): 668–90.

Cordell, D., J. Gregory and V. Piche (1996) *Hoe and Wage: A Social History of a Circular Migration System in West Africa*, Boulder, CO: Westview Press.

Cornwall, A. (2007) 'Of choice, chance and contingency: "career strategies" and tactics for survival among Yoruba women traders', *Social Anthropology*, 15(1): 27–46.

Cunningham, H. and P. Viazzo (1996) 'Child labour in historical perspective', Florence: UNICEF Innocenti Research Centre.

Davin, A. (1996) *Growing Up Poor: Home, School and Street in London 1870–1914*, London: Rivers Oram Press.

De Boeck, F. (2005) 'The divine seed. Children, gift and witchcraft in the Democratic Republic of Congo', in A. Honwana and F. de Boeck (eds), *Makers and Breakers. Children and Youth in Post-colonial Africa*, London: James Currey, pp. 188–214.

De Boeck, F. and A. Honwana (2005) 'Introduction: children and youth in Africa: agency, identity and place', in A. Honwana and F. de Boeck (eds), *Makers and Breakers. Children and Youth in Postcolonial Africa*, London: James Currey, pp. 1–18.

De Bruijn, M., R. van Dijk and D. Foeken (2001) 'Mobile Africa: an introduction', in M. de Bruijn, R. van Dijk and D. Foeken (eds), *Mobile Africa. Changing Patterns of Mobility in Africa and Beyond*, Leiden: Brill, pp. 1–7.

De Certeau, M. (1984) *The Practices of Every-day Life*, Berkeley: University of California Press.

De Haan, A. (1999) 'Livelihoods and poverty: the role of migration – a critical review of the migration literature', *Journal of Development Studies*, 36(2): 1–47.

De Lange, A. (2004) 'Child trafficking. Observations on Burkina Faso', in K. G. Lieten (ed.), *The Child Labour Problem. Issues and Solutions*, Amsterdam/Geneva: IREWOC and Defence for Children International, pp. 65–76.

— (2006) '"Going to Kompienga". A study on child labour migration and trafficking in Burkina Faso's south-eastern cotton sector', Research Report, Amsterdam: IREWOC.

— (2007) 'Child labour migration and trafficking in rural Burkina Faso', *International Migration*, 45(2): 147–67.

De Waal, A. (2002) 'Realising child rights in Africa: children, young people and leadership', in A. de Waal and N. Argenti (eds), *Young Africa. Realising the Rights of Children and Youth*, Trenton and Asmara: Africa World Press.

Devereux, S. (1992) 'Household responses to food insecurity in north-eastern Ghana', PhD thesis, University of Oxford.

Dietz, T. and D. Millar (eds) (1999) *Coping with Climate Change in Dryland Ghana: The Case of Bolgatanga*, Amsterdam/Tamale: ICCD.

Diouf, A., M. Mbaye and Y. Mactman (2001) 'L'éducation non-formelle au Senegal. Description, évaluation et perspectives, synthèse', UNESCO.

Diouf, M. (2005) 'Afterword', in A. Honwana and F. de Boeck (eds), *Makers and Breakers. Children and Youth in Post-colonial Africa*, London: James Currey, pp. 229–34.

Dottridge, M. (2002) 'Trafficking in children

in West and Central Africa', *Gender and Development*, 10(1): 38–42.

Dyson, J. (2008) 'Harvesting identities: youth, work, and gender in the Indian Himalayas', *Annals of the Association of American Geographers*, 98(1): 160–79.

Einarsdóttir, J. (2006) 'Relocation of children. Fosterage and child death in Biombo, Guinea-Bissau', in C. Christiansen, M. Utas and H. E. Vigh (eds), *Navigating Youth, Generating Adulthood. Social Becoming in an African Context*, Uppsala: Nordic Africa Institute, pp. 183–200.

Elmhirst, R. (2002) 'Daughters and displacement: migration dynamics in an Indonesian transmigration area', *Journal of Development Studies*, 38(5): 143–66.

Elson, D. (1982) 'The differentiation of children's labour in the capitalist labour market', *Development and Change*, 13(4): 490–92.

Ennew, J., W. E. Myers and D. P. Plateau (2005) 'Defining child labor as if human rights really matter', in B. H. Weston (ed.), *Child Labor and Human Rights*, Boulder, CO: Lynne Rienner.

Eriksen, T. H. (1995) *Small Places, Large Issues. An Introduction to Social and Cultural Anthropology*, London: Pluto Press.

Erulkar, A. S. and T. A. Mekbib (2007) 'Invisible and vulnerable: adolescent domestic workers in Addis Ababa, Ethiopia', *Vulnerable Children and Youth Studies*, 2(3): 246–56.

Evans, R. (2009) 'Young caregiving and HIV in the UK: caring relationships and mobilities in African migrant families', *Population, Space and Place*, published online, September.

— (2010) '"We are managing our own lives …": life transitions and care in sibling-headed households affected by AIDS in Tanzania and Uganda', *Area*, published online, 7 April.

Fall, P. D. (2007) 'La dynamique migratoire Ouest Africaine entre ruptures et continuités', Paper presented to the workshop 'Understanding migration dynamics in the continent', Oxford University and Centre for Migration Studies, University of Ghana, Accra, 18–21 September.

Fentiman, A., A. Hall and D. Bundy (1999)

'School enrolment patterns in rural Ghana: a comparative study of the impact of location, gender, age and health on children's access to basic schooling', *Comparative Education*, 35(3): 331–49.

Ferme, M. C. (2001) *The Underneath of Things. Violence, History and the Everyday in Sierra Leone*, Berkeley: University of California Press.

Fierlbeck, K. (1994) 'Accountability, consent and the articulation of "women's interests"', Paper presented to the IDS Workshop on 'Getting institutions right for women in development', Brighton, 3–5 November.

— (1997) 'Getting representation right for women in development: accountability, consent and the articulation of women's interests', in A. M. Goetz (ed.), *Getting Institutions Right for Women in Development*, London: Zed Books.

Finnegan, G. A. (1976) 'Population movement, labour migration, and social structure in a Mossi village', Unpublished PhD thesis, Brandeis University.

Fortes, M. (1938) 'Social and psychological aspects of education in Taleland', Supplement to *Africa*, 11(4), abridged version in R. A. LeVine and R. S. New (eds) (2008), *Anthropology and Child Development. A Cross-Cultural Reader*, Malden: Blackwell.

Foucault, M. (1978) *The History of Sexuality*, vol. 1: *An Introduction*, New York: Vintage.

Fréchette, L. and R. Aduayi-Diop (2005) 'La main-d'œuvre féminine chez les jeunes d'Afrique: regard sur trois situations aliénantes', Quebec: Centre d'étude et de recherche en intervention sociale (CÉRIS).

Glover, J. (1995) 'The research programme of development ethics', in M. Nussbaum and J. Glover (eds), *Women, Culture and Development: A Study of Human Capabilities*, Oxford: Clarendon Press.

GME (1999) 'Issue paper on the education sector for the National Network of Coordinating Group as input to the Comprehensive Development Framework', Accra: Ministry of Education.

— (2000) 'The official Ghana education home page', www.ghana.edu.gh/home.html, accessed 4 August 2003.

Goody, E. N. (1982) *Parenthood and Social Reproduction. Fostering and Occupational Roles in West Africa*, Cambridge: Cambridge University Press.

Gottlieb, A. (1998) 'Do infants have religion? The spiritual lives of Beng babies', *American Anthropologist*, 100(1): 122–35.

Grootaert, C. and R. Kanbur (1995) 'Child labor – an economic perspective', *International Labour Review*, 134(2): 187–203.

Grover, S. (2004) 'Why won't they listen to us? On giving power and voice to children participating in social research', *Childhood*, 11(1): 81–93.

GSS (2002) '2000 Population and Housing Census: summary report of final results', Accra: Ghana Statistical Service.

— (2003) 'Ghana Child Labour Survey', Accra: Ghana Statistical Service.

GSS and World Bank (1998) 'Ghana Core Welfare Indicators Questionnaire (CWIQ) survey 1997 main report', Accra/Washington, DC: Ghana Statistical Service/World Bank.

Gugler, J. and G. Ludwar-Ene (1995) 'Gender and migration in Africa south of the Sahara', in J. Baker and T. A. Aina (eds), *The Migration Experience in Africa*, Uppsala: Nordic Africa Institute.

Guichaoua, Y. (2006) 'Non-protected labour in one West African capital: characteristics of jobs and occupational mobility in Abidjan, Côte d'Ivoire', QEH Working Paper Series no. 132, University of Oxford.

Guyer, J. (1988) 'Dynamic approaches to domestic budgeting: cases and methods from Africa', in D. Dwyer and J. Bruce (eds), *A Home Divided: Women and Income in the Third World*, Stanford, CA: Stanford University Press.

Hannam, K., M. Sheller and J. Urry (2006) 'Editorial: mobilities, immobilities and moorings', *Mobilities*, 1(1): 1–22.

Harding, S. (1987) 'Is there a feminist methodology?', in S. Harding (ed.), *Feminism and Methodology*, Bloomington: Indiana University Press, pp. 1–14.

Hart, K. (1973) 'Informal income opportunities and urban employment in Ghana', *Journal of Modern African Studies*, 11(1): 61–89.

Hashim, I. (2004) 'Working with working

children: child labour and the barriers to education in rural northeastern Ghana', Unpublished DPhil thesis, University of Sussex.

— (2005) 'Research report on independent child migration from northeastern to central Ghana', Research report, Development Research Centre on Migration, Globalization and Poverty, University of Sussex.

— (2006) 'The positives and negatives of children's independent migration: assessing the evidence and the debates', Working Paper T16, Development Research Centre on Migration, Globalization and Poverty, University of Sussex.

— (2007) 'Independent child migration and education in Ghana', *Development and Change*, 38(5): 911–31.

— (2008) 'Children on the move: a discussion paper on protection issues for migrant children', London: Save the Children.

— (forthcoming) 'Learning and livelihoods: children's education in northeastern Ghana', *Cahiers de Recherche sur l'Education et les Savoirs*, Special issue on 'Out-of-school children and the school'.

Hasnat, B. (1995) 'International trade and child labour', *Journal of Economic Issues*, XXIX(2): 419–26.

Hendrick, H. (1997) 'Constructs and reconstructions of British childhood: an interpretive survey, 1800 to the present', in A. James and A. Prout (eds), *Constructing and Reconstructing Childhood: Contemporary Issues in the Sociological Study of Childhood*, 2nd edn, Basingstoke: Falmer Press.

Hertrich, V. and M. Lesclingand (2007) 'Transition to adulthood and gender: changes in rural Mali', Working Paper no. 140, Paris: INED.

Hirschfeld, L. (2002) 'Why don't anthropologists like children?', *American Anthropologist*, 104(2): 611–27.

Hoddinott, J. (1992) 'Rotten kids or manipulative parents: are children old age security in western Kenya?', *Economic Development and Cultural Change*, 40(3): 545–65.

Holland, D., W. J. Lachicotte, D. Skinner and C. Cain (1998) *Identity and Agency in Cultural Worlds*, Cambridge, MA, and London: Harvard University Press.

Holy, L. (1996) *Anthropological Perspectives on Kinship*, London: Pluto Press.

Honwana, A. and F. de Boeck (eds) (2005) *Makers and Breakers. Children and Youth in Postcolonial Africa*, London: James Currey.

Hopkins, P. E. and M. Hill (2008) 'Pre-flight experiences and migration stories: the accounts of unaccompanied asylum-seeking children', *Children's Geographies*, 6(3): 257–68.

Huisjman, R. (2008) 'Children working beyond their localities: Lao children working in Thailand', *Childhood*, 15(3): 331–53.

Ike, C. and K. Twumasi-Ankrah (1999) 'Child abuse and child labour across culture: implications for research, prevention and policy', *Journal of Social Development in Africa*, 14(2): 109–18.

ILO (1996) 'Child labour: targeting the intolerable', Report VI(1), International Labour Conference, 86th Session, Geneva: International Labour Office.

— (1997) 'Methodological child labour surveys and statistics: ILO's recent work in brief', Geneva: International Labour Office.

— (1999) 'Chart of ratifications of ILO Conventions on Minimum Age and Forced Labour by Country', ilo.org/public/english/comp/ child/standards/ratification, accessed 4 April 2000.

— (2002) 'Combat the trafficking of children', Geneva: International Labour Office, www.ilo.org/public/english/ standards/ipec/publ/childtraf/combat. pdf, accessed 23 February 2003.

— (2004) 'A comparative analysis: girl child labour in agriculture, domestic work and sexual exploitation. Rapid assessments on the cases of the Philippines, Ghana and Ecuador', vol. 2, Geneva: International Labour Office.

Imorou, A. B. (2008) 'Le coton et la mobilité: les implications d'une culture de rente sur les trajectoires sociales des jeunes et enfants au Nord-Bénin', Dakar: Plan-Waro, Terre des Hommes and Lasdel-Bénin.

INSD (2008a) 'Annuaire statistique. Edition 2008', Ouagadougou: Institut National de la Statistique et de la Démographie, www.insd.bf, accessed 26 June 2009.

— (2008b) 'Enquète nationale sur le travail des enfants au Burkina Faso (ENTE-BF) 2006', Ouagadougou: Institut National de la Statistique et de la Démographie, www.insd.bf, accessed 26 June 2009.

IOM (2003) 'Ghana trafficked children freed', Geneva: International Organization for Migration, www.iom.int/en/archive /pbn260803.shtml#item2, accessed 10 December 2004.

Isiugo-Abanihe, U. C. (1985) 'Child fosterage in West Africa', *Population and Development Review*, 11(1): 53–73.

— (1994) 'Parenthood in sub-Saharan Africa: child fostering and its relationship with fertility', in T. Locoh and V. Hertrich (eds), *The Onset of Fertility Transition in Sub-Saharan Africa*, Belgium: Derouaux Ordina Editions.

Iversen, V. (2002) 'Autonomy in child labor migrants', *World Development*, 30(5): 817–34.

Jackson, C. (1997) 'Post poverty, gender and development?', *IDS Bulletin*, 28(3): 145–53.

Jacquemin, M. Y. (2004) 'Children's domestic work in Abidjan, Côte d'Ivoire. The *petites bonnes* have the floor', *Childhood*, 11(3): 383–97.

— (2007) 'Sociologie du service domestique juvénile: "petites nièces" et "petites bonnes" à Abidjan', Doctoral thesis, Centre d'études africaines, Ecole des Hautes Etudes en Sciences Sociales.

— (2009) '"Petites nièces" et "petites bonnes" à Abidjan. Les mutations de la domesticité juvénile', *Travail, genre et sociétés*, 22: 53–74.

James, A. and A. Prout (1997) 'Introduction', in A. James and A. Prout (eds), *Constructing and Reconstructing Childhood: Contemporary Issues in the Sociological Study of Childhood*, 2nd edn, Basingstoke: Falmer Press.

Jenks, C. (2004) 'Many childhoods?', *Childhood*, 11(1): 5–8.

Johnson-Hanks, J. (2002) 'On the limits of life stages in ethnography: toward a theory of vital conjunctures', *American Anthropologist*, 104: 865–80.

Jonckers, D. (1997) 'Les enfants confiés', in M. Pilon, T. Locoh, E. Vignikin and P. Vimard (eds), *Ménages et Familles en Afrique. Approches des Dynamiques Contemporaines*, Paris: CEPED, pp. 193–208.

Journet, O. (1981) 'La quête de l'enfant', *Journal des Africanistes*, 51: 97–115.

Kabeer, N. (1999) 'Resources, agency, achievements: reflections on the measurement of women's empowerment', *Development and Change*, 30(3): 435–64.

— (2000) 'Inter-generational contracts, demographic transitions and the "quantity–quality" trade-off: parents, children and investing in the future', *Journal of International Development*, 12: 463–82.

— (2001) 'Deprivation, discrimination and delivery: competing explanations for child labour and educational failure in South Asia', IDS Working Paper 135, Brighton: Institute of Development Studies.

Kandiyoti, D. (1988) 'Bargaining with patriarchy', *Gender and Society*, 2(3): 274–90.

— (1998) 'Gender, power and contestation: "Bargaining with patriarchy revisited"', in C. Jackson and R. Pearson (eds), *Divided We Stand: Gender Analysis and Development*, London and New York: Routledge.

Katz, C. (2004) *Growing Up Global: Economic Restructuring and Children's Everyday Lives*, Minneapolis: University of Minnesota Press.

Kesby, M., F. Gwanzura-Ottemoller and M. Chizororo (2006) 'Theorising *Other*, "other childhoods": issues emerging from work on HIV in urban and rural Zimbabwe', *Children's Geographies*, 4(2): 185–202.

Khair, S. (2005) 'Preliminary report on child migrant workers in the informal sector in Dhaka', Dhaka/Brighton: RMMRU/Development Research Centre on Migration, Globalization and Poverty, University of Sussex.

Kielland, A. (2009) 'Child mobility as household risk management', *Forum for Development Studies*, 36(2): 257–73.

Kielland, A. and I. Sanogo (2002) 'Burkina Faso: child labor migration from rural areas, research report', Washington, DC: World Bank.

Kielland, A. and M. Tovo (2006) *Children at Work. Child Labour Practices in Africa*, Boulder, CO: Lynne Rienner.

King, R. (2002) 'Towards a new map of European migration', *International Journal of Population Geography*, 8(2): 89–106.

Klute, G. and H. P. Hahn (2007) 'Cultures of migration: introduction', in H. P. Hahn and G. Klute (eds), *Cultures of Migration. African Perspectives*, Münster and Berlin: Lit Verlag, pp. 9–30.

Koné, B. (2001) 'Monographie du Département de Tenkodogo', Projet de Développement Rural dans le Boulgou (PDR) et Direction Régionale de l'Economie et de la Planification du Centre-Est.

Konkobo, M. K. (2008) 'Place et rôle des cours du soir dans le système educatif Burkinabè', Women, Health, and Education Programme (WHEP), Groupe Inter-académique pour le Développement (GID), www.whep.info/spip.php?article100.

Kwankye, S. O., J. K. Anarfi and C. Addoquaye-Tagoe (2008) 'Sustainable return of independent child migrants to their home communities in northern Ghana', Paper presented to the workshop 'Children on the move in the developing world: sharing research findings', University of Sussex, 6–8 May.

Kwankye, S., J. Anarfi, C. Tagoe and A. Castaldo (2007) 'Coping strategies of independent child migrants from northern Ghana to southern cities', Working Paper T-23, Development Research Centre on Migration, Globalization and Poverty, University of Sussex.

Lachaud, J. P. (1994) 'Pauvreté et marché du travail urbain en Afrique sub-Saharienne: analyse comparative', Geneva: IILS.

Lambert, M. (2007) 'Politics, patriarchy, and the new traditions: understanding female migration among the Jola (Senegal, West Africa)', in H. P. Hahn and G. Klute (eds), *Cultures of Migration. African Perspectives*, Münster and Berlin: Lit Verlag, pp. 129–48.

Lancy, D. F. (2008) *The Anthropology of Childhood: Cherubs, Chattel, Changelings*,

Cambridge: Cambridge University Press.

Langevang, T. (2008) '"We are managing!" Uncertain paths to respectable adulthoods in Accra, Ghana', *Geoforum*, 39(6): 2039–47.

Lather, P. (2000) 'Reading the image of Rigoberta Menchú: undecidability and language lessons', *Qualitative Studies in Education*, 13(2): 153–62.

Le Jeune, G., V. Piché and J. Poirier (2004) 'Towards a reconsideration of female migration patterns in Burkina Faso', *Canadian Studies in Population*, 31(2): 145–77.

Leach, F. (2003) 'Practicing gender analysis in education', Oxford: Oxfam.

Leinaweaver, J. B. (2007) 'Choosing to move. Child agency on Peru's margins', *Childhood*, 4(3): 375–92.

Lesclingand, M. (2004) 'Nouvelles stratégies migratoires des jeunes femmes rurales au Mali: de la valorisation individuelle à une reconnaissance sociale', *Sociétés Contemporaines*, 55: 21–42.

LeVine, R. A. and R. S. New (2008) 'Introduction', in R. A. LeVine and R. S. New (eds), *Anthropology and Child Development: A Cross-Cultural Reader*, Malden: Blackwell.

Lund, R. (2007) 'At the interface of development studies and child research: rethinking the participating child', *Children's Geographies*, 5(1): 131–48.

Ly, B. (1985) 'La socialisation des jeunes dans les villes du Tiers-Monde – le cas de l'Afrique', *International Review of Education*, XXXI: 413–28.

Mahler, S. J. and P. Pessar (2006) 'Gender matters: ethnographers bring gender from the periphery toward the core of migration studies', *International Migration Review*, 40(1): 27–63.

Malhotra, R. and N. Kabeer (2002) 'Demographic transition, intergenerational contracts and old age security: an emerging challenge for social policy in developing countries', IDS Working Paper 157, Brighton: Institute for Development Studies.

Malkki, L. (1992) 'National geographic: the rooting of peoples and the territorialization of national identity among scholars and refugees', *Cultural Anthropology*, 7(1): 24–44.

Malkki, L. and E. Martin (2003) 'Children and the gendered politics of globalization: in remembrance of Sharon Stephens', *American Ethnologist*, 30(2): 216–24.

Mani, L. (1992) 'Multiple mediations: feminist scholarship in the age of multinational scholarship', in H. Crowley and S. Himmelweit (eds), *Knowing Women: Feminism and Knowledge*, Cambridge: Polity Press.

Massey, D. S., J. Arango, G. Hugo, A. Kouaouci, A. Pellegrino and J. E. Taylor (1993) 'Theories of international migration: a review and appraisal', *Population and Development Review*, 19(3): 431–66.

Mazzucato, V. and D. Niemeijer (2000) 'Rethinking soil and water conservation in a changing society. A case study in eastern Burkina Faso', PhD thesis, Wageningen Agricultural University.

McKay, D. (2005) 'Reading remittance landscapes: female migration and agricultural transition in the Philippines', *Geografisk Tidsskrift, Danish Journal of Geography*, 105(1): 89–99.

McKechnie, J. and S. Hobbs (1999) 'Child labour: the view from the north', *Childhood*, 6(1): 89–100.

Mead, M. (1928) *Coming of Age in Samoa. A Study of Adolescence and Sex in Primitive Societies*, Harmondsworth: Penguin Books.

Meinert, L. (2003) 'Sweet and bitter places: the politics of schoolchildren's orientation in rural Uganda', in K. F. Olwig and E. Gulløv (eds), *Children's Places. Cross-Cultural Perspectives*, London: Routledge.

Miles, A. (2000) 'Poor adolescent girls and social transformations in Cuenca, Ecuador', *Ethos*, 28(1): 54–74.

Mills, M. B. (2001) 'Auditing for the chorus line: gender, rural youth, and the consumption of modernity in Thailand', in D. L. Hodgson (ed.), *Gendered Modernities. Ethnographic Perspectives*, New York: Palgrave, pp. 27–51.

Minge-Kalman, W. (1978) 'The Industrial Revolution and the European family: the institutionalization of "childhood" as a market for family labour', *Comparative Studies in Society and History*, 20(3): 454–68.

Mohanty, C. T. (1991) '"Under Western eyes": feminist scholarship and colonial discourse', in C. T. Mohanty, A. Russo and L. Torres (eds), *Third World Women and the Politics of Feminism*, Bloomington and Indianapolis: Indiana University Press.

Montgomery, H. (2001) 'Imposing rights? – a case study of child prostitution in Thailand', in J. Cowan, M. Dembour and R. Wilson (eds), *Culture and Rights*, Cambridge: Cambridge University Press.

Moore, H. (1988) *Feminism and Anthropology*, Cambridge: Polity Press.

— (1994) *A Passion for Difference: Essays in Anthropology and Gender*, Cambridge: Polity Press.

— (2004) 'On being young', *Anthropological Quarterly*, 77(4): 735–46.

Moore, K. (2001) 'Frameworks for understanding the intergenerational transmission of poverty and well-being in developing countries', CPRC Working Paper no. 8, Chronic Poverty Research Centre.

Morice, A. (1982) 'Underpaid child labour and social reproduction: apprenticeship in Kaolack, Senegal', *Development and Change*, 13(4): 515–26.

— (1987) 'Ceux qui travaillent gratuitement: un salaire confisqué', in M. Agier, J. Copan and A. Morice (eds), *Classes Ouvrières d'Afrique Noire*, Paris: Karthala.

Muzvidziwa, V. (2001) 'Zimbabwe's cross-border women traders: multiple identities and responses to new challenges', *Journal of Contemporary African Studies*, 19(1): 67–80.

Myers, W. E. (1999) 'Considering child labour: changing terms, issues and actors at the international level', *Childhood*, 6(1).

Myers, W. E. and J. Boyden (1998) *Child Labour: Promoting the Best Interests of the Working Child*, 2nd edn, London: International Save the Children Alliance.

Ní Laoire, C., F. Carpena-Méndez, N. Tyrrell and A. White (2010) 'Introduction: childhood and migration – mobilities, homes and belongings', *Childhood*, 17(2): 155–62.

Nieuwenhuys, O. (1994) *Children's Lifeworlds: Gender, Welfare and Labour in the*

Developing World, London and New York: Routledge.

— (1995) 'The domestic economy and the exploitation of children's work: the case of Kerala', *International Journal of Children's Rights*, 3(2): 213–25.

— (1996) 'The paradox of child labor and anthropology', *Annual Review of Anthropology*, 25: 237–51.

Notermans, C. (2004) 'Sharing home, food and bed: paths of grandmotherhood in East Cameroon', *Africa*, 74(1): 6–27.

— (2008) 'The emotional world of kinship: children's experiences of fosterage in East Cameroon', *Childhood*, 15(3): 355–77.

Nussbaum, M. and J. Glover (1995) *Women, Culture and Development: A Study of Human Capabilities*, Oxford: Clarendon Press.

Nyambedha, E. O. and J. Aagaard-Hansen (2003) 'Changing place, changing position. Orphans' movements in a community with high HIV/AIDS prevalence in western Kenya', in K. F. Olwig and E. Gulløv (eds), *Children's Places: Cross-Cultural Perspectives*, New York: Routledge, pp. 162–77.

Nyamnjoh, F. B. (2002) '"A child is one person's only in the womb": domestication, agency and subjectivity in the Cameroonian grassfields', in R. Werbner (ed.), *Postcolonial Subjectivities in Africa*, London and New York: Zed Books, pp. 111–38.

O'Connell Davidson, J. (2003) 'Some reflections on the debates about child abuse and exploitation', Paper presented at the 'Conference on child abuse and exploitation: social, legal and political dilemmas', Onati, Spain, 29/30 May.

— (2005) *Children in the Global Sex Trade*, Cambridge: Polity Press.

O'Connell Davidson, J. and C. Farrow (2007) 'Child migration and the construction of vulnerability', Sweden: Save the Children.

Ofosu-Kusi, Y. and P. Mizen (2005) 'Adjusting to reality: the motivations of migrant street workers in Accra, Ghana,' Paper presented to the conference 'Childhoods. Children and youth in emerging and transforming societies', University of Oslo.

O'Laughlin, B. (1995) 'Myth of the African family in the world of development', in D. F. Bryceson (ed.), *Women Wielding the Hoe*, Oxford: Berg, pp. 63–91.

Panicker, R. (1998) 'Children's rights: challenges and future trust', *Indian Journal of Social Work*, 59(1): 276–90.

Payne, R. (2004) 'Voices from the street: street girl life in Accra, Ghana', CEDAR Research Papers no. 40, University of London.

Pilon, M. (2002) 'L'évolution du champ scolaire au Burkina Faso: entre diversification et privatisation', Paper presented at the conference 'Public et privé: éducation et formation dans les pays du Sud', Université Marc Bloch.

— (2003) 'Foster care and schooling in West Africa: the state of knowledge', Paper prepared for the UNESCO 2003 EFA Monitoring Report.

Ping, H. and F. N. Pieke (2003) 'China migration country study', Paper presented at the regional conference on 'Migration, development and pro-poor policy choices in Asia', Dhaka, 22–24 June.

Piot, C. D. (1999) *Remotely Global. Village Modernity in West Africa*, Chicago, IL: University of Chicago Press.

Punch, S. (2001a) 'Household division of labour: generation, gender, age, birth order and sibling composition', *Work, Employment and Society*, 15(4): 803–23.

— (2001b) 'Negotiating autonomy: childhoods in rural Bolivia', in L. Alanen and B. Mayall (eds), *Conceptualizing Child–Adult Relations*, London: Routledge.

— (2002a) 'Youth transitions and interdependent adult–child relations in rural Bolivia', *Journal of Rural Studies*, 18(2): 123–33.

— (2002b) 'Research with children. the same or different from research with adults?', *Childhood*, 9(3): 321–41.

— (2004) 'The impact of primary education on school-to-work transitions for young people in rural Bolivia', *Youth and Society*, 36(2): 163–82.

— (2007) 'Negotiating migrant identities: young people in Bolivia and Argentina', *Children's Geographies*, 5(1/2): 95–112.

— (2009) 'Moving for a better life: To stay

or to go?', in D. Kassem, L. Murphy and E. Taylor (eds), *Key Issues in Childhood and Youth Studies*, London: Routledge, pp. 202–15.

Pupavac, V. (2001) 'Misanthropy without borders: the international children's rights regime', *Disasters*, 25(2): 95–112.

— (2003) 'The children's rights and empowerment approach: social, legal and political dilemmas', Work-in-progress paper presented to the conference on 'Child abuse and exploitation: social, legal and political dilemmas', Onati, Spain, 29/30 May.

Qvortrup, J. (1985) 'Placing children in the division of labour', in P. Close and R. Collins (eds), *Family and Economy in Modern Societies*, London: Macmillan, pp. 129–45.

— (2007) 'Editorial: a reminder', *Childhood*, 14(4): 395–400.

Reenberg, A. and C. Lund (1998) 'Land use and land right dynamics – determinants for resource management options in eastern Burkina Faso', *Human Ecology*, 26(4): 599–620.

Reynolds, P. (1991) *Dance Civet Cat: Child Labour in the Zambezi River Valley*, London: Zed Books.

Reynolds, P., O. Nieuwenhuys and K. Hanson (2006) 'Refractions of children's rights in development practice: a view from anthropology – introduction', *Childhood*, 13(3): 291–302.

Riisøen, K. H., A. Hatløy and L. Bjerkan (2004) 'Travel to uncertainty. A study of child relocation in Burkina Faso, Ghana and Mali', Fafo Report no. 440, Oslo: Fafo Institute for Applied International Studies.

Robertson, A. F. (1991) *Beyond the Family: The Social Organization of Human Reproduction*, Cambridge: Polity Press.

Robertson, C. C. (1984) *Sharing the Same Bowl*, Bloomington: Indiana University Press.

Robson, E. (2004a) 'Children at work in rural northern Nigeria: patterns of age, space and gender', *Journal of Rural Studies*, 20(2): 193–210.

— (2004b) 'Hidden child workers: young carers in Zimbabwe', *Antipode*, 34(5): 227–48.

Robson, E., S. Bell and N. Klocker (2007) 'Conceptualizing agency in the lives and actions of rural young people', in R. Panelli, S. Punch and E. Robson (eds), *Global Perspectives on Rural Childhood and Youth*, New York and London: Routledge, pp. 135–48.

Rodgers, G. and G. Standing (eds) (1981) *Child Work, Poverty and Underdevelopment*, Geneva: ILO.

Roncoli, C., K. Ingram and P. Kirshen (2002) 'Reading the rains. Local knowledge and rainfall forecasting in Burkina Faso', *Society and Natural Resources*, 15(5): 409–27.

Rosemberg, F. and R. Freitas (1999) 'The participation of Brazilian children in the labor force and education', Paper presented to the IREWOC workshop on 'Children, work and education', Amsterdam, 15–17 November.

Roy, M. A. and D. Wheeler (2006) 'A survey of micro-enterprise in urban West Africa: drivers shaping the sector', *Development in Practice*, 16(5): 452–64.

Samuelsen, H. (1999) 'The topology of illness transmission. Localizing processes among the Bissa in Burkina Faso', PhD thesis, Department of Anthropology, University of Copenhagen and Danish Bilharziasis Laboratory.

Ṣaul, M. (1984) 'The Quranic school farm and child labour in Upper Volta', *Africa*, 54(2): 71–87.

Ṣaul, M. and P. Royer (2001) *West African Challenge to Empire*, Athens and Oxford: Ohio University Press and James Currey.

SC UK (2005) 'Participatory Action Research Report with migrant children and youth in northern provinces of Lao PDR bordering China, Myanmar and Thailand', London: Save the Children.

— (2006) 'Striving for good practices: lessons learned from community-based initiatives against trafficking in children in the Mekong sub-region', London: Save the Children.

— (2007) 'Children on the move: protecting unaccompanied child migrants in South Africa and the region', London: Save the Children.

SCF Canada (2003) 'Children still in the cocoa trade: the buying, selling and toiling of West African child workers in the multi-billion dollar industry', Canada: Save the Children Fund.

Schildkrout, E. (1981) 'The employment of children in Kano (Nigeria)', in G. Rodgers and G. Standing (eds), *Child Work, Poverty and Underdevelopment*, Geneva: ILO.

— (2002 [1978]) 'Age and gender in Hausa society. Socio-economic roles of children in urban Kano', *Childhood*, 9(3): 344–68.

Schrauwers, A. (1999) 'Negotiating parentage: the political economy of "kinship" in central Sulawesi, Indonesia', *American Ethnologist*, 26(2): 310–23.

Sheller, M. and J. Urry (2006) 'The new mobilities paradigm', *Environment and Planning A*, 38(2): 207–26.

Smith, L. C. and J.-P. Chavas (1999) 'Supply response of West African agricultural households: implications of intrahousehold preference heterogeneity', FCND Discussion Paper no. 60, Washington, DC: IFPRI.

Somerfelt, T. (ed.) (2001) 'Domestic child labour in Morocco', Fafo Report 370, Oslo: Fafo Institute of Applied Social Science.

Sudarkasa, N. (1977) 'Women and migration in contemporary West Africa', *Signs: Journal of Women in Culture and Society*, 3(1): 178–89.

Tan, E. and N. Gomez (1993) 'Beyond augmenting the family income', *Philippine Labour Review*, XVII(2): 34–73.

Terre des Hommes (2003) 'Les filles domestiques au Burkina Faso: traite ou migration?', Ouagadougou: Terre des Hommes.

Terrio, S. J. (2008) 'New barbarians at the gates of Paris?: prosecuting undocumented minors in the juvenile court – the problem of the "Petits Roumains"', *Anthropological Quarterly*, 81(4): 873–901.

Thomas, R. G. (1973) 'Forced labour in British West Africa: the case of the Northern Territories of the Gold Coast 1906–1927', *Journal of African History*, 14(1): 79–103.

Thorsen, D. (2002) 'We help our husbands! Negotiating the household budget in rural Burkina Faso', *Development and Change*, 33(1): 129–46.

— (2005) 'Sons, husbands, mothers and brothers. Finding room for manoeuvre in rural Burkina Faso', Unpublished DPhil thesis, University of Sussex.

— (2006) 'Child migrants in transit. Strategies to become adult in rural Burkina Faso', in C. Christiansen, M. Utas and H. E. Vigh (eds), *Navigating Youth, Generating Adulthood: Social Becoming in an African Context*, Uppsala: Nordic Africa Institute.

— (2007a) 'Junior–senior linkages. Youngsters' perceptions of migration in rural Burkina Faso', in H. P. Hahn and G. Klute (eds), *Cultures of Migration. African Perspectives*, Berlin: Lit Verlag.

— (2007b) '"If only I get enough money for a bicycle!" A study of childhoods, migration and adolescent aspirations against a backdrop of exploitation and trafficking in Burkina Faso', Working Paper T21, Development Research Centre on Migration, Globalization and Poverty, University of Sussex.

— (2009a) 'L'échec de la famille traditionnelle ou l'étirement des relations familiales? L'exode des jeunes Burkinabé des zones rurales vers Ouagadougou et Abidjan', *Hommes et migrations*, 1279: 66–78.

— (2009b) 'From shackles to links in the chain. Theorising adolescent boys' relocation in Burkina Faso', *Forum for Development Studies*, 36(2): 81–107.

— (2009c) 'Mobile youth with little formal education: work opportunities and practices', Development Research Centre on Migration, Globalization and Poverty, University of Sussex.

— (2010) 'The place of migration in girls' imagination', *Journal of Comparative Family Studies*, XXXXI(2): 256–80.

UN (1989) 'Convention on the Rights of the Child', www.unicef.org.

— (2000) 'Protocol to Prevent, Suppress and Punish Trafficking in Persons, Especially Women and Children', Supplementing the United Nations Convention against Transnational Organized Crime, available at untreaty.un.org/English/TreatyEvent2003/Texts/treaty2E.pdf, accessed 16 December 2008.

UNICEF (2002) 'Child trafficking in West Africa: policy responses', Florence: UNICEF Innocenti Research Centre.

— (2003) 'Trafficking in human beings, especially women and children in Africa', Florence: UNICEF Innocenti Research Centre.

— (2008) 'State of the world's children 2009: maternal and infant health', New York: UNICEF.

UNOWA (2006) 'Youth unemployment and regional insecurity in West Africa', United Nations Office for West Africa.

Valentine, G. (2003) 'Boundary crossings: transitions from childhood to adulthood', *Children's Geographies*, 1(1): 37–52.

Van Gennep, A. (1960) *The Rites of Passage*, Chicago, IL: University of Chicago Press.

Van Hear, N. (1984) '"By-day" boys and Dariga men: casual labour versus agrarian capital in northern Ghana', *Review of African Political Economy*, 31: 44–56.

Vandenbroeck, M. and M. Bouverne-de Bie (2006) 'Children's agency and educational norms: a tensed negotiation', *Childhood*, 13(1): 127–43.

Verhoef, H. (2005) '"A child has many mothers": views of child fostering in northwestern Cameroon', *Childhood*, 12(3): 369–90.

Vischer, L. R. (1997) *Mütter zwischen Herd und Markt. Das Verhältnis von Mutterschaft, sozialer Elternschaft und Frauenarbeit bei den Moose (Mossi) in Ouagadougou/Burkina Faso*, Basle: Universität und Museum den Kulturen.

Waage, T. (2006) 'Coping with unpredictability: "preparing for life" in Ngaoundéré, Cameroon', in C. Christiansen, M. Utas and H. E. Vigh (eds), *Navigating Youth, Generating Adulthood. Social Becoming in an African Context*, Uppsala: Nordic Africa Institute, pp. 61–87.

Werbner, R. P. (ed.) (2002) *Postcolonial Subjectivities in Africa*, London: Zed Books.

Whitehead, A. (1981) '"I'm hungry, mum": the politics of domestic budgeting', in K. Young, C. Wolkowitz and R. McCullagh (eds), *Of Marriage and the Market: Women's Subordination in International Perspective*, London: CSE Books.

— (1994) 'Wives and mothers: female farmers in Africa', in A. Adepoju and C. Oppong (eds), *Gender, Work and Population in Sub-Saharan Africa*, London/Portsmouth: James Currey/Heinemann.

— (1996) 'Poverty in northeast Ghana: a report to ESCOR', London: Economic and Social Committee on Research, Department for International Development.

— (1998) 'Gender, poverty and intra-household relations in sub-Saharan African smallholder households: some lessons from two case examples', Background paper prepared for the 1998 SPA report on poverty and gender in sub-Saharan Africa, Washington, DC: World Bank.

— (2006), 'Persistent poverty in north east Ghana', *Journal of Development Studies*, 42(2): 278–300.

Whitehead, A. and I. Hashim (2005) 'Children and migration: background paper for DfID migration team', London: Department for International Development.

Whitehead, A. and N. Kabeer (2001) 'Living with uncertainty: gender, livelihoods and pro-poor growth in rural sub-Saharan Africa', Working Paper 134, Brighton: Institute of Development Studies.

Whitehead, A., I. Hashim and I. Iversen (2007) 'Child migration, child agency and inter-generational relations in Africa and South Asia', Working Paper T24, Development Research Centre on Migration, Globalization and Poverty, University of Sussex.

Wilson, T. D. (1994) 'What determines where transnational labor migrants go? Modifications in migration theories', *Human Organization*, 53(3): 269–78.

Zelizer, V. (1994) *Pricing the Priceless Child: The Changing Social Value of Children*, revised paperback edn, Princeton, NJ: Princeton University Press.

— (2002) 'Kids and commerce', *Childhood*, 9(4): 375–96.

Zongo, M. (2003) 'La diaspora Burkinabè en Côte d'Ivoire: trajectoire historique, recomposition des dynamiques migratoires et rapport avec le pays d'origine', *Revue Africaine de Sociologie*, 7(2): 58–72.

Index

employment possibilities, 98; reliance on relatives for support, 79, 80, 83, 91; systems, among Bisa, 9; unpaid work for relatives, 86–7; work-finding networks of, 93; working for relatives, 88, 97

Koranic schools, 37–8

Kumasi, 90, 99

Kusasi ethnic group, 22–5, 27, 32, 40, 41, 48, 51, 60, 61, 62, 71, 85, 122

Laadi, 1

labour conscription, 26

labour migration, 2

Lamissi, 32, 106, 107

laziness, accusation of, 31, 82, 88, 89, 100

learning, 33–8; by doing, 36; migration as a process of, 86, 98, 126

learning work, 52–3

leisure time of working children, 101

literacy, 48, 89, 106

livelihoods, diversification of, 37

Luke, 30

Lutte contre le Trafic des Enfants en Afrique de l'Ouest (LUTRENA), 14, 78

Madi, 99–100, 101

Magid, 90–1

Mali: child migration in, 77; migration in, 89 (of children, 43, 77); school non-attendance in, 49

maltreatment of children at home, 43, 86

marriage, 39, 60, 61, 62, 97, 106, 121, 122; connection with migration, 63; consummation of, 63; delaying of, 61; good, facilitation of, 23; exogamy, 23; factor in boys' movement, 40

maturity of children, 8

Mbilla, Ayaraga, 20

Mead, Margaret, *Coming of Age in Samoa*, 2

Mende ethnic group, belief in learning, 50

metal recycling, children's work in, 92

methodologies of research, 44–6

migrant identity, production of, 70–1

migrant life, navigation of, 85–100

migration: as learning experience, 98, 126; as part of social fabric of lives, 120; as process of social learning, 86; as vital conjuncture, 119; chain migration, logic of, 74–5; concept of, vii, 1–19; contexts of, 20–41; educational need as driver of, 104–5; histories of, 25–8; initiated by children, 54, 112; models of, 11–13; of

children (as understood by children, viii; independent, 25, 92 (use of term, vii); of rural children, reasons for, 42–6; prevention of, 117; viewed as deviance and danger, 127; viewed negatively, 49); to cities, 26; viewed as rite of passage, 114 *see also* poverty, as driving factor in migration

Millennium Development Goals, 33

minimum age for admission into employment, 4

mobile phones, 62

mobilities paradigm, 44

mobility: and education, 49–53; and family crisis, 55–7; at destination, 99–103; central to West Africans' welfare strategies, 2; compulsion to, 54; concept of, vii, 11; inter-household, 18; negotiated, 60–3; offered to children, 10–11; to find work, 46–8; to 'help', 53–5

mobility–migration nexus, 11–13

money: extorted from migrants, 80; given by parents, 77; given for safekeeping, 85; of children, 32

moral panic about child welfare, 68

Moses, 1

Mossi, 90

mothers, children's concern for welfare of, 122

moving *see* mobility

na puure (aunt), 95, 96

negotiation, 95, 114; of social position of child, 99; of status, 123–5

networks of migrants, journeying within, 83–4

new social worlds, introductions to, 65–84

new spaces, arrival in, 81–3

Nokwende, 35, 50

non-payment of work, of girls, 97

Northern Region (Ghana), 105

orphans, 56, 85, 95

Ouagadougou, 39, 42, 47, 50, 68, 69, 70, 75, 78, 82, 84, 85, 91, 92, 93, 96, 97, 100, 101, 102, 103, 105, 108, 122; evening classes in, 105

Ousman, 73

parent–child relations, 3

parental migration, impact of, 13

parenthood, negotiation of, 10